CHURCH
God's
WAY

KATHLEEN HOLLOP

Copyright ©2024 by Kathleen Hollop.

ISBN 978-1-964097-71-8 (softcover)
ISBN 978-1-964097-75-6 (hardcover)
ISBN 978-1-964097-72-5 (ebook)

All rights reserved. No part of this book may be reproduced or transmitted in any form or by any means, electronic or mechanical, including photocopying, recording, or by any information storage and retrieval system without express written permission from the author, except in the case of brief quotations embodied in critical reviews and certain other non-commercial uses permitted by copyright law.

Printed in the United States of America.

INK START MEDIA
265 Eastchester Dr Ste 133 #102
High Point NC 27262

CHURCH
God's
WAY

KATHLEEN HOLLOP

TABLE of CONTENTS

CHURCH GOD'S WAY I
PROLOGUE IV

CHAPTER 1. ARE YOU REALLY SAVED OR
            DO YOU JUST HAVE RELIGION? 1
CHAPTER 2. BE FILLED WITH THE HOLY SPIRIT-BE
            BAPTIZED IN THE HOLY GHOST 18
CHAPTER 3. BE LED BY THE HOLY SPIRIT AND
            NOT YOUR FLESH OR INTELLECT 29
CHAPTER 4. SERMON PREPARATION GOD'S WAY 58
CHAPTER 5. WARNINGS OF THE HOLY SPIRIT 69
CHAPTER 6. THE FIVE FOLDS OF MINISTRY 81
CHAPTER 7. OBEY GOD'S COMMANDMENTS
            STAND ON HIS WORD, NO COMPROMISE ... 108
CHAPTER 8. SATAN'S PLAN TO DESTROY
            AMERICA'S YOUTH 116
CHAPTER 9. SPIRITUAL WARFARE AND CHRIST'S VICTORY
            OVER SATAN AND PRINCIPALITIES 139
CHAPTER 10. SATAN'S LIES AND FALSE THEOLOGIES THAT
            HAVE ENTERED THE BODY OF CHRIST 157
CHAPTER 11. DON'T ACCEPT A WRONG COVERING 238
CHAPTER 12. OUR WORDS HAVE SPIRITUAL POWER 244
CHAPTER 13. DON'T BE A FOOLISH VIRGIN,
            BE SANCTIFIED AND READY 260
CHAPTER 14. BE A FAITHFUL PRIEST TO GOD 266
CHAPTER 15. YOU ARE IN THE ARMY OF THE LORD
            STAND AND FIGHT. 278

ACCREDITATION 290
THANK YOU 291

CHURCH GOD'S WAY
(INSIDE COVER)

Are you tired of church as usual? Are you tired of the lack of signs, wonders and miracles that should be happening in the churches today, but are not? Are you tired of the enemy of your soul beating you up emotionally, physically, and spiritually?

Isn't it time to receive the Holy Spirit Baptism of Power and Anointing to "be bold and strong", "fight the good fight of faith" "be a good soldier in the army of the Lord", and "Be an Overcomer", instead of a victim?

Isn't it time we read, study and speak the Word of God into our situations, trust God and see Him be true to His Word to perform it?

Isn't it time that pastors recognize the other four folds of ministry called and chosen by God to feed God's sheep and to help the sheep to grow in their faith? Isn't it time for the prophets, the apostles, the teachers and the evangelists to have the pulpits and be able to impart their folds, into the Body of Christ? Isn't it time for the sheep to grow in the fulness of the faith and be prayed over and sent out of the church buildings and onto the highways and byways to reach the lost? Isn't it time that pulpit hogging pastors care more about the sheep, than their building projects and their own popularity? Isn't it time that pastors love the Word of God and the sheep enough to preach the entire Word of God from the pulpits; with the Power of the Holy Spirit accompanying the Word? Isn't it time that the "Fleshly, Intellectual Pastors" get out of the pulpits of America and Holy Spirit Filled Pastors minister to the Lord's sheep?

Isn't it time we stand in the Authority in Jesus' Name and in the Power of Holy Spirit to see and do the greater things Jesus said we will do, since he has gone to the Father?

Isn't it time we walk in the Victory that Our Jesus purchased and gave us; over the devil, over the demons, over the principalities, powers and rulers of darkness, and over spiritual wickedness in this world?

Isn't it time the Body of Christ rises up in the Glory of God to take our Nation and the Nations of the World back to Jesus Christ?

Isn't it time that the people of God take a stand against the wickedness of this world. Isn't it time we stop tickling the ears of sinners and tell them to REPENT?

Isn't it time that real teachers of God's Word disciple the body of Christ; so that their minds are transformed by the Word of God and not this wicked world?

Isn't it time that we stop pretending to be Christ Followers, and really be Christ Followers? Isn't it time we repent of doing our own will and surrender to God's Will and purpose for our lives?

Isn't it time for preachers to preach against sin, preach against the murders of innocent babies that Jesus is forming in their mother's wombs, preach against fornication, adultery, pornography, gayness, lust, perversion, gay marriage, transgender surgeries, drag queens, filth, and everything God does not approve of?

Isn't it time for preachers to fear God and not man? To preach God's Whole Bible and not just messages that make people feel good and entertain them on their way to hell? Isn't it time to preach messages that will get the foolishness and sin out of them, before they are locked outside of heaven's gate like the foolish virgins of Matthew 25? We Need God the Holy Spirit Back Into Our Churches Now. We need the Body of Christ taught the Word of God. We need the body of Christ instructed in the ways of God's righteousness and truth; to break the demonic mindsets of the world off of the people of God. We need to make disciples, not just converts.

THE WORLD IS SICK AND TWISTED BECAUSE THE CHURCH HAS BEEN SICK AND TWISTED. THE CHURCH MUST CHANGE AND CONFORM TO THE IMAGE OF JESUS CHRIST IN ORDER TO IMPACT THE WORLD. IF THE CHURCH DOES NOT CHANGE, THE WORLD WILL CONTINUE TO GET MORE DEPRAVED AND CORRUPT.

AMERICAS FORMER GREATNESS CAME FROM THE PULPITS AND THE FIERY SERMONS THAT RID PEOPLE OF SIN, WICKEDNESS, AND EVIL. PEOPLE WERE REPENTING, FOLLOWING THE BIBLE, OBEYING AND SERVING THE REAL GOD, AND GOD'S BLESSINGS WERE ON AMERICA. WE MUST TURN BACK TO GOD AND LOVE HIM WITH ALL OUR HEARTS, OUR SOULS, AND OUR MINDS. IF WE DON'T, THERE WILL BE NO GENUINE LOVE, JOY, PEACE, RIGHTEOUSNESS, TRUTH, LIGHT, FREEDOM, LIBERTY, AND GOODNESS LEFT ON PLANET EARTH. BLESSED IS

THE NATION WHOSE GOD IS THE LORD AND WHOSE HOPE THE LORD IS.

AMERICA MUST TURN BACK TO FATHER GOD, JESUS CHRIST, AND THE HOLY SPIRIT. AMERICA MUST REPENT, READ THE WORD OF GOD, AND LIVE LIVES THAT GLORIFY THE GOD OF HEAVEN AND EARTH. People say, "God Bless America." CAN GOD BLESS AMERICA IF AMERICA CONTINUES TO REBELL AGAINST GOD AND WALK IN EVIL AND MAN-MADE PRIDE? WE MUST OBEY GOD, IF WE WANT THE BLESSINGS OF GOD TO FLOW INTO OUR NATION AGAIN. GOD IS HOLY. HE CANNOT BLESS WICKEDNESS.

EITHER AMERICA WILL REPENT OF SIN AND RETURN TO THE GOD OF HEAVEN, WHO MADE US A GREAT NATION, OR AMERICA WILL CONTINUE IN IT'S WICKEDNESS. AMERICA HAS DONE THE FOUR THINGS THAT ANGER GOD THE MOST. America has forsaken the real god to serve the no god evolution lies, the Greek myth gods, and the vain philosophies. America has slain millions of innocent unborn babies-human beings that God was creating in the womb for His Divine Purposes. WE have shed innocent blood in our land. Our land is covered with blood. America has thrown traditional marriage between a man (born a man) and a woman (born a woman) under the bus to sanction gay marriage, pornography, fornication, adultery and all kinds of sexual lusts. America has caused Israel to give up land for so called peace. That land belongs to Israel. God gave it to Israel. IF we curse the people of Abraham, we will be cursed.

If America continues in it's FALSE GOD WORSHIP, IT'S SACRIFICE OF UNBORN BABIES TO FALSE GODS, IT'S WICKED ABOMINATIONS, LUST, PERVERSIONS, CORRUPTION, AND GREED; AMERICA WILL BE DESTROYED BY GOD HIMSELF. WE MUST REPENT AND STOP ALL WICKEDNESS AND PERISH BEFORE IT IS TOO LATE. GOD'S JUDGMENTS ARE ALREADY HAPPENING IN OUR LAND.

Kathleen Hollop

PROLOGUE

God has set some, in the Body of Christ, to be Apostles, Evangelists, Pastors, Teachers, and Prophets to grow the believers into unity of the Christian Faith, for the work of ministry. These five folds of ministry are all supposed to be imparting their fold of ministry to the sheep. Why is it that in most churches, the only fold functioning is the Pastor? Why is it that the Pastors are denying the sheep the ability to hear the teachings of the other four folds, and stunting their spiritual growth?

This is why the people in the pews are spiritually under fed, under nourished, and unable to live the Christian Walk Successfully. They are not skilled in hearing the voice of God, surrendering fully to the Lordship of Jesus Christ, being baptized and led by the Holy Spirit into Father God's Will for their lives, praying faith prayers, making God's Decrees into situations, Proclaiming God's Truths, operating in the signs, wonders, and miracles that Jesus said we will do, etc…

We have people sitting in churches for twenty years, and they are still baby Christians. They have not grown spiritually to be able to flee temptation, resist the devil, and fight a good warfare against the enemy. They do not know the authority they have in Jesus Christ and the Holy Ghost Power that is available for them to successfully live the Christian life. They are unskilled in the Word of God, don't know the promises that God has given to them, and don't believe that God is true to His Word to perform it. There are over 8,000 promises, of God , for the believers to tap into. If they don't read the Word and don't know what the promises of God are for them, how can they claim them and receive them?

The Bible says we are to be renewed in the spirit of our mind , and put on the new man, which after God is created in righteousness and true holiness. (Ephesians 4:23-24) Sadly, over eighty percent of Christians do not read their Bibles, and are seeped in old demonic, mindsets that are contrary to the Word of God. They approve and condone the wickedness of the world, because they do not know what God has to say about anything. They do what they feel is right in their own eyes, but they are spiritually and horribly wrong, in the sight of Almighty God.

Ephesians 5:26 says that God sanctifies and cleanses the church with the washing of the water by the word of God. IF pastors are not preaching the Bible, and if brethren are not reading their Bibles, they are still seeped in the lies of the devil, the old mindsets, the old ideas, the old thought patterns , public opinion, the secular news reports, and Hollywood. It is God's Truth, that we know, that will set us free from every lie of the devil. No lie is of the truth. WE MUST RENEW OUR MINDS WITH THE WORD OF GOD. It is our responsibility to grow spiritually by reading the Word of God.

When a person repents of their sins and welcomes Jesus into their heart and life, the Holy Spirit comes into their hearts and bears witness with their spirit that they are a child of God.(Romans 8:16). But their mind has to be renewed by the Word of God, or their mind area is not regenerated. Their mind has to be changed, to be the mind of Christ. Satan has had years to indoctrinate the person with lies, deceptions, false ideas, demonic thinking, believing that "Good" is "Evil" and "Evil" is "Good". The person must allow the WORD OF GOD AND THE HOLY SPIRIT OF GOD TO CORRECT, INSTRUCT, REPROVE, AND GIVE THEM SOUND DOCTRINE. If they don't, they say they are a "Christian" but don't believe and act like Christ at all. They approve things that are contrary to God, contrary to His Word, and contrary to His Holiness and His Nature, and they serve Satan by their mindsets and actions.

If we look at the Parable of the Ten Virgins in Matthew 25:1-12, we see people in the Churches that are not lights for Christ at all. They are looking for the Bridegroom, but they are not walking or living as the children of light. They are in darkness and their lamps have gone out. They were not accepted by the Bridegroom Jesus Christ, when He came. They were locked outside of heaven.

The Lord Jesus Christ and the Holy Spirit of God, have called me to write this book in the hope of bringing people into a REAL, TRUTHFUL, RELATIONSHIP WITH THE BRIDEGROOM, JESUS CHRIST. Many don't realize that if Jesus Christ came back today, they would be LEFT BEHIND.

It is time that Pastors, Ministers, Reverends, and Priests stop hogging the pulpits and let the other four folds of ministry give their folds of information, impartation, wisdom, knowledge, and testimonies, etc… to the sheep. The Apostles, the Evangelists, the Prophets, and the Teachers should all be allowed to function in the Churches and preach their part from the pulpits of America. These Ministries are all supposed to function and grow the sheep Spiritually to be able to stand against the temptations, the demonic influences, the peer pressure, and the evils of this world. Without these four folds of ministry, the sheep cannot be the OVERCOMERS THAT THEY SHOULD BE.

It is time that only the Bible is preached from the pulpits of America. Enough is enough of preacher's pedigree papers, vacations, myths, current events and other nonsense. People need the Word of God. People need the entire Bible preached to them, not just the gentle parts that tickle their ears and make them feel good on their way to hell.

We have people in the churches fornicating, committing adultery, practicing gayness, sodomy, pornography, sex trafficking with children, and all types of lust and perversion. No one is telling them to repent and stop it now. No one is preaching that sex outside of marriage is wrong. No one is telling them that the people of Sodom and Gomorrah were going after strange flesh. Men were having sex with men and women with women. They were also having sex with beasts and group sex.

God did not create them to be that way and then rain fire and brimstone upon them. They chose to use their entire body, soul, and spirit to rebel against God and the traditional marriage that God had set up. God gave Eve to Adam. God did not give Steve to Adam. God gave Eve to Adam. He didn't give Eve to Sharon. This wickedness caused the judgment of God to come on Sodom and Gomorrah. Even the children were sexually perverted. The herdsmen who moved with Lot to Sodom, and their families, also turned to the sins of Sodom. None of them or their families were saved when God destroyed Sodom. There are many scriptures in both the Old Testament and the New Testament that testify that traditional marriage between a man, (born a man) and a woman (born a woman) is God's idea of marriage. Nothing else is acceptable with God.

Church God's Way

God ordained marriage to reflect Christ's relationship to His Church. Ephesians 5:22-31 says, "Wives, submit yourselves unto your own husbands, as unto the Lord. For the husband is the head of the wife, even as Christ is the head of the church: and he is the savior of the body. Therefore as the church is subject unto Christ, so let the wives be to their own husbands in every thing. Husbands, love your wives, even as Christ loved the church, and gave himself for it: That he might sanctify and cleanse it with the washing of the water by the word. That he might present it to himself a glorious church, not having spot, or wrinkle, or any such thing; but that it should be holy and without blemish. So ought men to love their wives as their own bodies. He that loves his wife, loves himself. For no man ever yet hated his own flesh; but nourishes and cherishes it, even as the Lord the church." I am One Hundred Percent Sure that God's Traditional Marriage is the Only Marriage that God Recognizes and Will Accept. Anything else is not of God and is sin.

We have people in churches addicted to drugs, alcohol, cigarettes, lust, etc…Many are broken-hearted, wounded, abused, mis-treated, discouraged, depressed, angry, hurting, tormented by demons with hearts filled with rage, unforgiveness, and misery. When will God, The Holy Spirit/Holy Ghost be able to come back into the churches and minister to HIS PEOPLE FREELY? When will the Pastors STOP TRYING TO CONTROL, MANIPULATE, and Dominate the sheep? When will Pastors, Ministers, Reverends, Priests, stop Quenching and Grieving God the Holy Spirit? When will they STOP MAKING PEOPLE WORSHIP THEM, OVER GOD? WHEN WILL THEY STOP TRYING TO COVER EVERYONE AND CONTROL EVERYONE AND EVERYTHING? They practice witchcraft and need to REPENT.

Isaiah Chapter 30 verses 1-2 " Woe, to the rebellious children, saith the Lord, that take counsel, but not of me; and that cover with a covering, but not of my spirit, that they may add sin to sin; That walk to go down into Egypt, and have not asked at my mouth, to strengthen themselves in the strength of Pharoah, and to trust in the shadow of Egypt." God Himself must be the covering of the mature sheep. The Holy Spirit of God must be the One Directing their steps to fulfill Father God's Will for their lives. Pastors NEED TO STAND DOWN AND STOP TRYING TO CONTROL MATURE SHEEP AND THEIR WALK

WITH The HOLY SPIRIT. Once a person has matured, can hear the Voice of God, has surrendered to the Will of God, the pastor needs to let them go to follow GOD THE HOLY SPIRIT'S LEADING INTO FATHER GOD'S WILL AND PURPOSE FOR THEIR LIFE. Yes, baby Christians should be discipled and learn the Word of God. BUT there comes a time when they are Spiritually Grown Up and are fully accountable to God the Holy Spirit to do God's Will and purpose for their lives. They Must Obey God over man. They must serve God who has called them into the ministries that HE has trained them to do.

Personally, if I had listened to the Pastor over God the Holy Spirit, all the work the Lord used me to do and accomplish in Kenya, Columbia, Venezuela, Aruba, etc…would not have been done. I would have sat with Jesus and hung my head as He showed me all that HE had for me to do that was not done because I listened to a pastor instead of listening to God the Holy Spirit. I would have been ashamed as I realized I failed the Lord. IT would have been horrifying to see all the souls that went to hell because I refused to obey God and do the crusades He had called me to do. I would have been horrified to see all the people who kept unforgiveness in their heart and didn't get into heaven because I didn't get a chance to preach against harboring it.

IF I had relied on any church to sponsor the mission trips, I would still be waiting to go. People don't understand that God doesn't look at the outward appearance, God sees the hearts. Churches would have chosen a black man to do ministry in Africa, not a white woman. The Azusa Revival began with a black man who had been looked down upon, BUT GOD CHOSE HIM.

Churches look down upon anyone who didn't attend their "DENOMINATIONAL BIBLE COLLEGE." Someone who God the Holy Spirit taught the Word to, Who God Himself Called, trained up, anointed, appointed, empowered, and set apart for Himself, is devalued, their gifts are refused and denied, the Pastors try to sit on them, discourage them, smother them, refuse to release them into the ministries the Lord has Called them to, and imprison them inside their Church Buildings to serve them, instead of being FREE TO FOLLOW THE HOLY SPIRIT INTO THE WILL OF FATHER GOD. Then we wonder why the world is so wicked, people aren't reached with the Gospel of Christ, evangelists aren't released to Evangelize, teachers can't get the pulpit to Teach, Prophets of God can't prophesy, Apostles can't function in the local Churches because Pastors Want to Control and Cover Everyone with a witchcraft spirit of Diotrephes (The Third Epistle of John verses 9-11). Diotrephes wouldn't let the Apostles Preach or Teach in his church. He spoke against them with malicious words, would not receive them, and threatened to throw anyone out of his church that would have received them. As a result, the brethren in that Church couldn't grow spiritually the way God wanted them to grow. Even today, that wicked demonic spirit of Diotrephes is functioning, especially in the churches here in the Northeast. The lie that seeped into the Churches in the 1970's goes like this, "Everyone Has TO BE Under A Pastor". This lie has opened the door to a witchcraft spirit, Pastor Control of mature believers, Pastors ability to quench the giftings and spiritual walk of mature believers, Pastors ability to Control Everyone and deny the other four folds of ministry the ability to grow the sheep, use their giftings, and be led by the Holy Spirit of God. The devil has used Pastors mightily to curtail, stop or hinder the ministries that God has Called into being. These money loving, building project loving, materialistic, so called Pastors need to REPENT. They will be ashamed when they have to give an account to Jesus for all the brethren they have hurt, all the giftings in the brethren they refused and denied, all the ministries that never were able to exist because they blocked them, all the evangelical crusades that never happened because they fought the Evangelists, all the cities that were never REVIVED because they refused to release and cooperate with the Evangelists in the outreaches, etc...

Bible Colleges need to STOP teaching pastors to leave a gulf between themselves and the sheep, stop trying to Control everyone and cover everyone, stop building physical buildings that Jesus is not coming back for, stop running the Churches like a business, stop buying country clubs, apartment buildings to rent out, stop buying condos, stop trying to increase in material goods, AND START REACHING THE SOULS SO THEY CAN GO TO HEAVEN. REPENT OF YOUR MATERIALISTIC WICKEDNESS, LOVE OF MONEY, AND WORLDLY DESIRES. Love the Lord Jesus Christ, Love the Sheep, Feed the Sheep the Word of God and let others come and Feed Them Also. Let all the five folds impart their lessons and instruction to the sheep. Welcome God the Holy Spirit into your Church and let Him have the Freedom to Minister to His People. HE knows what they need, YOU DON'T.

Stop the Ridiculous Intellectualism that doesn't prosper anyone. Stop teaching sermon preparation classes that are VOID OF GOD THE HOLY SPIRIT. Intellectual Messages are DEAD< MAN-MADE MESSAGES that cannot get into the hearts and lives of the hearers. ONLY A HOLY SPIRIT FILLED MESSAGE WILL BE ABLE TO PENETRATE THE DARKNESS AND REACH THE EYES, EARS, MINDS, AND HEARTS OF THE HEARERS, AND BRING CHANGE. I will address this issue further in a Chapter of this book entitled, "Sermon Preparation God's Way."

I have two coverings. God the Holy Spirit and my Husband Paul are my coverings. I am an Evangelist called by God Himself. I am answerable to God Himself and my Husband Paul. The order of my life is this (1) God Himself, (2) my Husband Paul (3) Family (4) other people including Pastors. No Pastor will ever be my God or my Number 1. But many of them have tried to put me under them instead of under the Holy Spirit. Many have tried to put me, an Evangelist both to the lost and to the Body of Christ, under their board of elders (laypeople) that are supposed to serve the pastor. They are not in the Five Fold Calling of God. When asked where is it in the Bible that an Evangelist, Called and Trained by God Himself, has to submit to a board of elders, we were told, "Never Mind That." I said, "Never Mind The Bible?" Then the senior pastor began screaming that if we refused to put our ministry under his board of elders, we could no longer teach the men and women's Bible Studies, we could no longer be members of his church, and we should leave in haste. Needless to say, WE LEFT AND WILL NEVER GO BACK THERE.

This is the Witchcraft/Controlling/Manipulating Spirit that is operating in most of the Churches here in the Wappinger Falls, Poughkeepsie, Newburgh, area of N.Y. as well as in the island of Aruba calling itself (PROTOCOL). Many mature believers have recognized that it is a demonic spirit. They have left the Churches to worship and fellowship and study the Word of God at home, rather than sit under a witchcraft spirit that is in these Pastors. Not everyone who has left the "Traditional Churches is Backslidden". For the last four years, my Husband Paul, my Son Brian, a family friend and I have been worshipping, studying the Word of God, praying for each other, etc…at home. We also worship the Lord through the week, read scriptures, seek the Lord in prayer and are on several prayer calls to pray for our Nation. We, like many others, are Not Backslidden. We are disgusted with "Church As Usual."

Once a believer is rooted and grounded in the Word of God, can hear the voice of Holy Spirit and be led by Him, the pastor needs to stop trying to CONTROL THEIR WALK WITH GOD. The Holy Spirit is God, not the Pastor. IF you have been called by God to do something, and your Pastor won't let you obey God, you need to change Churches. For many years I attended a church that taught, "A woman can't preach. A woman can't teach men." The Lord had called me, trained me, chosen me, and appointed into the office of Evangelist not only to the lost souls but to the Body of Christ, to break the nonsense out of the churches. I couldn't stay in that Church. The Lord led me to leave.

I hear many people speak against (Church Hoppers), but there are times the Lord Himself will lead you out of a place where you cannot grow or use the Giftings that He has Given You. You are accountable to God to use the talents He has equipped you with to glorify Him. When you sit with Jesus, at the Judgment Seat of Christ, and HE looks at your life, You will either hear Him say, "Well Done My Good and Faithful Servant," or you will sit ashamed that you never fulfilled His Call and purpose for your life. You will be ashamed that you hid the talents He gave you and did nothing and accomplished nothing. I want to hear Him say, "Well done." Or just see Him Smile at me.

In the natural realm, once a child becomes an adult, they leave home to attend college, move out, find a job, get a skill, have a new life outside of the home they grew up in. They leave their parents, maybe their neighborhood and live a separate, mature life. WE cannot keep them babies, control them, hold them back from experiencing life, make them dependent upon us forever, etc… As it is in the natural realm, it is in the spiritual realm. Spiritually mature believers must be released to follow the leading of God the Holy Spirit into the will of Father God for their lives. Even in the Book of Acts, Churches prayed over the evangelists, the apostles, the teachers of the Word etc…and sent them out. They did not lock them in the four walls of the church and refuse to release them into what the Holy Spirit was calling them to do and accomplish. Mature believers must be released into the world to bring the Gospel of Jesus Christ to the lost. Souls are in the balance.

While in Kenya, the Holy Spirit used me to preach against the demonic tribalisms and show the people, from God's Word, that once they receive Jesus Christ as their Savior and Lord, they all belong to the Tribe of Judah. They disconnected themselves from the demonic, witchdoctor, tribes, and spiritually linked themselves into the Tribe of Judah. Pastors wrote me and said, "Now my people are in unity. There is no longer the tribal divisions. They love each other more, and love me more. Thank You for coming here."

Many repented and were delivered from demonic circumcisions that were done on them by witchdoctors, cuttings, oaths, covenants, etc… Many were in the churches, but had not repented of the demonic spiritual rituals, etc.. that they engaged in before they came to Jesus Christ. These things had to be dealt with, repented of, and broken off of them by the Blood of Jesus. They could not grow in Christ while the devil still had them by the foot.

Romans 8:14 "For as many as are led by the Spirit of God, they are the sons of God." Then who are those led by the Pastor, their flesh, or their intellect? Are they really of God? The most important thing is to be led by the Spirit of God. He knows the Father's Will for each person's life.

Isn't it time that Pastors, Ministers, Reverends, and Priests preach against the brutal murders of innocent unborn human babies? (Jeremiah 1:4, Psalm 139:13-17, and many other scriptures) show that God forms babies in their mother's womb according to His Divine Plan and Purpose for their lives. To rip them apart, poison them with salt, or stab them through the head when they are pulled out feet first, is a HORRIBLE DEMONIC CRIME. How anyone can claim to be a Christian (A CHRIST FOLLOWER) and be for MURDERING BABIES THAT JESUS CHRIST IS FORMING in the womb. They are no more Christian than Satan is. SATAN IS THE LIAR AND MURDERER FROM THE BEGINNING. THESE WICKED PASTORS NEED TO GET OUT OF GOD's PULPITS. THEY SERVE SATAN, NOT GOD. They are for sacrificing babies to Baal and other false gods, shedding innocent blood in our land and bringing a curse on America. May the Lord Remove These Wicked people out of the pulpits of America and replace them with God Fearing, Bible Believing, Holy Spirit filled Pastors who will preach the entire Bible.

Church God's Way

Margret Sanger was a KKK Member. I saw an interesting movie entitled "Hillary's America." In the movie there was Margaret Sanger sitting with group of KKK clan members with hoods over their heads discussing how they could kill black people. Margaret Sanger, the one who began Planned Parenthood said something like this, "We can't hang black people from trees anymore but we can put abortion clinics in all the black neighborhoods and decrease the population of blacks that way. Sadly four out of every five black babies are aborted. The movie showed Planned Parenthood, paying black pastors to lie to the black young women telling them that abortion wasn't a sin against God, it was ok. The movie only was shown two days in our local Regal Cinema. We rushed in to see it.

Isn't it time that REAL, GOD LED, HOLY GHOST PASTORS, PREACH WITH PASSION IN THE PULPITS OF AMERICA again? Isn't it time that the ear tickling, luke - warm, nonsense preachers step down, and REAL PREACHERS DO THE PREACHING OF THE WORD OF GOD.

Signs, Wonders, and Miracles accompany the Preaching of The Word of God. IF there are no signs, wonders, and miracles happening in your church, maybe your pastor isn't preaching the Word of God. Read God's Word, study God's Word, memorize God's Word, understand what Jesus Christ did for you on the cross. Get to know Him by reading the Gospels. Study the Word of God so you will understand right from wrong and good from evil.

People today are calling good, (Evil), and evil "Good." If you listen to the wicked media, Hollywood, public opinion, tabloids, social media, chat rooms, you will be pulled into a lot of things that God says are evil. Read the Word of God for yourself. Then you will know if that man or woman in the pulpit is preaching and teaching truth or error. Weigh everything you hear by, "What does God's Word say." Then the devil won't be able to deceive you through any fake preacher, fake prophet, fake teacher, fake ear tickler, the secular news, public opinion, CNN, Disney, MSNBC, ABC, etc…

Isn't it time that Pastors Preach against Sexual Sin? Isn't it time that the SEXUAL SINS OF FORNICATION, ADULTERY, PORNOGRAPHY, GAYNESS, LESBIANISM, RAPE, INCEST, MOLESTATION, SEX TRAFFICKING OF CHILDREN,

TRANSGENDER, ETC…IS PREACHED AGAINST FROM THE PULPITS OF AMERICA. Isn't it time that we stand on the word of God and preach the whole Bible. Isn't it time we preach about Sodom and Gomorrah and the surrounding cities – how they went after strange flesh and God destroyed them. The fact that they were so sexually wicked they wanted to rape the angels of God. Even when God smote them with blindness, they were still trying to get the door open to rape the angels.

Isn't it time that we preach the whole Bible, not only the Love of God, but the judgment of God upon the ungodly. Many people today believe the lies of the devil. We will cover the lies in one of the chapters of this book to expose them and bring people to repentance for believing them rather than God's Word of Truth.

Bible Colleges need to stop being intellectual institutions that operate in the flesh rather than in the Holy Spirit of God. They need to teach future Pastors HOW TO HEAR THE VOICE OF GOD, HOW TO FULLY SURRENDER THEIR OWN LIVES AND WILLS TO THE LORDSHIP OF JESUS CHRIST, HOW TO BE BAPTIZED IN THE HOLY GHOST, HOW TO BE LED BY THE HOLY SPIRIT, HOW TO SEE THE SPIRITUAL/SUPERNATURAL EVENTS THAT HAPPENED IN THE WORD OF GOD; HAPPEN IN THEIR CHURCHES, HOW TO ENCOURAGE THE SHEEP TO USE THEIR GIFTS, even if it means they leave your church to begin a ministry God is calling them to, HOW TO RELEASE MATURE BELIEVERS TO BE LED BY THE SPIRIT OF GOD? ISN'T IT TIME? Isn't it Time you stop building buildings and really BUILD THE BODY OF CHRIST, REACH THE LOST, RAISE THE DEAD, TAKE THIS WORLD BACK TO THE GOSPEL OF JESUS CHRIST? ISN'T IT TIME YOU STOP TRYING TO COVER EVERYONE AND LET GOD HIMSELF BE THEIR COVERING? ISN'T IT TIME YOU STOP TRYING TO BE GOD AND LET THE REAL GOD BE GOD to the BODY OF CHRIST? HE DIED FOR THEM. HE DESERVES THEIR OBEDIENCE, THEIR WORSHIP, THEIR SERVICE. LET THEM GO TO SERVE THE LORD WITH ALL THEIR BEINGS. LET THEM HEAR JESUS SAY IN THAT DAY, "WELL DONE MY GOOD AND FAITHFUL SERVANT," AMEN!

The real heart of a Pastor should be that the sheep grow up, stand strong in the faith and fully accomplish God's Will and purpose for their lives. A real Pastor will want the sheep to accomplish more than they have, in advancing the Kingdom of God on planet earth. A fake pastor will preach nonsense, keep the sheep as babies, never encourage them to use their gifts or really serve God. They will keep the sheep under their control so they can pay off their own building projects and advance their own will and worldly, materialistic kingdoms and ego trips. Are you a real one or a fake one? God Knows You!

CHAPTER ONE
ARE YOU REALLY SAVED OR DO YOU JUST HAVE RELIGION?

There are many people who attend a church every Sunday, try to lead "Good Lives", try to be "Good People", try to earn their way to heaven by doing what they believe to be "Good Works", and try to please God by their own way and means. IF we could do enough "Good Works" to earn our way to heaven, to atone for the bad things we have done, to make ourselves right with Father God; then Jesus Christ would not have had to leave heaven, take the form of a human being, suffer on a cross for your sins and mine, die, resurrect from the dead and ascend back into heaven to intercede for us. He would not have had to be the Sacrificial Lamb of God, the Perfect Lamb of God, who would be slain to redeem His Fallen Creation back to Himself, by His Own Sinless Blood.

John 14:6 Jesus said, "I am the way the truth, and the life; no man comes to the Father but by Me." In John 14:1-3, Jesus speaks of mansions in heaven and tells his disciples that he would go and prepare a place for them, come again, and receive them unto himself.

It is only those who receive Jesus Christ as their personal Savior and Lord in their heart and life who will be in heaven. People who worship other gods, and other religions, will not be in heaven. Jesus is THE WAY, THE TRUTH, AND THE LIFE. NO MAN CAN COME TO THE FATHER BUT BY JESUS.

If we look at Revelation Chapter 7 verses 9-17, There is a great multitude of people up in heaven; of every nation, kindred, people, and tongue, standing before the throne and before Jesus (the Lamb) clothed in white robes with palms in their hands. In verse 14, we see that "These are they which came out of great tribulation, and have washed their robes, and made them white in the blood of the Lamb.

This multitude were all believers in Jesus Christ from every nation, people group, kindred and tongue. There were NO OTHER GOD WORSHIPPERS, NO OCCULT PRACTICES, NO GREEK MYTH WORSHIPPERS, NO FAKE RELIGION WORSHIPPERS, ETC… IN HEAVEN. Only believers in Jesus Christ were up there. Their sins had been washed clean in the Blood of Jesus Christ shed for them on the cross. Because they had repented of their sins and received Jesus Christ as their Savior and Lord into their hearts and lives; the Blood of God shed for them on the cross was applied to them, they were cleansed from their sins, forgiven by Father God, and were allowed into heaven.

The crazy idea that "there are many ways to get right with God", has deceived many people. Many are in hell right now because they believed the lie that anything goes. They believed the lie that religion could save them, instead of a real, heart to heart relationship with Jesus (God Himself). Religion did not save the religious leaders, in the time of Christ, who trusted in their religion and refused to believe on the Savior, Jesus Christ Himself.

Jesus said to the religious Pharisees and Saducees, in John 5:39-40, "Search the scriptures; for in them you think you have eternal life: and they are they which testify of me. And you won't come to me, that you might have life."

> In John 5:46-47, Jesus said, "For had you believed Moses, you would have believed me: for he wrote of me. But if you believe not his writings, how shall you believe my words?"
>
> In John 8:56-59, Jesus said to the Jews, "'Your father Abraham rejoiced to see my day: and he saw it, and was glad." Then the Jews said, "You are not yet fifty years old, and have you seen Abraham?" Jesus said, "BEFORE ABRAHAM WAS, I AM." Then they took up stones to cast at him. Jesus was telling them that he is God; that he existed before Abraham ever was. That is why they wanted to stone him.
>
> In Matthew 22: 23-32, the religious Sadducees approached Jesus and told him that a woman had been married to one

brother and he died, the next brother married her, the next, etc… Seven of them had her to wife. They asked Jesus, " in the resurrection, whose wife will she be?" In verses 29-32 Jesus answered, "You err not knowing the scriptures, nor the power of God. For in the resurrection they neither marry, nor are given in marriage, but are as the angels of God in heaven. But as touching the resurrection of the dead, have you not read that which was spoken unto you by God, saying I am the God of Abraham, and the God of Isaac, and the God of Jacob? God is not the God of the dead, but of the living."

Notice here that Jesus did not say that human beings would turn into angels. He said human beings would not marry. The angels in heaven do not marry. Also notice that Jesus told them that Abraham, Isaac, and Jacob were alive, not dead.

In John Chapter 11:1-46, Jesus raised a dead man named Lazarus back to life after he had been dead four days and laid in a tomb. In verse 24, Martha, Lazarus' Sister said to Jesus, "I know that he shall rise again in the resurrection at the last day." Jesus said to her, "I AM THE RESURRECTION AND THE LIFE; HE THAT BELIEVES IN ME, THOUGH HE WERE DEAD, YET SHALL HE LIVE: AND WHOSOEVER LIVES AND BELIEVES IN ME, SHALL NEVER DIE."

Jesus went to the tomb, had them remove the stone away, and called, "Lazarus , come forth." And he that was dead came forth, bound hand and feet with graveclothes; and his face was bound about with a napkin. Jesus said to them, "Loose him, and let him go."

This event was done in front of the disciples. They saw Jesus raise a dead man back to life. They knew that if they died, while serving Jesus, Jesus could raise them up again too. They didn't have to fear death because the Author of All Life could give them new life again.

Here is a scripture that proves that Jesus always was and is God. Take a look at Daniel Chapter 3. Three Jews renamed Shadrach, Meshach, and Abednego refused to worship the image of gold that

King Nebuchadnezzar had set up. All of the princes, the governors, the captains, the judges. The treasurers, the counsellors, the sheriffs, and all the rulers of the provinces were supposed to bow and worship the image when they heard the musicians play. In verse 6, it says that whoever would not fall down and worship the golden image would be cast into the midst of a burning fiery furnace.

Chaldeans came near and accused the Jews of not worshipping the image. In verse 13, King Nebuchadnezzar gave the Jews a chance to bow down and worship the idol he had made. HE told them if they refused to worship the idol, they would be cast into the fiery furnace ; and who is that God that shall deliver you out of my hands?

> In verse 16-17, the Jews said, " If it be so, our God whom we serve is able to deliver us from the fiery furnace, and he will deliver us out of your hand, O king. But if not, be it known unto you O King, that we will not serve your gods, nor worship the golden image which you have set up."

The King was full of fury and commanded the furnace to be heated seven times hotter than it normally was heated. Then he commanded the most mighty men to bind the Jews and cast them into the midst of the fiery furnace. Because the furnace was exceedingly hot, the flame of the fire slew the king's mighty men who threw the Jews into the furnace.

The Jews fell into the fiery furnace. The king was amazed and said, "Did we not throw three men bound into the furnace in the midst of the fire?" The king's men said, "True O king." The king said, "I see four men loose, walking in the midst of the fire, and they have no hurt; and the form of the fourth is like the Son of God."

A fully grown Jesus Christ, as a man, was walking in the fiery furnace, before he ever was a seed planted in Mary's womb. He appeared as the fourth man in the furnace. Jesus Always Was. He protected the Jews in the furnace. The fire had no power over them. Their hair was not singed, neither was their clothing burnt, neither did they smell of smoke. It was a Miracle.

The part of the Godhead who walked with Adam and Eve in the Garden of Eden, was Jesus Christ. No one can see the face of Father God and live in our human bodies. The Holy Spirit is a Spirit. It was Jesus Christ who walked with Adam and Eve in the garden.

If you study John Chapter I, the Bible makes it very clear that Jesus Christ is God, that all things were made by Him, that He is the Light, and the Life of men, and that HE was in the world and the world was made by Him. HE came to the Jews first (his own) and they received Him not. But as many as received him, he gave the power to become the sons of God, even to them who believe on His Name. The Word is Jesus. HE became flesh and dwelt among us , and we beheld his glory, the glory of the only begotten of the Father, full of grace and truth. Notice that Jesus is begotten of the Father (not a created being).

> I Timothy 3:16 "And without controversy, great is the mystery of godliness: God was manifest in the flesh, justified in the Spirit, seen of angels, preached unto the Gentiles believed on in the world, received up into glory."

> Hebrews 7:1-3 "For this Melchisedec, king of Salem, priest of the most high God, who met Abraham returning from the slaughter of the kings, and blessed him; To whom also Abraham gave a tenth part of all, first being by interpretation King of righteousness, and after that also King of Salem, which is King of peace; Without father, without mother, without descent, having neither beginning of days, nor end of life; but made like unto the Son of God; abides a priest continually."

The point I am making here is that Jesus Always was, that He is God, that he created everything, that there was never a time when Jesus Wasn't, He was God, He is God, and He always will be God

> Isaiah 7:14 was prophesied many generations before Jesus came. "Therefore the Lord himself shall give you a sign, Behold, a virgin shall conceive, and bear a son, and shall call his name Immanuel." Immanuel means, "God With Us."

> Isaiah 9:6-7 "For unto us a child is born, unto us a son is given; and the government shall be upon his shoulder: and his name shall be called Wonderful, Counsellor, The mighty God, The everlasting Father, The Prince of Peace, OF the increase of his government and peace there shall be no end, upon the throne of David, and upon his kingdom, to order it, and to establish it with judgment and with justice from henceforth even for ever. The zeal of the Lord of hosts will perform this."

We see here that a virgin would be used to conceive a son who would be God in the flesh, dwelling among us. IT had to be a virgin of the lineage of King David, a Jew, that would be impregnated with the Messiah. Many people forget that both Joseph and Mary were Jews. The first disciples were Jews. The writers of the scrolls were Jews. The writers of both the Old Testament and the New Testament were Jewish holy men of God, as they were moved by the Holy Ghost.

IT was NOT JOSEPH'S SPERM NOR MARY'S EGG THAT BIRTHED JESUS. Jesus was Never an egg of the woman. He was the SEED OF THE WOMAN WHO WOULD CRUSH THE SERPENT'S HEAD.

> Luke 1:27-35 an angel appeared to Mary and told her she would conceive in her womb and bring forth Jesus. Mary asked "How shall this be, seeing I know not a man?" In verse 35, the angel said, "The Holy Ghost shall come upon you, and the power of the Highest shall overshadow you; therefore also that holy thing which shall be born of you shall be called the Son of God."

The Seed of the Word of God (Jesus), was implanted in Mary's womb by God the Holy Ghost. That is the reason Jesus spoke of the Parable of the Sower. The Sower sowed the Gospel of Jesus Christ unto Salvation. Some fell on the way side and the birds ate it. Some fell on rocky ground and didn't get rooted in deep. Some fell on thorny ground. The cares of this world choked the word and they became unfruitful. Some seeds fell on fertile ground that bore fruit.

People have a difficult time understanding the Trinity. We are a Trinity. We have a physical body, a soul (our emotions, feelings, will, etc…) and we have a spirit (our heart area-ability to love and receive love). Body, soul, and spirit equals one person. The Father, Son, and Holy Spirit equals one God.

The link between the Father and the Son is the Holy Spirit. It is the Holy Spirit who links the believer to the Godhead. The following scriptures emphasize the truth of this:

> Romans 8:6-9 "For to be carnally minded is death; but to be spiritually minded is life and peace, Because the carnal mind is enmity against God; for it is not subject to the law of God, neither indeed can be. So then they that are in the flesh cannot please God.

But you are not in the flesh, but in the Spirit, if so be that the Spirit of God dwell in you. Now if any man have not the Spirit of Christ, he is none of his." We see here that the Spirit of God the Father and the Spirit of Jesus Christ is the same Holy Spirit.

Also notice, that if any man does not have the Holy Spirit, he doesn't belong to God. Religion doesn't give anyone the Holy Spirit. It is repenting of your sins and receiving Jesus Christ into your heart and life, as your Savior and Lord, that gets the Holy Spirit into your heart. Until a person really receives Jesus Christ, they do not have the Spirit of God within them.

> Romans 8:10-14 "And if Christ be in you, the body is dead because of sin; but the Spirit is life because of righteousness. But if the Spirit of him that raised up Jesus from the dead dwell in you, he that raised up Christ from the dead shall also quicken your mortal bodies by his Spirit that dwells in you. Therefore, brethren, we are debtors, not to the flesh, to live after the flesh. For if you live after the flesh, you shall die: but if you through the Spirit (Holy Spirit) do mortify the deeds of the body, you shall live. For as many as are led by the Spirit of God are the sons of God."

Those who are not led by the Spirit of God are not the sons of God. God knows those who really belong to Him. They have God's Holy Spirit living in their hearts.

> Romans 8:15-17 "For you have not received the spirit of bondage again to fear; but you have received the Spirit of adoption, whereby we cry, Abba, Father. The Spirit Himself bears witness with our spirit, that we are the children of God. And if children, then heirs; heirs of God, and joint-heirs with Christ; if so be that we suffer with him, that we may be glorified together."

IF a person does not have the Holy Spirit living in their heart, they are not a child of God. They are not a member of God's Family. They have not repented of their sins and believed that Jesus Christ died on the cross for them personally and rose again.

> John 10:26-30 Jesus said, "You believe not, because you are not of my sheep, as I said unto you. My sheep hear my voice, and I know them, and they follow me; And I give unto them eternal life; and they shall never perish, neither shall any man pluck them our of my hand. My Father, which gave them to me, is greater than all; and no man is able to pluck them out of my Father's hand. I and my Father are one."

Notice here that Jesus is speaking of a relationship with His sheep, not a religion. He speaks to His sheep. They hear his voice and follow where He leads them. HE gives them eternal life and they shall never perish. No one can pluck them out of His hand. But they can fall into error and choose to walk away by their own will (Backsliding).

> I John 5:11-13 "And this is the record, that God has given to us eternal life, and this life is in His Son. He that has the Son has life; and he that has not the Son of God has not life. These things have I written unto you that believe on the name of the Son of God; that you may know that you have eternal life, and that you may believe on the name of the Son of God."

It will not matter what "Religion you were", what "Religious Denomination you were", "Where you went to church," "How many good works you did", "That you were a good person", "How much money you gave to a church," "How many religious classes you attended," "What religious degrees you possess," "How many trophies you won," etc… All these things will not get you into heaven. We all Need the Blood of Jesus to wash our sins clean. IF we steal a pen, we are a thief in the sight of God. If we tell a fib, we are a liar in the sight of God. If we have ever loved anyone or anything more than God, we have broken the first commandment. The Bible says we have all sinned and fallen short of the Glory of God. The ONLY PERFECT PERSON WHO EVER WALKED THIS EARTH IS JESUS CHRIST.

If we have the Son of God, His Holy Blood has washed our sin clean and we are forgiven. IF we reject the Son of God, we reject the Holy Blood shed for us on the cross and have to pay for our own sins in hell. The Main Thing the disciples Preached was THE CROSS OF CHRIST, THE GOSPEL OF JESUS CHRIST UNTO SALVATION. Many pastors, preachers, priests, ministers, and reverends, have never repented of their sins, do not personally know Jesus Christ in their hearts and lives as their Savior and Lord, and do not have the Holy Spirit (Holy Ghost), dwelling in them.

There are entire churches of people that do not have Jesus Christ living in their hearts and lives. They have "Religion" but not a Real Relationship with Jesus Christ Himself. They must be reached with the Gospel of Jesus Christ.

> I John 1: 8-10 "IF we say we have no sin, we deceive ourselves, and the truth is not in us. IF we confess our sins, he is faithful and just to forgive us our sins, and to cleanse us from all unrighteousness. IF we say that we have not sinned, we call God a liar, and his word is not in us."

> Romans 5:8-10 "But God commended his love toward us, in that, while we were yet sinners, Christ died for us. Much more then, being now justified by his blood, we shall be saved from wrath through him."

Notice here that Father God sent Jesus to die for us because He loves us. Through the blood of Jesus Christ, we are saved from wrath. Only the Blood of Jesus Christ can save a person from hell. There is no other sacrifice that we can offer to atone for our sins. There is no other name given among men by which we must be saved other that the name of Jesus. (Acts 4:9-12).

People tend to quote John 3:16-17 "For God so loved the world, that he gave his only begotten Son, that whosoever believes in him, should not perish; but have everlasting life. For God sent not His Son into the world to condemn the world, but that the world through him might be saved." Jesus is a Gift that Father God gave to the world. A gift has to be accepted by you in order to belong to you. IF you refuse to accept the gift of eternal life through Jesus Christ, you will die in your sins and have to pay for them yourself.

John 3:18-21 "HE that believes on him is not condemned: but he that believes not is condemned already, because he has not believed in the name of the only begotten Son of God. And this is the condemnation, that light is come into the world, and men loved darkness rather than light; because their deeds were evil. For every one that does evil hates the light, neither comes to the light, lest his deeds should be reproved. But he that does truth comes to the light , that his deeds may be made manifest, that they are wrought in God."

Have you ever repented of your sins and asked Jesus Christ to come into your heart and life and Save you? If not, you need to do it today. Also, you need to preach the Cross of Christ in your congregations and make sure the people know Jesus Christ and have eternal life through Christ, not eternal hell. Just pray this prayer:

"Father God, I am a sinner. I am sorry for my sins. I believe that Jesus Christ died on that cross to save me. Lord Jesus, come into my heart and life now. Be my Savior and my Lord. I receive you and ask that you will help me to know you more. Lead me into your will and purpose for my life. I surrender my life and will to you. Use this life to your glory. Thank you Jesus. Amen."

If you prayed that prayer, you have received Jesus, Father God who sent Him, and the Holy Ghost (Holy Spirit) who now dwells in your heart. You are a child of God by your faith in Christ. Read the Bible. The Gospel of John is a great place to start. Jesus will reveal Himself as the Good Shepherd, The Way, the Truth, the Life, the Door of the Sheep, the Light of the World, the Bread of Life, the Resurrection and the Life, and many other things. HE Loves You. The Angels in heaven rejoice over every sinner who repents and receives Jesus.

SURRENDER YOUR ENTIRE LIFE TO THE LORDSHIP OF JESUS

People in the Body of Christ wonder why they walk in defeat instead of Victory, why they go around the same mountain over and over again and why they keep going around in circles. Many quote a part of the scripture in Revelation Chapter 12, but leave out a vital and necessary part of it. IF they leave out the third part, they cannot overcome the devil in their lives. Lets examine this scripture.

> Revelation 12:7-9 "And there was war in heaven: Michael and his angels fought against the dragon; and the dragon fought and his angels, And prevailed not, neither was their place found any more in heaven, And the great dragon was cast out, that old serpent, called the Devil, and Satan, which deceived the whole world. He was cast out into the earth, and his angels were cast out with him."

WE see here that the devil, Satan, is called a serpent, and a dragon. Many Christians foolishly buy dragon statues and open their homes up to Satan and his demons. By having certain objects in your home, you could be welcoming demonic attacks. I will cover this in another chapter.

> Revelation 12:10-11 "And I heard a loud voice saying in heaven, Now is come salvation, and strength, and the kingdom of our God and the power of his Christ: for the accuser of our brethren is cast down, which accused them before our God day and night. "And they overcame him by the blood of the Lamb, and by the word of their testimony; and they loved not their lives unto the death." I hear many Christians say, "We overcame Satan by the Blood of the Lamb and the Word of our testimony." They forget the third part, "And they loved not their lives unto the death."

Any part of our lives that we refuse to surrender fully to the lordship of Jesus Christ, is under the Lordship of Self and Satan. If we are the Lord of our Life, Jesus Isn't.

Galatians 2:20, the disciple Paul said, "I am crucified with Christ nevertheless *I live; yet not I, but Christ lives in me, and the life which I now live in the flesh I live by the faith of the Son of God, who loved me, and gave himself for me."* Paul was saying, I am dead to myself, my own will, my own purposes, my own plans, and my own agendas. It is Jesus Christ living His Life in me and through me.

Mark 8:34-38 Jesus said ," Whosoever will come after me, let him deny himself, and take up his cross and follow me. For whosoever will save his life will lose it; but whosoever shall lose his life for my sake and the gospel's, the same shall save it. For what shall it profit a man, if he shall gain the whole world , and lose his own soul? Or what shall a man give in exchange for his soul? Whosoever therefore shall be ashamed of me and of my words in this adulterous and sinful generation; of him also shall the Son of Man be ashamed, when he comes in the glory of his Father and with the holy angels."

Jesus is telling us to deny ourselves and follow Him. IF we are following Jesus, Jesus must be the one leading our lives, not us. HE must be the Lord of Our Lives in order for us to fulfill the Father's Will for our lives. Jesus kept telling the people, "I and the Father are one." "I came here not to do my own will but the will of my Father who sent me. "The works Jesus did, he saw the Father do."

Matthew 26:42 "And Jesus went away again the second time, and prayed, saying, "Father, if this cup may not pass away from me, except I drink it, thy will be done." Jesus surrendered his own will to do the Father's Will.

Mark 14:36 Jesus said, "Abba, Father, all things are possible unto you; take away this cup from me; nevertheless not what I will, but what you wilt."

Luke 22:41-46 "And Jesus was withdrawn from them about a stone's cast, and kneeled down, and prayed, Saying, "Father, if you be willing, remove this cup from me; nevertheless not my will, but thine be done." And there appeared an angel unto him from heaven strengthening him. And being in an agony, he prayed more earnestly: and his sweat was as it were great drops of blood falling down to the ground."

For twelve years from 1984 (when I asked Jesus into my heart) until a CBN Tour of Israel in 1996, I tried to live a good life, please the Lord, and be obedient to His Word. BUT I HAD NEVER REALLY SURRENDERED MY ENTIRE LIFE, MY CHILDREN, MY FINANCES, MY PLANS, MY AGENDAS, MY OWN WILL, AND MY OWN LIFE TO HIM.

I was in the Church of The Nations, in Israel with the CBN Tour Group. There was a flat rock, on the floor of the church, that was roped off with ropes around it. The Holy Spirit led me to go under the ropes and touch the rock. Immediately I felt the Presence of the Lord and was convicted that I had been living for me. I had not asked Him for His Will for my life. I had not fully surrendered myself and my life to Jesus. He was My Savior, but Not My Lord. I stood there repenting of living for myself. I said, "Jesus I give you my heart, my soul, my body, my emotions, my feelings, my plans, my agendas, my family, my finances, my entire life and my will. They are all yours. Use this life to Your Glory. Amen."

I was weeping, crying, surrendering, and was enveloped in His Presence. I was not aware of anything going on around me. The tour had left and headed for the bus. When they counted the people, I was missing. My Son Brian had to come back in and get me. I believe that when Jesus sweated the drops of blood, some of the blood must have fallen on that rock. It was the only flat rock in the garden.

After I surrendered fully to the Lordship of Christ, I began having dreams. I saw myself on a platform preaching to a sea of people. Shortly after that, the Lord sent me on two mission trips with Marilyn Hickey Ministries and then opened the door for me in Africa to do crusades, revivals, preach in many churches, do Pastor's Conferences, preach on Jesus is Lord Radio (Nakuru, Kenya) and Sayre (Voice of Mercy) radio and T.V. out of Eldoret, Kenya. Many souls were saved, many people were healed, and many were delivered of tribal hatred, unforgiveness, sin, depression, fear, etc…as the Holy Spirit led me into Father's Will for my life. IT is not my life. It belongs to Him. HE is Amazing.

Before the Lord began sending me on mission trips, I received a phone call from the Crisis Pregnancy Center in Poughkeepsie, N.Y. They said, "we could train you to be a crisis pregnancy counselor. We have an opening. " I said, "Let me ask the Lord if this is His Will for me."

Before the week was over, I got another phone call from TBN, who was in Fishkill, N.Y. They wanted to know if I would be a prayer call counselor for TBN, when people would call in for prayer. I said, "Let me ask the Lord if this is what He has for me."

When I prayed and asked the Lord, He said, "No." to both things. These were both good ministries. These were both Christian Ministries. BUT GOD HAD ORDAINED OTHER PEOPLE TO TAKE THOSE POSITIONS, NOT ME. If I had said YES, to either of these two "Good Things," I would have been tied up and unable to go on the Mission Trips that the Lord really had for me. Also, I would have been taking the position of someone else that the Lord had really called to those positions. This is why we should ALWAYS ASK THE LORD BEFORE WE AGREE TO ANYTHING. When I saw Marilyn Hickey on the television looking for people to go on a mission to China and the Philippines and then to Africa, the Lord sent me on both of those missions and then back to Africa myself.

One time I was in a place called Gilgal, Kenya. I asked the Lord, "Where is your Isaiah 60 Glory? Darkness is covering the earth and gross darkness the people. Why haven't you given us the Isaiah 60 Glory?" The Lord said, "ASK MY PEOPLE THIS QUESTION. HOW CAN I TRUST YOU WITH MY GLORY IF YOU WON'T TRUST ME WITH YOUR LIFE?" We need the Body of Christ to Trust Jesus with their entire lives and surrender fully to His Lordship. There are not enough people that are fully surrendered to carry His Glory into all the Nations.

Unless a person is fully surrendered to the Lordship of Jesus, they would misuse His Glory and die. If we look at the man who touched the ark on the ox cart to steady it, he died. If we look at two of Aaron's Sons who offered strange fire in the temple, fire came down from God and they died. If God were to trust a person who hasn't surrendered fully, with His Glory, they would sell miracles, glorify themselves and not God, and want people to worship them.

IF we want the Isaiah 60 Greater Glory to come upon the Body of Christ, we must trust God with our entire lives (holding nothing back) and surrender our lives and wills to Him fully.

The areas of our lives that we refuse to surrender fully, are under the Lordship of Self and Satan. We cannot defeat the devil if he controls parts of our lives, with our permission. Anything not surrendered to Jesus is not under the Lordship of Christ. We will not have total victory over the devil until we fully surrender everything to Jesus Christ. If God is in control, the devil isn't.

Jesus surrendered everything to Father God. He gave it all, paid it all, laid it all down for us. We need to be willing to lay it all down for Him. He Loved us enough to Die for Us. Do we love Him enough to live for Him- To Let Him Live Big In Us-To die to self -To possibly die physically for Jesus?

Do we love Him enough To let Him work in us and through us to continue the Father's Will on planet earth? Surrender your entire life to Jesus. Be led by the Holy Spirit and fulfill Father's Will for your life. Do It Today!

Years ago I heard a tape of Kathryn Kuhlman. She said, "If you decide to follow Jesus, it will cost you everything." At the time, I was a baby Christian and didn't understand what she meant. After many years passed, I realized the full extent of what she meant. When the Lord called me to do mission trips in Africa, six weeks at a time, 23 trips, I left my family, my house, my bed, my creature comforts, my friends, my running water, electricity, my comfort zone, my security, and everything comfortable and usual; to plunge into the unknown with the Lord. I gave up everything and surrendered everything including my entire life, safety, family, friends, finances, health, etc…into His Hands and trusted Him with it ALL.

I got on a plane, in 1997, to do crusades in Kenya, when I had never preached a message in front of people before. The Word of God was in me. The devil kept saying, "What if the Africans don't meet you at the airport? What if you get on that platform and get tongue tied? What if this? What if that?" I said, "I can do all things through Christ who strengthens me. Shut up Satan, in Jesus Name." The devil even sent two women I had known as close friends to try to discourage me with a strange doctrine of "Extra Special Covering." When I asked them where it was in the Bible, they couldn't show me because it wasn't there. I went with the Lord God's Covering and my Husband Paul's Covering. Biblically, that was the only covering I needed. I saw many souls saved, people healed of sicknesses and diseases, barren wombs opened, demoniacs delivered, entire villages set free of false prophets and their nonsense, a village in a Uganda set free of a witchdoctor and his bags of bird claws, drunks saved and delivered, at once, from years of alcoholism, broken bones healed, whole Churches set free of unforgiveness, tribal rituals that were grieving the Holy Spirit, dead ancestor worship, tribal hatreds, fear, discouragement, etc…I saw a legion run out of a woman by the Power of God. I saw a dead boy raised in Butere, Kenya. The Lord put me on Jesus is Lord Radio out of Nakuru, Kenya and Sayre Voice of Mercy radio and television out of Eldoret, Kenya as well as on Cable T.V. here in N.Y., as Fishers of Men Ministries.

My Fishers of Men Ministry Programs were on every week before God T.V. came into Kenya in 2003. Despite all the missionary work and messages the Lord has given me to preach to the Body of Christ, the local Pastors, here in N.Y. believe "A Woman Can't teach" "A woman can't preach", "A Woman Can't teach Men", and because God the Holy Spirit Taught me the Word of God and not their particular Bible Colleges, they won't even give me a chance to minister to the people. The sheep are being denied all of the Teachings, Ministry and Blessings the Lord had for them through my ministry because of selfish, ungodly Pastors, in our area. The Book of Acts Can and Does Happen Now. There are many things the Lord has for the people here in N.Y. but the Pastors are in the way of it all. May the Good Lord who I serve, get them out of the way and may I deliver God's messages to the Body of Christ here in N.Y. and beyond, in Jesus Name. Amen.

I got on the airplanes with God the Father, God the Son (Jesus), and God the Holy Spirit. I know the Lord also sent two angels with me that He hand picked. A man, who sees angels, saw My Jesus go down a row of angels and pick the two He sent with me.

There were times when I was in serious danger, but the Lord Protected me and returned me back home safely. There were times Holy Spirit warned me not to walk through the field, not to go to Congo, not to trust certain people, not to take certain objects with me.. etc…

IF anyone should doubt that the Lord has chosen me and called me, the fact that I, a white woman, made 23 trips six weeks at a time, into Africa, alone with God and came back safe, should prove that God Has Chosen and Called Me to be an Evangelist both to the lost and to the entire Body of Christ. If the Proof is in the Pudding, I have a lot of Pudding to the Lord's Glory and Credit.

Have you ever slept in rooms with roaches climbing the walls, or bats flying in the rafters of the Pastor's house where you are sleeping, or rats squeaking and shaking plastic bags all night looking for food, or been bitten by bed bugs, bitten by roaches, bitten by big black spiders and had a welt on your neck, been without indoor plumbing, had no water to wash your face, your hair, your clothes, suffered with road dust flying into your eyes as the bus kicked it up on the dirt roads? Have you ever been in villages with no electricity, no way to call home, no contact with the outside world? Have you ever had to go to the outhouse in the middle of the night and had a panther claw at the wooden door trying to get at you? Have you ever been in the Garissa Desert where the temperatures are so hot your feet would swell if you wore closed shoes? Have you ever traveled into the Narek Mountains of Kenya, during rainy season when the roads are full of mud, the cold and rain seeps through your clothing and you freeze continually for days and can't get warm, the Masai tribe is up there four hours from civilization and need the Word of God. Have you ever been in an African town, where people are being slashed to death because of a Presidential Election that angered the slashers? Have you ever had to hide in a bus station that was smaller than a garden shed, under a counter from the police curfew and the slashing cult members who were murdering people? In order to catch the bus for Uganda where people were expecting you to preach? Yes, I Follow Jesus and IT Has Cost ME Everything. HE Is the Pearl of Great Price. I Must Serve Him and Be Faithful to Him Forever. He is Worth The Cost.

Trust in the Lord with all your heart and lean not into your own understanding. My Husband Paul had to trust the Lord in order to release me to obey God. The funds for the mission trips came mostly from our retirement account. We paid the coordinator to go to villages and towns, speak to Pastors and see if they would welcome an evangelist from America, make up posters for the meetings, see that crusade platforms were built, sometimes give them some money for food for the people who had to travel many kilometers to attend the meetings, pay for my airfare, the coordinators and the interpreter's food, hotel rooms or lodging as well as my own, pay their travel expenses on public transport vehicles, buses, etc… But it was all worth every dollar we spent. How can you put a price tag on souls coming to Jesus, Churches being set free of demonic rituals, unforgiveness, fear, false doctrines, witch doctor threats, etc…Our treasures are not on this earth. We are storing our treasures in heaven.

Christians are not wimps. We are bold as lions. We are to step out in faith and see what the Lord will do when we line up with Him and obey His Call for our lives. IF the Lord has called you to do something, do it. There were three men the Lord had called to do what I did in Africa. They all said, "No." I was the Lord's fourth choice. People sing, "Here I Am Send Me," but they don't really mean it. When I sang, "Here I am Send ME." I meant every word. So God sent Me.

People sing, "I Surrender All," but refuse to surrender their entire hearts, bodies, souls, spirits, emotions, feelings, families, finances, wills and lives to the Lordship of Jesus Christ. In reality, they honor God with their mouths but their hearts are far from Him. The things they hold onto, keep them from ever fulfilling the plan and purpose of God for their lives. If you want to hear the Lord say, "Well done, my good and faithful servant," fully surrender everything to Jesus and see the amazing things He will do in you and Through You. If HE can use me, HE can use you. Surrender Fully and Be Victorious.

CHAPTER TWO
BE FILLED WITH THE HOLY SPIRIT-BE BAPTIZED IN THE HOLY GHOST

Every Gospel mentions the Holy Ghost Baptism. When a person repents of their sins and receives Jesus Christ into their heart and life as their Savior and Lord, the Holy Spirit comes into their heart and bears witness with their spirit that they are a child of God. (Romans 8:14-17). That is just the beginning of the person's walk with God.

After you receive Jesus, you should be water baptized as a public confession that you have believed on the Lord Jesus Christ. As the person is water baptized, they are submerged into the water symbolizing that their old man is dead in the water, and they are raised in newness of life.

> Romans 6:1-6 "What shall we say then? Shall we continue in sin, that grace may abound? God forbid. How shall we that are dead to sin, live any longer therein? Do you not know that so many of us as were baptized into Jesus Christ were baptized into his death? Therefore we are buried with him by baptism into death: that like as Christ was raised from the dead by the glory of the Father, even so we also should walk in newness of life. For if we have been planted together in the likeness of his death, we shall be also in the likeness of his resurrection. Knowing this, that our old man is crucified with him, that the body of sin might be destroyed, that henceforth we should not serve sin."

As we confess Jesus Christ as our Savior and Lord and go into the baptismal tank, pool, bath tub, or river, and are submerged, we are symbolizing the death of Jesus Christ for our sins. We are demonstrating that we are putting to death the old person we used to be and coming out of the water as a new person in Jesus Christ. WE are declaring that we will no longer serve sin, but we will serve Jesus. IT is a Spiritual, Public Declaration that our lives will be different and new.

The next step for the person is to read the Word of God that they can spiritually grow. In Romans 12: 2 "And be not conformed to this world; but be transformed by the renewing of your mind, that you may prove what is that good and acceptable, and perfect will of God."

> Ephesians 4:21-23 "If so be you have heard Jesus, and have been taught by him, as the truth is in Jesus. That you put off concerning the former conversation the old man, which is corrupt according to deceitful lusts: And be renewed in the spirit of your mind." We are told here, that our mind can have a wrong spirit. We have to allow the Word of God and the Holy Spirit to work in us to get rid of the "stinking thinking". For years the enemy of our souls has implanted wrong ideas, wrong values, wrong thought patterns, etc… into your mind. When you come to Jesus Christ, it is your responsibility to get into the Bible and renew your mind with the Word of God and the mind of Jesus Christ.

> Ephesians 4:24-30 "And that you put on the new man, which after God is created in righteousness and true holiness, Wherefore putting away lying, speak every man truth with his neighbor: for we are members one of another. Be angry, and sin not, let not the sun go down upon your wrath; Neither give place to the devil. Let him that stole steal no more, but rather let him labor with his hands the thing which is good, that he may have to give to him that is in need. Let no corrupt communication proceed out of your mouth, but that which is good to the use of edifying, that it may minister grace to the hearers. And grieve not the Holy Spirit of God, whereby you are sealed unto the day of redemption."

Begin reading the Bible in the Gospel of John. John was the disciple who clung to Jesus the most. John wanted to know more and Jesus revealed

Himself to John in ways He didn't reveal himself to the others. The others saw Jesus as "The Son of God," the "Son of Man," the "Messiah"; But John saw Jesus as the Creator of all things seen and unseen, the Way, the Truth, the Life, the Light, the Life Giver, the Door of the sheep, the Good Shepherd, the True Vine, the Resurrection and the Life, the Bread of Life, and more. Then read the other Gospels. See what Jesus said, who He said it to, what He did, how He related to people, His Love, His Miracles, His Healing Power, etc…

While reading and studying the Gospels and the Word of God on my security posts 6, 7, and 8 hours a night for nine years, the Holy Spirit showed me, there was much more for me.

Every Gospel tells us there is more. John the Baptist baptized people with water, but Jesus Christ Baptizes them with the Holy Ghost and with fire. The Baptism of the Holy Ghost is the Power of God the Holy Ghost, released in the believer, so they can have boldness to witness the Gospel of Jesus Christ with power, signs, and miracles accompanying the Preaching of the Word. Without the Baptism of the Holy Spirit, the believer has no spiritual power to walk and live the Christian life.

> Matthew 3:11 John the Baptist said, "I indeed baptize you with water unto repentance: but he that comes after me is mightier than I, whose shoes I am not worthy to bear; he shall baptize you with the Holy Ghost, and with fire."

> Mark 1:6-8 "And John was clothed with camel's hair, and with a girdle of a skin about his loins; and he did eat locusts and wild honey; And preached saying, "There comes one mightier than I after me, the latchet of whose shoes I am not worthy to stoop down and unloose. I indeed have baptized you with water; but he shall baptize you with the Holy Ghost."

> Luke 3:15-16 "And as the people were in expectation, and all men mused in their hearts of John, whether he were the Christ, or not; John answered, saying unto them all, "I indeed baptize you with water; but one mightier than I comes, the latchet of whose shoes I am not worthy to unloose: he shall baptize you with the Holy Ghost and with fire."

Luke 3:21-22 Now when all the people were baptized, it came to pass, that Jesus also being baptized, and praying, the heaven was opened, And the Holy Ghost descended in a bodily shape like a dove upon him, and a voice came from heaven, which said, "Thou art my beloved Son, in you I am well pleased."

John 1:24-34 And they which were sent of the Pharisees asked John, and said to him, " Why baptize you then, if you be not that Christ, nor Elias, neither that prophet?" John answered them saying, "I baptize with water, but there stands one among you whom you know not; He it is, who coming after me is preferred before me, whose shoe's latchet I am not worthy to unloose. These things were done in Bethabara beyond Jordan, where John was baptizing. The next day John saw Jesus coming unto him, and said, "Behold the lamb of God which takes away the sin of the world. This is he of whom I said, After me comes a man which is preferred before me: for he was before me. And I knew him not : but that he should be made manifest to Israel, therefore am I come baptizing with water. And John bare record, saying, I saw the Spirit descending from heaven like a dove, and it abode upon him.

And I knew him not: but he that sent me to baptize with water (Father God), the same said unto me ,"Upon whom you shall see the Spirit descending, and remaining on him, the same is he which baptizes with the Holy Ghost. And I saw, and bare record that this is the Son of God."

After reading and studying the Gospels, I wanted the Holy Ghost Baptism. I went to one of the men who led me to Jesus and said, "I want that Holy Ghost Baptism. I want Jesus to Baptize me in the Holy Ghost." The man said, "I'll go to my security booth and ask Jesus to Baptize you in the Holy Ghost. You go to your security booth and ask Him for the Baptism." So I got to my security booth and asked Jesus to baptize me in the Holy Ghost. Immediately I began speaking in tongues as the Holy Spirit gave me utterance. No man laid hands on me to impart the Baptism into me. Jesus Christ Himself touched me in that booth.

The speaking in tongues comes in very handy at times. Here is an example of why praying in tongues is so important:

I was sponsoring a Christian Missionary in India. One night, the Lord woke me up and I had a burden in my heart for him. I knew he was in some kind of trouble, but I didn't know how to pray , or what to pray for him. I didn't know whether he was sick, or his wife or his children, or whether a group of hostile people were attacking him, or if he had been jailed for his faith in Jesus, or what was going on with him. He was in India. I was in the U.S.A. So I asked the Lord to give me a prayer in tongues for him. I prayed in tongues until I had peace in my heart and knew I had prayed through what was needed to help him. The Holy Spirit knows everything. We don't. He is the Best Friend we can have here on planet earth. He is the part of the Godhead who is actively in us and with us; If we receive the Baptism of the Holy Ghost and want Him.

There are many things going on in this nation and all over the world, behind closed doors. We do not know about all of the devil's plans to destroy this Nation, but God does. When we pray in tongues for this Nation, we are praying exactly what is needed, when it is needed. Of course I pray in the natural, and I pray in the Spirit, in tongues. I sing in the natural and I sing in the Spirit, in tongues.

> Romans 8:26-27 "The Spirit also helps our infirmities: for we know not what we should pray for as we ought; but the Spirit Himself makes intercession for us with groanings which cannot be uttered. And he that searches the hearts knows what is the mind of the Spirit, because he makes intercession for the saints according to the will of God."
>
> 1 Corinthians 14:15 "What is it then? I will pray with the spirit, and I will pray with the understanding also; I will sing with the spirit, and I will sing with the understanding also."
>
> 1 Corinthians 14:18 Paul said, "I thank my God, I speak with tongues more than you all." As we can see here, the disciples both spoke in tongues and sang in tongues. Tongues is just one of the many Holy Spirit Giftings that the Lord has given to His People. Many other gifts are listed in 1 Corinthians

Chapters 12 and 14, Ephesians 4:10-15, and other places in scripture. Read the Bible and study them for yourself. Allow the Holy Spirit to teach you and show you which gifts He has given you. But first, ask Jesus to Baptize you in the Holy Spirit. Without the Holy Ghost Baptism, the gifts are not released to function in you and through you. Many Christians walk around saved, but powerless to walk the walk, powerless to stand firm in the faith, powerless to combat the powers of darkness in this world, etc…All because they either believe the lie that the gifts aren't for today, or don't desire to get out of their comfort zones and allow God to use them, or are satisfied to just be saved themselves but don't care about the lost around them. Let's see what happened when the disciples were Holy Ghost Baptized.

In Acts Chapter 1:8 Jesus said, "But you shall receive power, after the Holy Ghost is come upon you, and you shall be witnesses unto me both in Jerusalem, and in all Judaea and in Samaria, and unto the uttermost part of the earth."

In Acts Chapter 2:1-13 Pentecost happened. The disciples were in an upper room, in unity, in one accord when the sound of a mighty rushing wind filled all the house where they were sitting. And cloven tongues of fire sat upon each of them and they were all filled with the Holy Ghost and began speaking with other tongues as the Spirit gave them utterance. People who were in the town all heard the disciples, who were all Galileans, speaking in other languages the mighty works of God. Peter preached a message to the crowd, as the Holy Spirit led him, and over three thousand people received Jesus. (Acts 2:41). HE had the Power of Holy Spirit in what he said to the people. That is why his sermon was so effective.

In Acts 3:1-26, Peter and John prayed for a man who was lame from his mother's womb and the man walked in the name of Jesus. Crowds of people gathered. Peter, led by the Holy Spirit, spoke to the crowds of people. In Acts 4:4 Many of them which heard the word believed , and the number of the men was about five thousand.

In Acts 4:1-18 Peter and John were grabbed by the Sadducees and the priests of the temple. They were threatened not to preach or teach in the Name of Jesus. In Acts 4:19-21 "But Peter and John answered and said to them, "Whether it be right in the sight of God to listen to you more than to God, judge you. For we cannot but speak the things which we have seen and heard. And they called them, and commanded them not to speak at all nor teach in the name of Jesus."

In Acts 4:23-29, they prayed to the Lord and asked for more boldness to speak God's Word. In verse 31, God answered their prayers by shaking the place where they were assembled together and filling them all with the Holy Ghost again, and they spoke the word of God with boldness. In verse 33 it says, "And with great power gave the apostles witness of the resurrection of the Lord Jesus and great grace was upon them all."

IF the early disciples and apostles of Jesus Christ needed the Holy Ghost Baptism to have boldness to preach the Gospel of Jesus Christ, even under adversity, WE NEED THE BAPTISM OF THE HOLY SPIRIT ALSO. Without Him, we have no real power to witness, no power to cast out demons, heal the sick, raise the dead, and do the supernatural works of God on planet earth. The enemies of Jesus Christ are wicked people operating in evil, demonic power of witchcraft, wizardry, Satanism, etc… This evil Harry Potter Wizardry is being taught in our schools, as well as Greek Myths and false gods, the atheist Lie of Evolution, and Baal Worship. When is the Body of Christ going to STOP THIS WICKEDNESS by warring against these thing in the Spiritual Realm?

Ephesians Chapter 6:12 "For we wrestle not against flesh and blood, but against principalities, against powers, against the rulers of darkness of this world, against spiritual wickedness in high places." If we are not equipped to war against this spiritual wickedness, the enemy of our souls will totally destroy Christianity and the future of our children, our grandchildren and this Nation. WE MUST GET INTO THIS WAR, STAND ON THE WORD OF GOD WITH NO COMPROMISE, FIGHT THE GOOD FIGHT OF FAITH, BE GOOD SOLDIERS IN THE ARMY OF THE LORD, WAR A GOOD WARFARE, STAND ON GOD'S WORD AND HIS PROMISES, DECREE HIS WORD INTO THE ATMOSPHERE, BIND THE FORCES OF DARKNESS, LOOSE GOD'S ANGELIC HOSTS TO WAR WITH US AND SEE THE VICTORY IN JESUS NAME. We cannot SHUT UP, STAND DOWN, GIVE UP, OR ALLOW THIS EVIL TO CONTINUE By BEING SILENT AGAINST IT. GET A VOICE, GOD'S VOICE, AND SPEAK LOUD AND CLEAR-WE WILL NOT TOLERATE THIS WICKEDNESS AND THIS EVIL ANY MORE. God will hold us accountable for what we do or don't do now.

Acts 8:14-17 "Now when the apostles which were at Jerusalem heard that Samaria had received the word of God, they sent unto them Peter and John: Who, when they were come down, prayed for them, that they might receive the Holy Ghost; (For as yet he was fallen upon none of them: only they were baptized in the name of the Lord Jesus.) " We see here clearly, that these people had believed on the Lord Jesus Christ and were water baptized in the name of Jesus BUT HAD NOT BEEN BAPTIZED IN THE HOLY GHOST. Peter and John were sent to see that they received the Holy Ghost Baptism also. "Then they laid their hands on them, and they received the Holy Ghost."

Acts 10:1-48 A man named Cornelius who prayed to God, and gave alms to help the poor, was heard by the God of heaven. God gave this man a vision and sent an angel to speak to him. HE was instructed by the angel to send to Joppa and call for Simon Peter. The angel even told him that Simon Peter was staying in the house of Simon a tanner by the sea side. In obedience, Cornelius sent three people to seek Simon Peter.

In the meantime, Peter was up on the roof of the housetop, praying. HE became very hungry , and would have eaten, but fell into a trance. He saw the heavens opened and saw a great sheet, knit at the four corners , come down to earth. On the sheet were all manner or four footed beasts, and wild beasts, and creeping things, and fowls of the air. God spoke to him and said, "Rise, Peter; kill, and eat." Peter responded by saying, "No Lord. Since my youth I have never eaten anything common or unclean." God said, "What God has cleansed, don't call it common." This happened three times.

Peter doubted what this all meant. While Peter thought on the vision, the Spirit (Holy Spirit) said unto him, "Three men seek you. Arise and go down, and go with them, doubting nothing; for I have sent them."

IF Peter had not been Baptized in the Holy Spirit, he would not have fallen into the trance, seen the vision, heard the Voice from Heaven, Heard the Holy Spirit speak to Him to go with the men, etc… The Supernatural Workings of God would not have been present in his life. IF we look at the three men's arrival , immediately after Peter had experienced the trance, a vision, an angel, a Voice from heaven, and a Holy Spirit direction, etc… The Timing was God's Perfect Timing.

Peter went down, spoke to the three men, learned that Cornelius was a man of prayer and alms, who sought God, and went with the men. At that time, it was unlawful for a Jew to enter the house of a Gentile and eat with them. Gentiles were deemed unclean. In Acts 10: 24-48, Peter and his companions arrived at the house of Cornelius. Cornelius had gathered his family and friends inside his house to hear the Word of God, from Peter's mouth. Cornelius told Peter about the angel who spoke to him and why he sent the men for Peter.

> In verse 34 Peter opened his mouth and said, "Of a truth I perceive that God is no respecter of persons: But in every nation he that fears him, and works righteousness is accepted with him." Peter preached Jesus Christ, his birth, death on the cross, and his resurrection from the dead. In Acts 10:44 While Peter was speaking these words, the Holy Ghost fell on all of them which heard the word. And the Jewish believers, who accompanied Peter, were astonished because that on the Gentiles also was poured out the gift of the Holy Ghost. For they heard them speak with tongues, and

magnify God. Then Peter said, "Can any man forbid water that these should not be baptized, which have received the Holy Ghost as well as we?" And he commanded them to be baptized in the name of the Lord.

We see here that the Gentiles believed the Gospel that Peter preached to them and immediately they were baptized with the Holy Ghost/Holy Spirit. They hadn't been water baptized yet, but they were Holy Ghost Baptized first and then water baptized. Both baptisms are vital and important for the believer in Christ.

As we can ask for more wisdom, more understanding, more peace, more comfort, more angels, more funds needed to pay our bills, or for ministry purposes, and for direction, for open doors of ministry, more anointing, more revelation into His Word, etc…WE CAN ASK FOR MORE OF THE HOLY SPIRIT.

> Luke 11:9-13 "And I say unto you, Ask, and it shall be given you; seek, and you shall find, knock, and it shall be opened unto you. For everyone that asks receives: and he that seeks finds; and to him that knocks, it shall be opened. If a man shall ask bread of any of you that is a father, will he give him a stone? Or if he shall ask for a fish, will he for a fish give him a serpent? Or if he shall ask an egg, will he offer him a scorpion? If you then, being evil, know how to give good gifts to your children: how much more shall your heavenly Father give the Holy Spirit to them that ask him?"

IF we ask our heavenly Father for more of the Holy Spirit, WE WILL RECEIVE MORE OF THE HOLY SPIRIT. WE WILL NOT RECEIVE A DEMON, OR ANY OTHER SPIRIT.

In the Old Testament, Elisha asked for a double portion of the Spirit that was on Elijah and he received the double portion of the Holy Spirit that he asked for. He did not receive a demon or another spirit. We can ask for an unlimited amount of Holy Spirit. IF we are willing to submit ourselves to the Lordship of Jesus Christ and ask for more of the Holy Spirit to empower us and use us to do Father's Will on this earth, we will receive more of the Holy Spirit.

People in the Body of Christ tend to settle for Less Than The Lord Has For Them. People pray, " Lord, give me mustard seed faith that moves mountains." My Prayer is, "Lord Give Me Mountainous Faith that Shakes Kingdoms."

People pray, "Lord make me a vessel that can reach a few souls for your kingdom." I Pray, "Make ME a Vessel That Can Reach Millions of People for your Kingdom." Through T.V. and Radio Broadcasts in Kenya, I may have already reached millions of people. Now I am praying, "Lord Make Me A Vessel To Reach Billions of People with your Gospel, in Jesus Name. Amen!

We serve a BIG GOD. ASK BIG. BELIEVE FOR The BIG. BELIEVE THAT NOTHING IS IMPOSSIBLE FOR OUR GOD. SURRENDER FULLY TO THE LORDSHIP OF CHRIST, RECEIVE THE HOLY GHOST BAPTIZM, LET THE HOLY SPIRIT LEAD YOU INTO FATHER GOD'S WILL AND PURPOSE FOR YOUR LIFE AND THE LIVES OF YOUR SHEEP. THEY ARE GOD'S SHEEP. BE A GOOD SHEPHERD. GROW THE SHEEP.

CHAPTER THREE

BE LED BY THE HOLY SPIRIT AND NOT YOUR FLESH OR INTELLECT

Romans 8: 1-2 "There is therefore now no condemnation to them which are in Christ Jesus, who walk not after the flesh, but after the Spirit." Notice here, that there is no condemnation to those who have believed in the Lord Jesus Christ (they are in Christ), that are not walking after their flesh but after the Holy Spirit.

If a believer obeys the Holy Spirit and follows Him, they will not be sinning against the Lord. They will not be condemned, feel condemned, and the devil will have nothing to attack them with. They will be doing nothing wrong to be condemned about.

IT is when a believer listens to their flesh nature and allows fleshly thoughts to take root, or fleshly lusts, or fleshly attitudes to have a place, that they sin. It is possible to go many days without sinning. If we walk in the Holy Spirit, we will not fulfill the lusts of the flesh, the lusts of the eyes, and the pride of life. If The Holy Spirit shows us we have sinned we need to repent speedily and continue our walk with the Lord.

Romans 8:2-4 "For the law of the Spirit of life in Christ Jesus has made me free from the law of sin and death. For what the law could not do, in that it was weak through the flesh, God sending his own Son in the likeness of sinful flesh, and for sin, condemned sin in the flesh. That the righteousness of the law might be fulfilled in us, who walk not after the flesh, but after the Spirit."

Again, we see that we are not to walk after our flesh but after the Holy Spirit. Everywhere in the Bible where the word "Spirit," is capitalized, it is referring to God the Holy Spirit/Holy Ghost. IF we obey the Holy Spirit/Holy Ghost, we will not sin against God because God's Holy Spirit does no sin. HE is as Perfect as Father God and our Lord Jesus Christ is.

> Romans 8 :5-8 "For they that are after the flesh do mind the things of the flesh; but they that are after the Spirit, the things of the Spirit. For to be carnally minded is death; but to be spiritually minded is life and peace. Because the carnal mind is enmity (an enemy) against God; for it is not subject to the law of God, neither can be. So then they that are in the flesh cannot please God."

A fleshly Christian is not pleasing to God. IF a person has accepted Jesus Christ into their heart as Savior and Lord, they need to be led by the Spirit of God and live a life that is pleasing to God. If they, their flesh, and the devil is ruling their life, then Jesus isn't ruling their life. If they remain in their old mindsets, old lusts, old patterns and refuse to renew their minds with the Word of God and allow Holy Spirit to lead them into Father's Will, they will never fulfill the call of God on their lives.

Sadly, many pastors, ministers, priests, reverends, lay people, etc… have never put away their fleshly sins and lusts. They have never left their old ways. That is why we have people in Church Leadership Positions falling into sexual sin, stealing Church funds, lying to the Congregations, not preaching against the abortion murders of innocent babies, not preaching against adultery, fornication, gayness, lesbianism, homosexuality, bestiality, transgender, orgies, pornography, etc…Many Church leaders are into these things and need to repent and be delivered from these generational curses, lust, and wickedness. The statistics of Church Leaders that are into Pornography is somewhere around 45%. This should not be.

> Romans 8: 9-10 "But you are not in the flesh, but in the Spirit, if so be that the Spirit of God dwell in you. Now if any man have not the Spirit of Christ, he is none of his.

> And if Christ be in you, the body is dead because of sin; but the Spirit is life because of righteousness." Notice here that the Spirit of Father God and the Spirit of Jesus Christ is the same Spirit. He is the Holy Spirit. The trinity is linked together by the Holy Spirit.
>
> Romans 8:11-14 "But if the Spirit of him that raised up Jesus from the dead dwell in you, he that raised up Christ from the dead shall also quicken your mortal bodies by his Spirit that dwells in you. Therefore, brethren, we are debtors, not to the flesh, to live after the flesh. For if you live after the flesh, you shall die; but if you through the Spirit (Holy Spirit/Holy Ghost) do mortify the deeds of the body, you shall live. For as many as are led by the Spirit of God, they are the sons of God."

Here is a promise, that if the Holy Spirit dwells in us, He will quicken our mortal bodies by His Holy Spirit that dwells in us. We can mortify the deeds of the body through the Holy Spirit. IF we obey Holy Spirit, we will not be living like the fleshy, lustful, worldly people, who do not know God. WE will truly be living for Jesus Christ, honoring Him in how we live, how we act, what we think, what we do, and what we say.

Verse 14 says, "For as many as are led by the Spirit of God, they are the sons of God." If we are not led by the Spirit of God, we are not sons of God. The sons of God allow the Holy Spirit to lead them into Father's Will and purpose for their lives. They are not living fleshly lives of selfishness, self-gratification, self-will, greed, love of money, materialism, lusts, sexual sin, perversion, lying, stealing, envy, and all other types of wickedness.

> Romans 8:15 "For you have not received the spirit of bondage again to fear; but you have received the Spirit of Adoption, whereby we cry, Abba, Father." The Spirit Himself bears witness with our spirit , that we are the children of God. And if children, then heirs of God, and joint-heirs with Christ; if so be that we suffer with him, that we may be glorified together."

IT is through God the Holy Spirit, that we become a son of God, a joint-heir with Jesus, and inherit all the promises of eternal life. Those who just have "Religion", a "Denomination," a "Religious Background," "Try to Lead a good life," "Try to be a good person," and do not have the Holy Spirit, are not yet sons of God.

Notice also, that the Holy Spirit is NOT A SPIRIT OF BONDAGE TO FEAR. HE IS THE SPIRIT OF ADOPTION WHEREBY WE CAN CALL GOD OUR FATHER.

> John 14:15-17 Jesus said, "If you love me keep my commandments. And I will pray to the Father, and he shall give you another Comforter, that he may abide with you for ever. Even the Spirit of Truth; whom the world cannot receive, because it sees him not, neither knows him; but you know him; for he dwells with you, and shall be in you.

WE see here that the believers had the Holy Spirit dwelling in them and with them. The people in the world do not have the Holy Spirit. He is Only for the Believers in Christ. HE is described here as the COMFORTER, AND THE SPIRIT OF TRUTH. Also notice that Jesus said if you love me you will keep my commandments. The commandments are still in effect in the New Testament. We are still accountable to obey them.

> John 14: 23-24 Jesus said, "If a man love me, he will keep my words; and my Father will love him, and we will come unto him, and make our abode with him. HE that loves me not keeps not my sayings; and the word which you hear is not mine, but the Father's which sent me."

The test of how much you really love Jesus; is How Much Are You Obeying Him. The Ten Commandments are still in effect today. We do not need to sacrifice animals to atone for our sins now, because Jesus Christ was and is the Perfect Lamb of God who died to take away the sins of the world. But we are still required to put sin out of our lives. WE can do this with the help of Holy Spirit.

> John 14: 26 "But the Comforter which is the Holy Ghost, whom the Father will send in my name, he shall teach you all things, and bring all things to your remembrance whatsoever I have said unto you.

IT is the Holy Spirit/Holy Ghost who will teach you the Word of God as you read it, if you ask Him. IT is the Holy Spirit/Holy Ghost who brings the scriptures to our remembrance when we need them. But we have to study the Word of God to provide the Holy Spirit the scriptures to bring to our remembrance. If we don't study the scriptures, we have no sword to stand with against the devil. The Holy Spirit has no ability to bring something we haven't read or studied to our memory banks. WE must get the word of God into us by reading the Word. Read it out laud so while you are seeing it, and saying it, your ears are hearing it , and faith is growing up in you. "Faith comes by hearing the Word of God." READ IT, SPEAK IT, HEAR IT, AND GROW IN YOUR FAITH.

> John 16:7-11 Jesus said, "Nevertheless I tell you the truth; IT is expedient for you that I go away; for if I go not away, the Comforter will not come unto you, but if I depart, I will send him unto you. And when he is come, he will reprove the world of sin, and of righteousness, and of judgment: Of sin, because they believe not on me; Of righteousness, because I go to the Father, and you see me no more; Of judgment, because the prince of this world is judged."

Notice here that it is the Comforter/Holy Ghost/Holy Spirit who reproves the world of sin. Reproof is Conviction of Sin. IF a Believer sins, IT is the Holy Spirit who will convict the believer; so that they will repent and get their relationship with Father God back into right alignment.

Some horribly mistaken pastors and preachers have attributed this 'conviction' work of God the Holy Spirit to the devil. They have been preaching lies by saying that "CONVICTION" and "CONDEMNATION' Both come from the devil. They have been telling people that 1 John 1:9 "If we confess our sins, he is faithful and just to forgive us our sins; and to cleanse us from all unrighteousness," is only for the unbelievers to come to Christ. They have been saying that "Everything is Under the Blood" and " We don't have to repent any more." IF the Body of Christ doesn't have to "REPENT ANY MORE', THEN WHY DOES THE HOLY SPIRIT IN REVELATION CHAPTERS 2 AND 3 TELL FIVE OF THE SEVEN CHURCHES TO REPENT? Conviction is a work of

God the Holy Spirit, while Condemnation is the work of the devil. These mistaken preachers are in danger of BLASPHEMY AGAINST THE HOLY SPIRIT OF GOD. They need to REPENT and stop preaching lies, in Jesus Name. Amen.

IF God the Holy Spirit shows you that you have sinned, repent right away and get things right with God. Don't let unconfessed sin pile up until you doubt your salvation and are totally backslidden. None of us is perfect. But we must put sin out of our lives. IF we need help we can ask the Lord to deliver us from whatever bondage or addiction we have been ensnared into. WE have to be willing to stop it. God will not deliver anyone from something they want to do. He will not go against a person's free will. In order to be free, you have to really want to be free. And those who the Son of God sets free are free indeed.

> John 16:13 "Howbeit, when he, the Spirit of truth, is come, he will guide you into all truth: for he shall not speak of himself; but whatsoever he shall hear, that shall he speak; and he will shew you things to come."

The Holy Spirit guides us into the Truth of the Word of God. HE hears what Father God and Jesus Christ are saying in heaven and tells it to us. HE reveals Father's Will to us so that we can do it. The Holy Ghost/Holy Spirit, Father God, and Jesus Christ are One God in Three Persons. The Spirit of God directs us and guides us into the will of God the Father. Without His guidance, we could never know the Father's Will and Purpose for our lives. Our flesh profits nothing. The Spirit is life.

This scripture in John 16:13 says that the Holy Spirit shows us things to come. IF we look at the Old Testament Scriptures of God's Prophets, we see many scriptures about the coming of the Christ. Isaiah 53, Psalm 22, Isaiah 9:6-7, Isaiah 7:14, Micah 5:2, are just some of the prophesies about Jesus Christ that He fulfilled hundreds and thousands of years later. The Book of Revelation has many more prophesies that have been fulfilled, are being fulfilled, and will be fulfilled in the future. How did these prophets know all the Messiah would suffer, in complete detail, but by the Holy Spirit showing them things to come.

> John 16:14 Jesus said, "He shall glorify me: for he shall receive of mine, and shall shew it unto you. All things that the Father has are mine: therefore said I, that he shall take of mine, and shall shew it unto you." The Holy Spirit shows us what Jesus and Father God want.

As Jesus' custom was, he went into the synagogue on the sabbath day, and stood up to read. And there was delivered unto him the book of the prophet Esaias (Isaiah). And when he had opened the book, he found the place where it was written, "The Spirit of the Lord is upon me, because he has anointed me to preach the gospel to the poor; he has sent me to heal the brokenhearted, to preach deliverance to the captives, the recovering of sight to the blind, to set at liberty them that are bruised, To preach the acceptable year of the Lord." Jesus closed the book, and gave it to the minister, and sat down. And he began to say unto them, "This day is this scripture fulfilled in your ears." The people got angry and wanted to cast him down from the hill.

As we look at this scripture, we see that Jesus's commission was outlined in it. IF we are His hands and feet, we must continue to do the works of Jesus. WE need the Spirit of the Lord God to come upon us, as HE did Jesus. Without God the Holy Spirit/Holy Ghost coming upon us, residing in us, filling us, anointing us with power; we cannot possibly continue the works of Jesus Christ, on planet earth. Our flesh profits nothing. The Spirit is life.

If Jesus Himself was led by the Holy Spirit, we also must be led by the Holy Spirit in order to fulfill Father God's Will for our lives. In Matthew 4:1 "Then was Jesus led up of the Spirit into the wilderness to be tempted of the devil." It was the Holy Spirit of God who led Jesus into the wilderness. Jesus was directed and guided by the Holy Spirit when He was in human form. He was tempted by the devil, But He did not sin. The words Jesus spoke were Father God's Words. The works Jesus did were the works of Father God. The will that Jesus operated In, was Father God's Will. HE did not come to do his own will but the will of Father God, who sent him.

> John 16:13 "Howbeit when he the Spirit of truth, is come, he will guide you into all truth: for he shall not speak of himself: but whatsoever he shall hear, that shall he speak,

and he will shew you things to come." Holy Spirit led Jesus into the wilderness because Holy Spirit knew it was the will of Father God for Jesus to be tempted of the devil. Jesus hearkened to the Holy Spirit and went where he led him.

God the Holy Spirit/Holy Ghost is the part of the Godhead who is here with us every day. Father God is in heaven and Jesus Christ is in heaven, at the right hand of the Father. IT is God the Holy Ghost/Holy Spirit who is here to change us from glory to glory to be like Jesus.

11 Corinthians 3:17-18 "Now the Lord is that Spirit: and where the Spirit of the Lord is, there is liberty." Notice that the Holy Spirit of the Lord brings liberty from bondage, whether it be to drugs, alcohol, lust, perversion, cigarettes, etc…

11 Corinthians 3:18 "But we all, with open face beholding as in a glass the glory of the Lord, are changed into the same image from glory to glory even as by the Spirit of the Lord."

IT is the Holy Spirit/Holy Ghost who changes us from glory to glory to be more like Jesus. Why then, are Pastors refusing to let the Holy Spirit/Holy Ghost minister to the Sheep? How are the sheep to be changed from glory to glory by the Holy Ghost/Holy Spirit, if the pastors have locked the Holy Ghost/Holy Spirit out of their churches? When are they going to get out of the way and let God The Holy Spirit/Holy Ghost touch the Body of Christ and change them into the people God wants them to be?

There are multitudes of people, sitting in church pews, full of bondages to drugs, alcohol, lust, perversions, pornography, adultery, fornication, etc…and the Spirit of God/Holy Spirit could set them free, if He were allowed to minister to these people the way He wants to. Many Pastors, Elders, Deacons, Church Leaders are into pornography, wife stealing among themselves, false doctrines, false theology contrary to God's Word, etc…and have compromised with the world and its ungodly lusts, greed, materialism, filth, vile affections, etc…Many Church Leaders need to allow God the Holy Spirit/Holy Ghost to convict them of their own wickedness, bring them to repentance, and get their hearts right with the Lord. They need Deliverance as much as the people in the pews need it. The reason many of them refuse to let

God the Holy Spirit/Holy Ghost into their churches is that they don't want anyone to know about their own sins and wickedness. They want to continue in what they are doing and don't want to give it up and let God deliver them from it. If the Church Leaders are not walking in righteousness and truth, how will the people in the pews walk in righteousness and truth?

There are people in the churches with unconfessed sin in their lives and generational curses that keep them in bondage. The Holy Ghost/Holy Spirit could set them free, if He was allowed to minister to them.

The Pastors of many denominational Churches have failed to preach and teach and disciple the people in the Word of God. There is NOW A FAKE CHRISTIANITY THAT MOST OF THE POLITICAL LEADERS OF AMERICA ARE WALKING IN. THEY HAVE A "religious Christianity" WITHOUT A RELATIONSHIP WITH JESUS CHRIST. If you want proof of this, the National Legal And Policy Center publishes a UNITED STATES CONGRESS DIRECTORY every year. If you look at the people who are promoting ABORTION GAYNESS, TRANSGENDER, DRAG QUEENS, FILTH, VILE AFFECTIONS, WICKED BILLS CONTRARY TO GOD AND HIS WORD, etc…most of them claim to be BAPTIST, METHODIST, EPISCOPAL, CHRISTIAN, PRESBYTERIAN, CATHOLIC, JEWISH, LUTHERAN, UNITED METHODIST, etc.

Obviously, Abortion is contrary to Jesus Christ who is forming these babies in the womb of their mothers for His Divine Plan and Purposes. (Jeremiah 1:4-5, Psalm 139:13-18 KJV, Psalm 22:9, Isaiah 44:1-2, Isaiah 49:1-2, Luke 1:41-42, and many other scriptures make it clear that God forms babies in the womb of their mothers. Abortion is the Sacrificial Murder of Innocent Human Beings to false gods-to Baal. Yet, all these people "Claiming to Be Christians" or "Claiming To Belong to A Denomination of Christianity" are for THESE WICKED MURDERS OF INNOCENT HUMAN BABIES. They stand for the wickedness of the LGBTQ and Transgender Surgeries that mutilate children's bodies and minds.

Titus 1:15-16 "Unto the pure all things are pure: but unto them that are defiled and unbelieving is nothing pure; but even their mind and conscience is defiled. They profess that they know God; but in works they deny him, being abominable, and disobedient, and unto every good work reprobate." This describes these WICKED PEOPLE. They are NOT REAL CHRISTIANS. THEY SERVE SATAN, NOT GOD.

The Prophet Micah asks a question in Micah 6:7b "Shall I give my firstborn for my transgression, the fruit of my body for the sin of my soul?" When women are full of lust, fornication, and adultery, they sin against God by having sex with people they are not married to. Then they Murder their babies to Baal, the gods of convenience, etc…Sexual sin Needs To Be Preached Against From the Pulpits of America Again. IF people stop their sexual sins, the abortions would stop. There are many childless couples who would love to be able to have and raise these children. Why can't they have them?

Psalm 127:3 "Children are a heritage of the Lord and the fruit of the womb is his reward." Why are people Murdering the Children that the Lord is Forming in the Womb?" How can anyone who claims to be a Christian (A Christ Follower) be Murdering the Children that Jesus Christ is Forming, for His Divine Purposes?

The answer is: THEY HAVE A FAKE CHRISTIANITY WITHOUT A RELATIONSHIP WITH JESUS CHRIST HIMSELF. AS A RESULT, THEY SERVE SATAN AND NOT GOD. WITHOUT JESUS CHRIST LIVING IN THEIR HEARTS AND LIVES, THEY DO NOT KNOW FATHER GOD, AND THEY DO NOT HAVE THE HOLY SPIRIT OF GOD LIVING IN THEIR HEARTS. They have a godless, Christless religion, like the Pharisees and Scribes, and Sadducees had. They DO NOT HAVE GOD , OR KNOW GOD, HIMSELF.

How can anyone foolishly believe that God makes mistakes when HE makes a boy a boy, or a girl a girl? IT is Almighty God who Created Heaven and Earth and Everything Seen and Unseen that has formed that baby. Who is man to change the gender of the person God formed for His Divine Purposes.? Mutilating little children's bodies, with Transgender Surgeries, is DEMONIC AS HELL AND NEEDS TO BE STOPPED, IN JESUS' NAME.

The drag queens need to be banned from our schools along with their filthy sexual actions with ducks and other beasts. This Wickedness Must Stop Now. Wicked Lustful Transgender Books MUST BE TAKEN OUT

OF SCHOOL LIBRARIES AND ALL PUBLIC LIBRARIES. Why should little children and teens be instructed to embrace these wicked, reprobate, life styles, ideas, and filth. GAYNESS IS NOT A MINORITY. I REPEAT, GAYNESS IS NOT A MINORITY. IT IS A SEXUAL SIN. IT SHOULD NOT BE ENCOURAGED OR PROMOTED TO OUR CHILDREN AND TEENS OR ANYONE ELSE.

Have we so soon forgotten the Biblical account of God's Judgment on Sodom and Gomorrah and the surrounding cities? The people of Sodom and Gomorrah wanted to have sex with the angels. Take a look at Genesis Chapter 19:1-28. The Lord sent two angels into Sodom to see if the city was as wicked as God saw from heaven. Lot took the angels into his house because he knew if they were outside, the men of Sodom would rape them. In verse 4, the men of Sodom surrounded Lot's house and they called to Lot, "Where are the men which came into you house this night? Bring them out unto us, that we may know them." They didn't want to just be introduced to them. To know them meant they wanted to have sex with them. Lot tried to reason with the men of Sodom, but they would not turn from their desire to rape the angels. In verse 11, the angels smote the men at the door with blindness, both small and great: so that they wearied themselves to find the door. Even when God's angels smote them with blindness, they didn't repent or stop trying to get at the angels inside the door. The angels took Lot, his wife, and his daughters out of Sodom. Verse 24 says, "Then the Lord rained upon Sodom and upon Gomorrah brimstone and fire from the Lord of heaven; And he overthrew those cities, and the plain, and all the inhabitants or the cities, and that which grew upon the ground." Is this what we want to happen to America?

> Jude verses 5-8 "I will put you in remembrance, though you once knew this, how the Lord. Having saved the people out of the land of Egypt, afterward destroyed them that believed not. And the angels which kept not their first estate, but left their own habitation, he has reserved in everlasting chains under darkness unto judgment of the great day.

Even as Sodom and Gomorrah, and the cities about them in like manner, giving themselves over to fornication, and going after strange flesh, are set forth for an example; suffering the vengeance of eternal fire. Likewise also these filthy dreamers defile the flesh, despise dominion, and speak evil of dignities."

> Romans 1:20-28 "For the invisible things of him (God) from the creation of the world are clearly seen, being understood by the things that are made, even his eternal power and Godhead; so that they are without excuse: Because that, when they knew God, they glorified him not as God, neither were thankful; but became vain in their imaginations, and their foolish heart was darkened.

Professing themselves to be wise, they became fools. And changed the glory of the uncorruptible God into an image made like to corruptible man, and to birds, and four-footed beasts, and creeping things. Whereby, God also gave them up to uncleanness through the lust of their own hearts, to dishonor their own bodies between themselves.

Who changed the truth of God into a lie, and worshipped and served the creature more than the Creator, who is blessed for ever. Amen. For this cause God gave them up unto vile affections for even their women did change the natural use into that which is against nature.

And likewise also the men, leaving the natural use of the woman, burned in their lust one toward another; men with men working that which is unseemly, and receiving in themselves that recompence of their error which was meet.

And even as they did not like to retain God in their knowledge, God gave them over to a reprobate mind, to do those things which are not convenient,"

> THEN HE DESCRIBES A REPROBATE MIND IN Romans 1:29-32 "Being filled with all unrighteousness, fornication, wickedness, covetousness, maliciousness; full of envy, murder, debate, deceit, malignity; whisperers, Backbiters, haters of God, despiteful, proud, boasters, inventors of evil things, disobedient to parents, Without understanding, covenant breakers, without natural affection, implacable, unmerciful:

Who knowing the judgment of God, that they which commit such things are worthy of death, not only do the same, but have pleasure in them that do them."

IS THIS THE WICKEDNESS THAT WE WANT OUR CHILDREN TAUGHT TO DO IN SCHOOL? DO WE WANT OUR CHILDREN TO BE WICKED ENEMIES OF GOD AND ALL TRUTH? WE MUST FIGHT AGAINST THIS EVIL NOW, LEST WE BE DESTROYED LIKE SODOM AND GOMORRHA.

God has not changed His Mind about these sexual sins and wickedness. Do we want our children to serve God, or Satan? A gay church is a demonic, Satanic Church. IT promotes this wickedness in the sight of God. You Cannot live a gay lifestyle and be right with God. You are using your whole body, soul, and spirit, to rebel against God, God's Word, God's Truth and God Ordained Marriage Between a Man Born a Man and a Woman Born a Woman. There is No Such Thing As A Gay Christian. God set apart the marriage covenant to show forth His relationship and covenant with The Body of Christ. Gayness is a total affront to the God of Heaven and His Plans. IF you are involved in this wickedness, REPENT AND ASK GOD TO DELIVER YOU FROM IT. You may want to find a good DELIVERENCE MINISTRY TO CAST OUT THE DEMONS OF GAYNESS, LESBIANISM, PERVERSION, UNGODLY AFFECTIONS, etc…You can be set free if you want to be set free.

There are many people who are suffering with guilt, self-hatred, shame, unforgiveness, emotional pain, heartbreak, wounded spirits, etc…They continue suffering needlessly because the One Who Could Minister Healing (The Holy Spirit/Holy Ghost) is being denied them, by the Pastors who refuse to let the Holy Spirit/Holy Ghost Minister to Them.

Generational Curses are Very Real. They can influence Christians, if they are not stood against and broken off of their lives, by the Blood of Jesus. I will give you some examples of Generational Curses.

> Exodus 20: 3-6 "Thou shall have no other gods before me. Thou shall not make unto yourself any graven image, or any likeness of any thing that is in heaven above, or that is in the earth beneath, or that is in the water under the

earth: Thou shall not bow down yourself to them, nor serve them; for I the Lord thy God am a jealous God, visiting the iniquity of the fathers upon the children unto the third and fourth generation of them that hate me; And shewing mercy unto thousands of them that love me and keep my commandments."

King David's Great Grandmother was Rehab the harlot. IF we look at Matthew 1:5-6 "And Salmon begat Booz of Rehab, and Booz begat Obed of Ruth; and Obed begat Jesse; And Jesse begat David the king; and David the king begat Solomon" AS most of us know, Rehab was a harlot who hid the spies of Israel when they went to Jericho. She and her family members put the scarlet cord in her window and their lives were spared when Joshua took Jericho.

The spirit of lust and harlotry entered the family tree. David sinned with Bathsheba committing adultery and fornication. Then he had Bathsheba's husband put into the hottest battle and had the men withdraw and allowed him to be slain. Then he married Bathsheba. Their first son, conceived in David's lust for Bathsheba, died. Then David repented (Psalm 51) and God gave him another son, by Bathsheba, named Solomon.

David's Son, Amnon raped his half sister Tamar. Absalom, Tamar's brother by the same mother, plotted to slay Amnon. David never made the situation right by making Amnon marry Tamar. Tamar lived a life alone and disgraced because of what Amnon did to her.

I Kings 11:1-3 "But King Solomon loved many strange women, together with the daughter of Pharaoh, women of the Moabites, Ammonites, Edomites, Zidonians, and Hittites: OF the nations concerning which the Lord said unto the children of Israel, You shall not go in unto them, neither shall they come in unto you; for surely they will turn away your heart after their gods; Solomon clave unto these in love. And he had seven hundred wives, princesses, and three hundred concubines: and his wives turned away his heart." WE see here that King Solomon lusted after many women. The spirit of lust functioned in him and through him. One Thousand women and he still wasn't satisfied.

When I think about how awful it was for a wife, to have to share her husband with nine hundred ninety nine other women , I would never have wanted to be one of Solomon's wives. Some of them he had only once, in bed, and never went to their bed again. In the meantime, those women were stuck in his harem and were never able to marry anyone else. I believe that due to this fact, there were many fights among the women over who would sleep with their Husband Solomon. WE get a clue about this when we read verses in Proverbs written by Solomon.

> Proverbs 21:9 "IT is better to dwell in a corner of the housetop, than with a brawling woman in a wide house."

> Proverbs 21:19 "IT is better to dwell in the wilderness, than with a contemptuous and an angry woman."

I'm sure there were many fights and disagreements, and arguments among the thousand wives of Solomon.

In Kenya, the men are allowed to take up to ten wives by the law. Many men have taken multiple wives. I counseled with many of these women. First wives were complaining that their husbands didn't love them because they took another wife. Second and third wives were complaining that wife number one hated them and did all she could to make their lives a misery. I said, "How would you feel if you were the first wife and your husband took on more wives? Would you be happy, or would you feel unloved, unwanted, betrayed, and angry? IF you knew he was married, then why did you marry him? My advice to all of them was to "Forgive each other and make peace."

IT was common, in the villages, to see one cows dung hut in the center, for the husband, and many cows dung huts around it for all of the wives to live in. The husband would visit whatever wife he wanted, when he wanted them. Because of the multiple wife law, there were many parentless children roaming the streets of Kenya or being taken care of by elderly grandparents.

IF a man had three wives and had children by them and decided to take a fourth wife (who happened to have AIDS), he would infect the other wives and the adults would die off leaving all the children parentless. IT was a very serious problem. Many of the teens left alone would become street thugs, in order to survive.

Pastors came to me with a question. "A man came to Christ with his wives and children. They are all now in my church. What am I supposed to tell him to do about his multiple wives? Do I tell him to keep only the first one and to throw the others out? Or what?"

I said, "Let me ask the Lord to tell me the answer. Give me five minutes." I walked away and inquired of the Lord. The Lord said, "Tell that man he cannot take any more wives. He must be responsible for the wives and children he already has. But he can never be a Pastor, an Elder, or a Deacon in the Church because of the multiple wives. We cannot have the young men believing that taking multiple wives is fine.

Later on, I saw the great wisdom in what the Lord told me to tell them. By letting the man keep his family members, the women were not thrown out to be prostitutes. The children grew up having a dad figure. Other men with multiple wives would not be hindered from believing in Jesus. They knew they could keep their families intact.

The above example of King David's Family, which shows all the lust, adultery, fornication, rape, murder, envy, etc. is just one example of a generational curse that can plague a family. If we look at the family of the author, Ernest Hemmingway, we can see a clear generational curse. His dad committed suicide, his daughter committed suicide, and he committed suicide. The spirit of suicide ran through three generations and all committed suicide. IF they had known the Lord, and the Power of the Blood of Jesus to break curses, their lives would not have ended in such a tragic way.

Generational curses of sickness, diabetes, cancers, anger, unforgiveness, rage, divorce, suicide, false god worship, paganism, witchcraft, occult practices, addictions, alcoholism, ungodly lusts, incest, raving and ranting, strife, bitterness, fear, etc… can go on through generations. They can skip a generation and hit the next, or the next generation. They travel through family blood lines and continue to operate until someone comes to faith in Jesus Christ and breaks them by the Blood of Jesus.

Does a Christian need to be delivered from generational curses? Yes! IF you are saved, but you are having a problem with drugs, alcoholism, lust, anger, fear, etc…and IF YOU HATE WHAT YOU ARE DOING, BUT YOU CANNOT GET THE VICTORY OVER IT,

TO STOP IT, there is probably a GENERATIONAL CURSE ON YOUR FAMILY TREE THAT HAS TO BE BROKEN. It can be broken off of your family tree if you PLEAD THE BLOOD OF JESUS INTO YOUR FAMILY TREES ALL THE WAY BACK TO ADAM AND EVE , REPENTING OF ANY SINS THAT OPENED THE DOOR TO THE GENERATIONAL CURSES AND BREAKING THESES GENERATIONAL CURSES OFF OF YOUR FAMILY TREES, BY THE BLOOD OF JESUS. Until Christ's Blood is applied to your family trees and any generational sins repented of, the enemy still has a hold on you and future generations because your ancestors sinned and opened the door to the demonic activity operating in your life and the lives of future generations in your family tree or blood line.

> Galatians 3: 13-14 Christ has redeemed us from the curse of the law, being made a curse for us; for it is written, Cursed is every one that hangs on a tree; That the blessing of Abraham might come on the Gentiles through Jesus Christ; that we might receive the promise of the Spirit through faith."

Because Christ took our curse upon Himself, generational curses can be broken off of us, when we apply the Blood of Jesus to them and to the sins in our family blood lines that opened the door to them.

I'll give you some examples in my own life. After I was saved and baptized in the Holy Ghost, the Holy Spirit showed me that I was operating in a generational curse of raving and ranting. As a child, if something angered my mother, she would rave about it for hours and hours. I hated listening to that, when I was a child, but I found myself doing the same thing to my husband and children. The very thing that I hated, I was doing. I realized that there was some kind of generational curse in operation, so I said, "In the Name of Jesus, I rebuke the spirit of raving and ranting. I repent of the sins of my ancestors who opened the door to this spirit and I plead the Blood of Jesus to all my family trees, to destroy it off of myself and future generations, in Jesus Name. Amen. After that, I had no more raving and ranting problem.

My ancestors, some of them were American Indians. I know they worship the spirit of the wind, the spirit of the water, the spirit of this and the spirit of that. Other ancestors were from Germany. I don't know if they persecuted the Jews or helped the Jews. Other ancestors were Irish. I don't know if they liked to fight or liked to drink a lot of alcohol, or what they were into. Other ancestors were English. Others were Swedish. I do not know what kinds of sins, bondages, addictions, etc…were operating in and through them.

To be safe, I prayed and pled the Blood of Jesus through all my generational trees on all sides of the family and repented of all their sins, and broke all generational curses off of me, my children, grandchildren, etc…I did the same for my Husband Paul and his family trees.

THERE ARE NAME CURSES THAT EFFECT FAMILY MEMBERS

For many years, my Husband Paul had a problem with alcohol. He drank a lot of beer from the time he got home from work to the time he went to bed at night. On weekends he drank after noon. He never got nasty with me or the children, but he was addicted to alcohol. I would also find bottles of gin and rum under the kitchen sink, and under the bathroom cabinets. He received Jesus as his personal Savior in 1990. He was water baptized and Holy Spirit Baptized. But he still had a drinking problem. One day, the Holy Spirit showed me that Paul's problem stemmed from his name. He had been named after his Uncle Paul, who was an alcoholic, who died of liver problems. When his Uncle Paul died, the demons of alcoholism left his dead body and looked for someone else to inhabit. Because my husband had the same name and was in the same blood line, they came right for him. He wanted to stop drinking but had no power to stop it, because of the name curse that was attached to him.

I prayed and said, "In the Name of Jesus, my Husband Paul Hollop is not connected to his dead uncle Paul anymore. I break the name connection by the Blood of Jesus and change his name to Andrew Smith, in the spiritual realm. I rebuke the demons of alcoholism and command them to get out of my Husband Paul, forever, in the name of Jesus." OF course my husband still goes by his natural name, but in the Spiritual Realm, his name is different. Right after I did that, my husband came home from work, dumped all the beer into the sink along with the gin and rum he had hidden under the sinks. That was back in 2000. He hasn't touched a drop of alcohol for 23 years. HE never had any shakes or withdrawal symptoms either. The Holy Spirit is So Good to us.

While in Kenya, we came upon the case of a doctor who couldn't stop beating his wife. We asked him how he felt about his wife and he would say, "I love her very much." Then, later, with uncontrollable anger, he would beat her up. Afterwards he would be very sorry.

HE hated what he was doing to his wife, But he couldn't stop. IT turned out that his name in Swahili, meant "Anger." Because his name meant anger, uncontrollable anger was manifesting through him to attack his wife. We prayed and first broke any generational curses of anger off of his family trees all the way back to Adam and Eve, by the Blood of Jesus. Then we said, "In the name of Jesus we remove and refuse this Swahili name of anger off of this man (we named him) and then said, "We change his name, in the spiritual realm, to the name "Love" in Swahili. His name now means love and he will love his wife as Christ loves the church and gave himself for it, in Jesus Name, amen." After that, the man was able to love his wife.

While doing deliverance ministry in Kenya, a woman came up to me. She said, "I was named after my aunt who could only have one child. My husband and I have only one child. WE want more children, but I have not been able to get pregnant with more children. Can you help me. I believe this is some kind of name curse. Can you break it off my life? In the spiritual realm, I disconnected her from her aunt and changed her name, in the spiritual realm, to a different name. The Holy Spirit came upon her and she was on the floor in God's Presence. He showed her a window with two more children looking out at her and told her she would have these children. She got up off the floor and told me what the Lord had shown her.

One time I had a cat that we named "Bear". Every time a dog chased him, he would run up a tree 60 feet and stay in the tree crying for days. Bears climb trees. He did not know how to get down once he ran up the tree. Once, he climbed up further until a branch broke and he fell out of the tree. WE had to take him to the vet to stitch up his torn chin, etc… The next time, I had to pay a bucket truck driver to go up and get him down. A tree climber used his special shoes to climb up and get him, another time. Finally I said to the cat, "In the Name of Jesus, your name is no longer Bear in the Spiritual Realm. Your name is now "GROUND HOG. YOU WILL STAY ON THE GROUND FROM NOW ON AND NEVER CLIMB A TREE AGAIN, IN JESUS NAME. AMEN. After that, I saw a dog chase Bear, but he ran around the tree trunk and kept running on the ground. HE never climbed another tree.

> Jeremiah 7:32-33 "Therefore, behold, the days come, saith the Lord, that it shall no more be called Tophet, nor the valley of the son of Hinnom, but the valley of slaughter: for they shall bury in Tophet, till there be no place. And the carcasses of this people shall be meat for the fowls of the heaven, and for the beasts of the earth, and none shall fray them away." This was the result of the people burning their sons and daughters in fire to false gods. There was a place where railroad tracks were being laid, in Kenya. Unfortunately, the name of the place, in "Swahili", meant "Valley of slaughter". Because the place had that name, lions were attacking the people who were trying to lay the train tracks, to the point, that no one wanted to work for the railroad. Quite a few of the workers were eaten by lions there.

If you were named for a relative and you find yourself having the same problems and issues, in your life, that they had, you need to pray and change your name in the spiritual realm to a different name. When we look at the times when the Lord changed people's names, it was very significant. Sari was changed to Sarah. Abram was changed to Abraham. The Prophet Hosea was told what to name his children in order for them to be messages, to God's people. Saul was changed to Paul, the disciple. Names are important. Isaac means child of laughter because both Abraham and Sarah laughed when they were told they would have a baby at their ages.

My advise to you is: Don't Name Your Children after any relative, in your family. It is better to give them a different name altogether, that is not spiritually and bloodline connected to anyone.

CAN CHRISTIANS HAVE DEMONS FOM THEIR PASTS EFFECTING THEIR LIVES NOW?

While in Kenya, a man and a woman came forward. They had been married weeks earlier, But had not consummated the marriage.

The woman had been in a girl's boarding school and had had a lesbian affair with another girl. Years later, she became a Christian, met this Christian man, fell in love, and married him. Every time he tried to get romantic with her, she would scream, "Get away from me. I hate You. Don't Touch Me." When she was asked how she felt about her husband, she would say, "I love him very much. He is a good man. " But every time he tried to have sex with her, she would scream at him, "Don't Touch ME." She needed to repent of that lesbian relationship she had years earlier. A demonic spirit, of lesbianism, had entered her at that time. IT WAS SCREAMING THROUGH HER, every time her husband tried to consummate the marriage. IT had to be cast out, in Jesus Name. Then they were able to consummate their marriage after it was cast out.

There were many Pastors and Brethren, in Kenya, who needed deliverance from tribal hatreds, demonic tribal covenants and rituals they had engaged in (before they got saved), witchdoctor circumcisions, witch doctor cuttings on their bodies (blood sacrifices) to other gods, unforgiveness, depression, discouragement, sex with beasts, lusts, perversions, addictions to alcohol, fornication, adultery, gayness, stealing, etc…

In Kenya, young men were not circumcised on the eighth day (like a Biblical Circumcision). Many of them were circumcised at ages 13-16, by witch doctors in a circle of wheat. The circle of wheat constitutes a Covenant. The circumcision, by a witch doctor, in the circle of wheat, was a blood sacrifice to Satan. The witch doctor had the young boys sing songs glorifying fornication and adultery. He also gave them alcohol to drink.

Years later, many of these boys became men and came to faith in Jesus Christ. Although they were in the churches, they were having trouble with the sins of fornication, adultery, alcoholism, etc… The rituals they had partaken of, had given Satan a hold on them. Even though they were Christians, their ability to live a Christian life and walk the Christian walk, was hindered. If Satan has you by your foot, because of covenants you made with him before you came to Christ, you must fully repent of these things and render them null, void, and of no effect, in Jesus Name." You must totally renounce Satan and his hold on your life. Otherwise, your walk with Jesus Christ will be hindered.

IT was necessary to have a "Deliverance Service" where people could Repent of witch doctor circumcisions, cuttings on their bodies to false gods, sexual sins, perversions, unnatural affections for beasts, hatred, Unforgiveness, anger, demonic tribal rituals they had done or were involved in, etc…

At a camp meeting at Joyland School in Kisumu, Kenya, for a week, with over three thousand Pastors, Elders, Deacons, and brethren, there were over 300 people who needed deliverance ministry. Many of them were Church Pastors and Church Leaders. Most of them were having problems with things they got involved with before they repented of their sins and came to Christ. Any occult practices (things done to glorify false gods, rituals to false gods, sacrifices to false gods, etc)…need to be individually repented of because of the serious nature of them. Since we cannot sit at the table of the Lord and the table of devils, and we cannot drink the cup of the Lord and the cup of devils, these former wicked practices must be totally renounced and repented of, because they were things that directly linked us to Satan, in worship of him as our god. They were not just regular sins done in ignorance. They were a total affront to the Lord of Heaven and Earth.

There are Word Curses that also need to be broken off people. Maybe your mother said, "You were an accident. I didn't want another child." How would that make you feel? Or if someone says, "You are so ugly, you will never find a husband." "You are stupid." "You are nothing" "You shouldn't have been born. You are no good." "You will never amount to anything." Can you imagine how that destroys the person who is receiving these hateful words into their spirit and soul? Words can cut a person deeper than if you used a knife on them.

Proverbs 18:21 "Death and life are in the power of the tongue; and they that love it shall eat the fruit thereof." You can either speak words of encouragement, life, light, love and truth into a person's life, to build them up; or you can speak discouragement, anger, death, darkness, hatred, and lies into a person's life. Depending upon what you speak, you are putting fruit into their life. You are either putting good fruit into their soul and spirit or you are putting evil fruit into their soul and spirit, by what you speak. Words have spiritual power. God spoke the world into existence. HE said, "Let there be" and everything was as HE spoke it into existence. The Bible says we will give an account to God for every idle word we speak. May God help us to speak what is right in His Sight.

Years ago, someone phoned and told me that a sixteen year old boy wanted to kill himself. They asked if I would speak to him. Before he came to the house, I asked Holy Spirit to help me to know what to say to this young man. Holy Spirit gave me the words to speak to him. Out of my mouth came, "Did anyone ever tell you that you are worthless, useless, and would never amount to anything?" He began crying. HE said, "My dad used to tell me that all the time, from the time I was four years old." I showed him Psalm 139:13-18 (KJB). I showed him that God wanted him. God first wrote him in His book and then fashioned him in his mother's womb according to God's plan and purpose for his life. God doesn't make any useless, worthless people. I showed him how Jesus came to this earth to die on the cross for his sins, because he loved him.

I was able to lead him to Jesus. Then I broke every negative word his dad or anyone else said over him or his life, by the Blood of Jesus, and rendered those words powerless, in Jesus Name. He became a cab driver in Poughkeepsie. I heard he got married and has some children.

We see here, that his dad's words, spoken over the years, had a horrible effect on his life. HE had dropped out of school and was living in store doorways. HE was believing the hateful lie that his dad had spoken to him, that he was useless and worthless. The lie was destroying his life and making him want to die. Once the lie was exposed, removed and broken off of his life, the word curse was gone and he had the will to live. HE no longer wanted to kill himself.

The Bible says we are to be renewed in the spirit of our mind. A person's mind can have a wrong spirit. Sadly, many Pastors and Churches refuse to believe that a Christian can have a demon. What is lust, fear, depression, discouragement, unforgiveness, rage and hatred? They are all Spiritual Things that operate in the minds of human beings. We cannot look at an object and say, "this is Love." Or "This is Fear", or "This is Discouragement." These things are all Spiritual. We have Galatians Chapter 5 which lists the fruit of Holy Spirit and also lists the wickedness of the flesh (demonic spiritual activity). We are either operating in God's Holy Spirit Fruit, or we are operating in Satan's demonic spiritual fruit. A real Christian cannot be possessed but they can certainly be oppressed by spirits of fear, hatred, unforgiveness, bitterness, lust, pornography, etc…in their mind and body. That is why we are to be renewed in the spirit of our minds. That is why we must stand on the healing scriptures because Satan does attack people's physical bodies with sicknesses. While our Spirit Man has God the Holy Spirit bearing witness that we belong to Jesus, our minds must be renewed because they can have wrong ideas, wrong concepts , and wrong attitudes and agendas. How many Christians walk in "FEAR?" FEAR IS A SPIRIT THAT doesn't come from God. (II Timothy 1:7) I rest my case.

A DESCRIPTION OF A TYPICAL HOLY GHOST/HOLY SPIRIT SERVICE FOLLOWS

Back in 1993-1996, there was a Holy Ghost/Holy Spirit Revival happening at the Airport Church in Toronto, Canada. Two Pastors from Kingston, N.Y. and one Pastor from Albany attended the revival. They were in Canada a week letting the Holy Ghost/Holy Spirit touch them and minister to them. They were filled with God the Holy Spirit and returned to their churches with Holy Fire. They conducted Holy Ghost/Holy Spirit Anointing Services, which I attended.

Personally, I was a shy person. As a child I was teased because of my Boston accent and kept quiet all through school. I never volunteered to speak because I was afraid of being made fun of. I hated oral reports because I didn't want to get up in front of anyone to speak. I couldn't sleep for days before an oral report was due. I even hid behind a poster when I gave my report, out of fear of public speaking. I had a "fear of man," "fear of what people would think of me," and "fear of speaking to people." These fears I had carried with me from my childhood.

While at the revival meetings, on the floor , in the Presence of God, He removed all of my fear and gave me boldness. From that day on, I could speak to people with no fear at all. In 1997, He sent me to Africa to do crusades in Kenya and Uganda. I could never have done that if the fear hadn't been removed by God the Holy Spirit. I preached to 3,000 pastors and brethren from all over Kenya, did Pastor's Conferences for Kenya City Mission Churches, preached on Jesus is Lord Radio from Nakuru, Kenya and Sayre "Voice of Mercy" T.V. and radio out of Eldoret, Kenya. The Holy Spirit had delivered me from years of walking in fear, and gave me the boldness I needed to be the Evangelist God Wanted Me To BE. He did amazing things in each person's life, as they attended these meetings, and were touched by God the Holy Ghost/Holy Spirit.

WHY DO PEOPLE FALL DOWN AT HOLY GHOST/HOLY SPIRIT REVIVAL MEETINGS?

Most people do fall over when the Holy Spirit/ Holy Ghost comes upon them. IF we look at the account of Solomon's Temple Dedication, we will see similar falling down.

Look first at 11 Chronicles 5:13-14 "It came even to pass, as the trumpeters and singers were as one, to make one sound to be heard in praising and thanking the Lord; and when they lifted up their Voice with the trumpets and cymbals and instruments of music and praised the Lord, saying, for he is good; for his mercy endures for ever; that the house was filled with a cloud, even the house of the Lord; So that THE PRIESTS COULD NOT STAND TO MINISTER BY REASON OF THE CLOUD; FOR THE GLORY OF THE LORD HAD FILLED THE HOUSE OF GOD." They couldn't stand up. They were on the floor.

> 11 Chronicles 7:1-3 "Now when Solomon had made an end of praying, the fire came down from heaven, and consumed the burnt offering and the sacrifice and the glory of the Lord filled the house. And the priests could not enter into the house of the Lord, because the glory of the Lord had filled the Lord's house. And when all the children of Israel saw how the fire came down, and the glory of the Lord upon the house, they bowed themselves with their faces to the ground upon the pavement, and worshipped, and praised the Lord, saying, For he is good, for his mercy endures for ever." They were all bowed down on the pavement with their faces to the ground and worshipped.

The accounts written in the book "Azusa Street They told Me Their Stories" by Tommy Welchel mention similar accounts of fire coming down, glory clouds appearing, all kinds of healings taking place, people on the floor in the Presence of God, etc…just like the accounts of Solomon's Temple. God is the same yesterday, today, and forever.

WHY DO PEOPLE LAUGH, CRY, SCREAM, SHAKE, ROAR WHEN THE HOLY SPIRIT COMES?

Personally, there were three different times , while in the Presence of Holy Spirit, that I wept. One time, I felt the Love of God pour into my heart and soul in such a loving, personal way that I just wept and thanked Him.

Another time I wept as HE showed me I had some resentment against my Husband Paul and needed to repent of harboring it. I wept as I repented.

Another time, HE took the pain and hurt of my childhood to the surface and healed me as I wept. The music, the sermon, the prophecy was all fine-tuned to minister to me. The tears flowed and my broken heart, and emotional and spiritual pain was removed by God the Holy Ghost/Holy Spirit.

No psychiatrist/psychologist/or human being, could have gotten into my wounded spirit man and taken out the years of childhood pain and hurt; BUT GOD THE HOLY SPIRIT DID.

Another time the Holy Spirit filled me with such joy that I laughed and laughed and laughed. IT was a wonderful, refreshing laughter that came up from the depts of my being as all tension, stress, and discouragement left me. Many people, in the room, also burst out with Holy Ghost Laughter that took their stress, depression, discouragement, and fears away.

Other times I had wonderful visions of My Jesus. In a vision, I danced with My Jesus in a beautiful flower garden. I was in a white wedding gown and He was My Bridegroom. Another time, I had a vision of a picnic with My Jesus by the ocean. Another time I saw my Jesus riding a white horse through the heavenlies with the army of God following Him on white horses. I was riding one of them.

Every person ,who wanted God to touch them , received individual attention from God the Holy Spirit each time they attended the revival meetings. God deals with each of us as individuals. There are no carbon copies.

One time, before I left for Africa to begin missions, the Holy Spirit came upon me as a current, like electricity, and I knew He was giving me an anointing for ministry. I shook and shook as I laid there on the floor feeling super charged. IT didn't hurt. It was some kind of Holy Ghost Power running through my body. He was preparing me for the Africa Mission Trips He was sending me on.

Sometimes people shriek as the Holy Spirit delivers them from demons. Let them shriek. It is better that they be delivered from the demons then leave the building with them still tormenting them.

There was a man laying on the floor, roaring like a lion. He was a Chinese Christian. He was having a vision of the Lion of Judah fighting against the red dragon of the Chinese People. There are scriptures that call Jesus the Lion of the Tribe of Judah. There are other scriptures that say, "The Lord roars out of Zion." He saw, in the spirit, the battle going on.

God, the Holy Spirit, knows what each person needs at any given time. He comes at our invitation. People sing, "Holy Spirit, You are welcome in this place; Holy Spirit you are welcome in this place." Then when He comes to touch His Sheep; His People, the pastors close the meeting. You are grieving the Spirit of God. You are Wounding the Spirit of God. He comes to work in the hearts, emotions, bodies, souls, and spirits of His Children. Let Him have the Freedom to Minister in your churches.

HOW TO CONDUCT A HOLY GHOST/ HOLY SPIRIT SERVICE OR MEETING

First Give a Short teaching on how to receive from the Holy Spirit. I call it my DON'T BE, INSTRUCTIONS AS FOLLOWS:

Don't Be A Looker. Don't look around the room, watching everyone else. Your focus needs to be on Jesus, with your eyes closed, seeking Him. If you are not seeking Him, you will not be touched by His Holy Spirit.

Don't Be A Boxer. Don't stand there with your feet apart saying to yourself: "God is Not Going to Knock Me Down." While you are concentrating on not toppling over, you are not open to receive anything from God. Your focus must be on Jesus and you must be willing to receive whatever the Holy Spirit wants to minister to you.

Don't Be a Judge. Don't look around and say, "That is God." "That over there may not be God." "What is going on over there? Can that be of God?" Who made you a judge over God the Holy Spirit/Holy Ghost? Stop trying to Judge God and open your heart to receive from God what he wants to bless you with.

Don't Be a Chatterer. This is not the time to be telling God what you need or what you want Him to do. This is the time to be still, and know He is God. HE knows what you need, at any given time. Be Quiet, be open, focus on Jesus, and be willing to receive from God the Holy Spirit/Holy Ghost exactly what God wants to give you.

First instruct the Ushers to just stand in back of the people, catch them and lay them on the floor and leave them alone, in the presence of God. Instruct them Not to go near them, once they lay them down. Reverence God the Holy Spirit and leave Him to minister to the person the way He wants. Otherwise you will wound and grieve the Holy Spirit and interrupt what HE wants to do in that person's heart and life.

Clear the room of the benches, seats, or pews , if possible. IF you have stationary pews mounted into the floor, use the aisles to pray for the people. Play beautiful worship music either live music with worship team members or piped in beautiful worship music , with soft lyrics, welcoming the Holy Spirit to come and minister to His People. As people are touched by the Holy Spirit, they are simply caught by the ushers and laid on the floor.

Anoint the people with olive oil, or other anointing oil as you pray over them. Oil is symbolic of the Holy Spirit. When Samuel anointed David to be King, the Holy Spirit came upon David from that day forward. (1 Samuel 16:13). Later on, David, who was anointed and filled with the Holy Spirit, fought the giant Goliath. The Holy Spirit gave him boldness to stand against a huge giant, and win.

Don't close the meeting. Let God the Holy Spirit minister to His people as long as HE wants. Some people will be on the floor a half hour, others an hour, still other will be there for hours. You may have to just leave them there, and lock up the building with them still there , in God's Presence. God can do more in a human heart, soul, and spirit, than years of man-made counseling can do. Let God the Holy Spirit/Holy Ghost into your churches. People need Him Desperately. They need Him to heal their wounded emotions, their wounded spirits, their deep seated wounds from sexual abuse, physical abuse, or mental abuse.

Many need the Holy Spirit to deliver them from addictions, generational curses, and things they have not been able to overcome, by themselves. Many have secret sins, unconfessed sins, hidden personal problems that they will not discuss with any human being, BUT GOD THE HOLY SPIRIT KNOWS AND CAN HELP THEM. IT is God the Holy Ghost/Holy Spirit who changes us from glory to glory into the image of Christ. How are we to be changed in our minds, hearts, emotions, feelings, etc…unless we allow Holy Spirit to change us? How are we to be ready for the Return of Our Bridegroom if we don't allow Holy Spirit to get us ready? We need to cooperate with God the Holy Spirit and allow Him to mold us and make us like Jesus. Without His Divine Help, we will fail to become everything God has created us to be. We will fail to do and accomplish everything God created us to do and accomplish. We need God the Holy Spirit/Holy Ghost back into our churches NOW.

Kathleen Hollop

CHAPTER FOUR
SERMON PREPARATION GOD'S WAY

Once I heard about a Berean Sermon Preparation Course offered at a local Faith Assembly of God Church. Out of curiosity, I decided to attend a few classes to see what was being taught. I was shocked at how much intellectualism and fleshly ideas had gotten into the Sermon Preparation. Where, in the Bible, are the sermons by the early Church, labeled Topical, Textual, and Expository? Where did these terms come from and how can messages to the Body of Christ be prepared and labeled these things? Shouldn't the sermons be given to the Pastors by God the Holy Ghost? How many Pastors actually pray and ask the Lord to give them His Messages to preach to the congregations?

Matthew 28:18-20 "And Jesus came and spoke unto them, saying, All power is given unto me in heaven and in earth. Go ye therefore, and teach all nations, baptizing them in the name of the Father, and of the Son, and of the Holy Ghost; Teaching them to observe all things whatsoever I have commanded you; and, lo, I am with you always, even unto the end of the world. Amen."

The people of God need to be taught all things Jesus commanded us. How many pastors are really preaching and teaching the Bible? How many pastors deny the teachers and refuse to allow them to teach the Body of Christ the Word of God? How many pastors refuse to let a Holy Spirit filled evangelist have the pulpit to bring some correction into their churches and to impart their fold? How many pastors are actually preaching and teaching the Word of God from the pulpits of America? How many pastors are consumed with the things of this world and live for the tithe money and don't care about the sheep? How many love mammon, and not Jesus Christ?

I have been to many churches in Africa, in Columbia, in Venezuela, in Aruba, in the Philippines, and here in America. The Lord has had me visit many local churches in the Hudson River Valley of N.Y. to see what is going on in the churches. I have heard pastors preach their vacations, preach public events, compare Father God to the wizard of Oz, to compare the Christian walk to a roadrunner cartoon, preach dry messages that could never change a heart or a life, and even preach their building projects, ask for money to build their new parking lots, etc…on Sunday mornings. I have seen how pastors want to keep the entire Body of Christ locked inside their church buildings. I have seen pastors deny the ability of people to use their God given; Holy Spirit gifts, deny the calling of God on people's lives, discourage women and put them down, attack Holy Spirit filled brethren from the pulpits, cast Holy Spirit filled people out of their churches, and never allow anyone Holy Spirit filled to have the pulpit.

Every time I would leave for Africa, I had an empty notebook. When I arrived at the first village, town, slum area, mountain or desert, I would ask the Lord to give me His Messages for His People. I would pray, "Lord you know the hearts and lives of these people. You know where they are in their walk with you. You know what they need to hear. I don't. Please give me Your Messages to Your People every day, in Jesus Name. Amen."

Every night, in the wee hours of the morning, Holy Spirit would wake me up and give me the messages for the three messages for the two morning services and the after lunch service. I would have all three messages within an hour and a half. He, the Holy Spirit, would remind me of the scriptures and link them together the way He wanted them to come forth. IF I couldn't remember exactly where the scriptures were, I would look them up in my concordance. The Word of God is in me. I have read and studied my Bible six, seven, and eight hours a day for many years and am still reading the Word of God and He is still teaching me things. His Word is always fresh and new as He reveals it to us in deeper ways.

WE wouldn't give a physical baby meat to eat. They get the milk/formula. As they grow some cereal is mixed into the formula. After they can digest that, they get to taste fruit and vegetables. When they get enough teeth, they get some soft meats cut up in very small pieces. Gradually they can eat everything.

IT is exactly the same for a spiritual baby who just repents of their sins and receives Jesus Christ into their heart and life believing Jesus died on the cross for them personally. As they read their Bible, preferably the Gospel of John, and then Matthew, Mark and Luke they learn who Jesus is, what Jesus said, What Jesus did, and how Jesus related to people. Once they grow in God's wisdom and understanding with the Holy Spirit teaching them, the Holy Spirit can teach them more. As they read the Book of Acts and study the early church, and the signs, wonders, and miracles the disciples could do in Jesus' Name, they grow stronger spiritually. As they continue studying God's Word with the Holy Spirit teaching them, they can spiritually grow up and grasp the meat of the Word which is for mature believers that have their senses in tune to discern good and evil. The mature believers can help to grow the rest of the Body of Christ. IF people don't spiritually grow, they tend to fall back into the world, into the ungodly lusts, into the same ungodly mindsets, and the same life style that they had before they turned to Jesus. This is why we are to be RENEWED IN THE SPIRIT OF OUR MIND BY READING THE WORD OF GOD. We grow spiritually to the extent that we read God's Word-The Holy Bible and apply it to our everyday lives.

When I would preach the messages that Holy Spirit gave me to preach, hearts and lives were touched and changed. People would come to the altar and get right with God – Whether they needed to repent of some sin or whether they needed to surrender fully to Jesus- or whether they needed to forgive or stop the tribal hatred. Whatever they needed, Holy Spirit gave me the messages and the anointing to pray over them and see them saved, delivered, and healed, as they responded to the sermons. Pastors would come up to me all the time and say, "I want to go to the Bible College You Attended. What Bible College did you learn from?" I would reply, I went to the College of God the Holy Spirit and He taught me His Word."

> II Peter1:20-21 "Knowing this first, that no prophecy of the scripture is of any private interpretation. For the prophecy came not in old time by the will of man: but holy men of God spoke as they were moved by the Holy Ghost."

I Peter 1:7-12 "That the trial of your faith being much more precious than of gold that perishes, though it be tried by fire, might be found unto the praise and honor and glory at the appearing of Jesus Christ; Who having not seen, you love; in whom, though now you see him not, yet believing, you rejoice with joy unspeakable and full of glory: Receiving the end of your faith, even the salvation of your souls. Of which salvation the prophets have enquired and searched diligently, Who prophesied of the grace that should come unto you: Searching what, or what manner of time the Spirit of Christ which was in them did signify, when it testified beforehand the sufferings of Christ and the glory that should follow. " We see here, that the Holy Spirit of Jesus Christ testified to the prophets of Jesus Christ's coming hundreds of years before Jesus came and fulfilled those prophecies.

John 16:13 "Howbeit when he, the Spirit of truth is come, he will guide you into all truth: for he shall not speak of himself; but whatsoever he shall hear, that shall he speak; and he will shew you things to come." The Holy Ghost/Holy Spirit hears what Jesus Christ and Father God are saying in heaven. He can reveal what they are saying, to us, so that we can line up with Father God's Will and Purpose for our lives. IT is God the Holy Spirit who links us to Father God and Jesus Christ. It is the Holy Spirit who can show us the future-things to come. It is the Holy Spirit who changes us from glory to glory to be more like Jesus.

The real author of the Bible is God the Holy Ghost. This is why the prophet Isaiah knew of the birth of Jesus Christ, who He was, and how He would be despised and rejected and crucified, hundreds of years before Christ came. The Holy Ghost revealed all of this to the Prophet Isaiah and then Jesus Christ came and fulfilled it. (Isaiah 7:14) describes the virgin birth.

Isaiah 9:6-7 "For unto us a child is born, unto us a son is given: and the government shall be upon his shoulder; and his name shall be called Wonderful, Counselor, The Mighty God, The

Everlasting Father, the Prince of Peace. OF the increase of his government and peace there shall be no end, upon the throne of David, and upon his kingdom, to order it, and to establish it with judgment and with justice from henceforth even for ever. The zeal of the Lord of hosts will perform this."

Jesus was planted in Mary's Womb by God the Holy Ghost. HE is the "Seed of The Woman who would bruise the devil's head, mentioned in Genesis 3:15." Jesus was planted in Mary's womb by God the Holy Ghost. Mary was the relative of King David , a virgin, and chosen by God to implant Jesus as the Seed of The Word of God, into her womb. Jesus was NEVER AN EGG OF THE WOMAN. IF Jesus was Mary's egg, He would have had original sin. He was never an egg. He was a "SEED."

Hebrews Chapter 7:1-3 "For this Melchisedec, king of Salem, priest of the most high God, who met Abraham returning from the slaughter of the kings, and blessed him: To whom Abraham gave a tenth part of all, first being by interpretation King of Righteousness, and after that also King of Salem, which is, King of peace; Without father, without mother, without descent, having neither beginning of days, not end of life; but made like unto the Son of God; abides a priest continually." We see here that Jesus Always Was and Is God. There was never a time that Jesus didn't exist.

Isaiah 53 describes the rejection Jesus suffered, the griefs and sorrows he bore, the wounds he endured for our transgressions, bruises for our iniquities, the stripes he bore on his back for our healing, the affliction he suffered, the fact that he was silent and didn't try to defend himself, he was put in prison, he was cut of from life for our transgressions, he made his grave with the wicked(he was crucified between two thieves) and with the rich in his death (he was placed in a rich man's tomb), his soul was made an offering for our sins, he bare our sins, etc… Read Isaiah 53 and see for yourself. Keep in mind, this was written hundreds of years before Jesus left heaven and came to earth. It was God the Holy Ghost who revealed these things to the Prophet Isaiah.

The Prophet Micah prophesied that the Messiah would be born in Bethlehem. Look at Micah 5:2 "But thou, Bethlehem, Ephratah, though you be little among the thousands of Judah, yet out of you shall he come forth unto me that is to be ruler in Israel ; whose goings forth have been from of old, from everlasting."

Many people don't realize that Jesus Christ is God. HE always was. There was Never a Time when Jesus wasn't. If we look at Daniel Chapter 3, the story of Shadrach, Meshach, and Abednego, it will prove my point. King Nebuchadnezzar made an image of gold and demanded that everyone fall down and worship the idol he had made. Shadrach, Meshach, and Abednego refused to bow before Neb's idol. They stood before the king and said in Daniel 3:17 "If it be so, our God whom we serve is able to deliver us from the burning fiery furnace, and he will deliver us out of your hand, O king. But if not, be it known unto you, O king, that we will not serve your gods, nor worship the golden image which you have set up."

> Daniel 3:19 "Then was Nebuchadnezzar full of fury. HE commanded that they should heat the furnace seven times more than it would normally be heated. Then he commanded the most mighty men that were in his army to bind Shadrach, Meshach, and Abednego, and to cast them into the burning fiery furnace. Because the furnace was so hot, the flame of the fire slew the army men who threw them in. In verse 23, they fell down bound into the midst of the burning fiery furnace. Then the king was astonished because he saw four men walking around in the midst of the fire. In verse 25 He said, I see four men loose, walking in the midst of the fire, and they have no hurt; and the form of the fourth is like the SON OF GOD." Jesus Christ was there, in the furnace walking with them AS A MAN, BEFORE HE WAS EVER A BABY IN MARY's WOMB. Jesus Always Was God.

When we think about the Garden of Eden, it was Jesus who walked with Adam and Eve in the midst of the garden. No one can see the face of God the Father and live in an earthly body. God hid Abraham in the cleft of a rock and passed by; letting Abraham only see His back, after

He passed by. God the Holy Spirit/Holy Ghost is a Spirit. IT was not Him in the garden either. It was Jesus Christ, in human form , as a man, who walked with Adam and Eve in the Garden of Eden.

> John 4:23-24 "But the hour comes, and now is, when the true worshippers shall worship the Father in spirit, and in truth; for the Father seeks such to worship him. God is a Spirit: and they that worship him must worship him in spirit and in truth."

How can we worship God in Spirit and in Truth if we deny the work of God the Holy Spirit and revert to our own devices, man-made intellectualism, man-made ideas, man-made programs, man-made schedules, and man-made sermons? The Bible says in John 15:5 "I am the vine, you are the branches, He that abides in me, and I in him, the same brings forth much fruit: for without me you can do nothing."

When we revert to our flesh to make a man-made sermon, instead of asking the Holy Spirit to give us the message for His People, the message is dead, lifeless, and could never change anyone's heart or life. IF a message does not have the Holy Spirit moving in it and through it, it is a useless, ridiculous piece of man-made nonsense that shouldn't even be preached at all. Our flesh profits nothing. The Spirit is Life, and Light, and Truth.

There are many unfaithful pastors preaching their vacations, Greek myths, new age philosophies, their pedigree papers, their degrees, their popular public opinions, their ear tickling messages that will never correct anyone, their non-Biblical current event messages, and anything but the Word of God, from the pulpits of America. Many twist the Word of God into lies by taking what God really said out of context, adding manmade meanings that God didn't say, and distorting God's Holy Bible into half-truths and lies. "No lie is of the truth." The Holy Spirit is not obligated to bring to pass man's words that are contrary to God's Real Words. The Holy Spirit will only accompany the real Word of God. Many phony Bibles leave out key scriptures on the Blood of Christ, the Trinity, the Deity of Jesus Christ, and the exact words God really said. I'll give you some examples of this:

> Matthew 4:4 Jesus said, "It is written, Man shall not live by bread alone, but by every word that proceeds out of the mouth of god."(KJV Bible)

Some other Bibles say, "IT is written, man shall not live by bread alone." People who read the phony Bibles will never know that there is more to the scripture, "But by every word out of the mouth of God." They will get the idea that they need to eat vegetables, fruit, and meat.

Scripture pulled out of the context is equally dangerous. A Baptist Church leader did not understand 1 Corinthians 13:10. They said, "But when that which is perfect is come, that which is in part shall be done away." "The Bible is here. The Bible is perfect. No need for the gifts." I said, "Are you telling me that if someone was sick, you wouldn't pray for their healing, believing the Lord could heal them? Or if someone demon oppressed came into your church you wouldn't try to deliver them?" They said, "Believe Me. The Gifts Are Not For Today!"

I looked up that scripture and read the entire chapter of 1 Corinthians 13:12 which says "For now we see through a glass darkly; but then face to face: now I know in part; but then shall I know even as I am known." It is obviously speaking of when we are face to face with Jesus Christ, in heaven, there will be no need for the gifts. There certainly is a real need for healings, salvations, and deliverances, here on earth. Because they took one scripture out of the context in which it was written , they did away with whole chapters of 1 Corinthians 12, 1 Corinthians 14, the Book of Acts, Mark 16:15-18, and many other scriptures.

WE must be a people who "Rightly Divide the Word of Truth." IF we don't we will be deceived. IF there is no need for the gifts, there would be no need for preaching gifts, evangelism gifts, teaching gifts, apostolic giftings, prophetic giftings, etc…There is certainly a need for all these gifts and other gifts that include healings, and deliverances, miracles, signs, wonders, and everything the Lord has given to the Body of Christ to further His Plan and His Kingdom, here on earth as it is in heaven.

> Mark 16:15-18 (KJV) Jesus said, "Go ye into all the world, and preach the gospel to every creature. HE that believes and is baptized shall be saved; but he that believes not shall be damned. And these signs shall follow them that believe;

> In my name shall they cast out devils; they shall speak with new tongues; They shall take up serpents; and if they drink any deadly thing; it shall not hurt them, they shall lay hands on the sick, and they shall recover."

These signs shall follow the Believers – US. We are the current Believers in Jesus Christ. These signs shall follow us. We shall cast out devils. We shall speak in tongues (Holy Ghost Prayer Languages). We will have victory over snakes (Demonic spirits, demonic people, demons,) This goes along with Luke 10:19 Jesus said, "Behold, I give unto you power to tread on serpents and scorpions, and over all the power of the enemy: and nothing shall by any means hurt you." Jesus is speaking about Satan's agents, calling them snakes and scorpions. No where in the Bible are we told to deliberately play with poisonous snakes and scorpions. We are not to put the Lord our God to the test. We are not to deliberately drink poison either. But there have been cases where witches tried to poison missionaries and the poison had no effect, when the missionaries stood on the Word of God. There have been other cases where a hospital gave a child a wrong dose of medicine that could have killed the child, but the parents stood on the Word of God and the medicine had no ill effect on their child.

People who listen to a sermon may have demonic mindsets, barriers, mis-information, mistaken ideas, wrong attitudes, etc…that only the Holy Spirit can break through with the truth of the Word of God. A dead sermon, without the Holy Spirit, will do and accomplish NOTHING in the Hearts and Lives of the people. It takes God the Holy Spirit, accompanying the Word of God, that gets the Word of God through the obstacles of the enemy; right into the hearers minds and hearts to bring about spiritual change.

> John 14:26 "But the Comforter which is the Holy Ghost, whom the Father will send in my name, he shall teach you all things, and bring all things to your remembrance, whatsoever I (Jesus) have spoken unto you." As the Word of God is being preached, it is the Holy Spirit who brings that Word into our mind and spirit so He can remind us of the Word later on when we need it. HE reminds us of what Jesus Christ has said to us.

It is the Holy Spirit who knows what messages the people need to hear in order to deliver them, heal them, minister to them, and get them to spiritually grow into the Father's Will and Purpose for their lives. His Messages bring Life, Light and Truth that penetrates the darkness and gets deep inside the minds, hearts, and souls of the people of God, to bring them lasting change.

On the way to the crusades, in Kenya and Uganda, I would ask the Holy Spirit for a scripture to start with. He would give me one scripture. I would speak that scripture and Holy Spirit would come upon me and continue speaking the scriptures He knew would draw people to Jesus. The Holy Spirit knew who would attend the crusade each day and what scriptures would touch their heart and draw them to faith in Jesus Christ. I would continue until Holy Spirit told me to give an altar call to receive Jesus. People would come forward and get saved. If you were to ask me what the other scriptures I used at the crusade were, I could not tell you. I could only tell you the first one. IT was God the Holy Spirit, on that platform, ministering the Gospel to His People. I was just a delivery girl (like UPS or the Postal Service). The messages were God's Messages to His People, given to me by the Holy Spirit according to the will of Father God and Jesus Christ. To God be the Glory, Honor and Praise Now And Forever. Amen.

Once I was in Garissa, Kenya preaching to many Christian Churches that came together for a joint meeting. I thought everyone attending was saved. The Holy Spirit knew there was one man sitting among us who was not yet saved. The message, I was preaching, was swung into a Salvation Message by the Holy Spirit. I gave an altar call and one Muslim man came running forward to get saved. Everyone thought everyone was a Christian, but God the Holy Spirit knew that man was ready to receive Jesus. Then the Holy Spirit swung the message back to the original message and it continued . That Muslim man began working with the local pastors and churches to bring the Gospel of Jesus Christ to many Muslim people. IT amazed me that the message flowed so perfectly into that salvation message and then so perfectly back into the original message. The Holy Spirit is Amazing. He knows what needs to be preached at any given time.

Acts 20:28-31 "Take heed therefore unto yourselves, and to all the flock, over which the Holy Ghost has made you overseers, to feed the church of God, which he has purchased with his own blood. For I know this, that after my departing shall grievous wolves enter in among you, not sparing the flock. Also of your own selves shall men arise, speaking perverse things, to draw away disciples after them. Therefore watch, and remember, that by the space of three years I ceased not to warn every one night and day with tears." Luke was warning them of false teachers, false preachers, wolves pretending to be of God, but not of God. Any Pastor, Minister, Preacher, Teacher, Priest, Apostle, Prophet, Evangelist, who preaches things contrary to the Word of God is one of these wolves. That is why it is **VITAL TO WEIGH EVERYTHING THEY SAY BY THE WORD OF GOD.** IF they are condoning all the wickedness of the world and refuse to preach God's Truth, they need to step down or be thrown out of the churches. They will be held accountable for what they preach, and for what truth they refuse to preach.

When we look at the messages preached by Peter who was filled with the Holy Ghost, we see that three thousand people received Jesus. In another account five thousand people came to faith in Jesus Christ. Peter was a vessel used by God the Holy Spirit to reach many souls for Jesus. We can also be powerful witnesses for Jesus if we allow the Holy Spirit/Holy Ghost to fill us and use us. Without God the Holy Ghost/Holy Spirit, we can accomplish nothing. Let Holy Spirit give you His sermons, His messages for His People. Your Church will come alive and fulfill the call of God, if you let God be in control, and work in the people's hearts, souls and lives to do His Perfect Will. As you release people into Father's Will for their lives, Father will bring more people into your church for you to grow.

CHAPTER FIVE
WARNINGS OF THE HOLY SPIRIT

There have been many times that God the Holy Spirit has warned me of physical danger, spiritual danger, and the enemies plans and schemes. IF I failed to listen to His Warnings, I would have been kidnapped, raped, robbed, or murdered . If we study the Book of Acts, there are many times that the Holy Spirit guided the disciples as to who should go on a mission, what direction they should go, what they should take with them, and what to do with the situations they faced. Lets first look at some of these examples and then how the Holy Spirit has worked in my life and can work in your life if you are willing to listen to Him.

> In the account of Acts 8:26-39, First the angel of the Lord spoke to Phillip and told him to go down from Jerusalem unto Gaza, which was desert. Phillip immediately arose and went. He saw a man of Ethiopia, a eunuch of great authority under Candace queen of the Ethiopians returning from worshipping in Jerusalem. The man was sitting in his chariot reading the prophet Isaiah (Esaias). The HOLY SPIRIT SAID unto Phillip, "Go near, and join yourself to this chariot." Phillip ran to the eunuch and heard him reading Isaiah. Phillip asked him if he understood the scriptures. The man said, "How can I unless someone guide me." The man was reading Isaiah 53 (the sufferings of Jesus Christ for our transgressions). The eunuch wanted to know who the scriptures were speaking about. Phillip was able to share faith in Jesus with the man and the eunuch believed. They came to WATER in the desert and the eunuch wanted to be water baptized. Phillip said if he believed with his whole

heart he could be baptized. The eunuch said, "I believe that Jesus Christ is the Son of God." Phillip and the eunuch went into the water and Phillip baptized him. As they were coming out of the water, the Spirit of the Lord caught away Phillip, and the eunuch saw him no more. "But Phillip was found at Azotus, and passing through he preached in all the cities, till he came to Caesarea."

When we look at this account, we see that both an angel of the Lord, and the Holy Spirit, worked together, and spoke to Phillip. WE also see that both the angel of the Lord and the Holy Spirit knew that the Ethiopian eunuch was there, in the desert, at that time. What if the eunuch had left the day before? What if the eunuch had decided to wait in Jerusalem another week? What if Phillip didn't leave right away and told himself he would rest first and leave tomorrow for the desert.? The timing of this entire recorded meeting was GOD'S PERFECT TIMING. That eunuch worked for the queen of Ethiopia. HE was able to witness to the queen and the people of Ethiopia that Jesus Christ is the Son of God. We have no way of knowing how many people received faith in Jesus Christ because of that eunuch's testimony. HE was the chosen evangelist for the people of Ethiopia.

WE cannot ignore the fact that the Holy Spirit caught away Phillip (Phillip was transported-whisked away by the Spirit of the Lord) and was found several towns away. What a Way to Travel!

In Acts 20:22-28 The Disciple Paul said, "And now, behold, I go bound in the spirit, unto Jerusalem, not knowing the things that shall befall me there: Save that the Holy Ghost witnesses in every city, saying that bonds and afflictions abide me. But none of these things move me, neither count I my life dear unto myself, so that I might finish my course with joy, and the ministry, which I have received of the Lord Jesus, to testify the gospel of the grace of God. And now, I know that you all, among whom I have gone preaching the kingdom of God, shall see my face no more. Wherefore, I take you in record this day, that I am pure from the blood of all men. For I have not shunned to declare unto you all the counsel of God. Take heed therefor unto yourselves, and to all the flock, over which the Holy Ghost has made you overseers, to feed the church of God, which he has purchased with his own blood."

We see here that prophets had warned Paul of the bonds and afflictions that awaited him in Jerusalem, but he chose to obey the Holy Spirit and go, trusting God with his life and future. IF Paul did not obey the Holy Spirit, many books of the New Testament would not have been written for us to live by.

In Acts 21:3-4 Paul was warned by some prophetic disciples not to go up to Jerusalem. In Acts 21:8-12 a prophet named Agabus took Paul's girdle, and bound his own hands and feet, and said, "Thus says the Holy Ghost, So shall the Jews at Jerusalem bind the man that owns this girdle, and shall deliver him into the hands of the Gentiles." And when we heard these things, both we, and they of that place, besought him not to go up to Jerusalem. Then Paul answered, "What do you mean to weep and to break my heart? for I am ready not to be bound only, but also to die at Jerusalem for the name of the Lord Jesus." And when he would not be persuaded, we ceased, saying, "The will off the Lord be done."

The Prophet Agabus gave Paul more information than he had before. Agabus said he would be delivered into the hand of the Gentiles. Paul chose to TRUST AND OBEY THE HOLY SPIRIT/HOLY GHOST, rather than man.

In 1999, I was going back to Africa to preach in Kenya, Uganda, Tanzania, Rwanda, Burundi, and Zaire/Congo. It would be a 2 ½ month trip. One day, before I left for Africa, I was praying about these African Nations and got a check in my spirit over Zaire/Congo. Holy Spirit was warning me not to go there. I wrote my coordinator in Kenya a letter telling him not to schedule anything in Zaire. He never got my letter. When I arrived in Kenya and looked at the schedule, Zaire was on it. Immediately I got a check in my spirit about Zaire. After preaching the weeks in Kenya, Uganda, Tanzania, Rwanda and Burundi, Holy Spirit spoke to me. An overwhelming feeling of grief hit me and I knew if I went to Zaire, I would never see my family again on planet earth. I would die.

The Kenyan pastors, I was traveling with, were going to Zaire. I said, "Please drive me to the Burundi airport. I'll take a plane back to Kenya. God is warning me that if I go to Zaire I will be killed." They all decided to drive back to Kenya with me. The next day, they heard a report that three Americans and five Uganda college students were murdered in the forest, by Congolese Terrorists who fled back into the Congo. They were studying the gorillas, in the forest, when they were murdered. If we went to Zaire, we would have had to pass through that forest. We would have been among the dead. Holy Spirit saved Our Lives.

> Acts 16: 6-10 "Now when they (Paul and Silas) had gone throughout Phrygia and the region of Galatia, and were forbidden of the Holy Ghost to preach word in Asia. After they were come to Mysia, they purposed to go into Bithynia, but the Spirit suffered them not. And after passing by Mysia came down to Troas. And a vision appeared to Paul in the night: There stood a man of Macedonia, and prayed him, saying, "Come over into Macedonia and help us."

As we can see here, they were guided by Holy Spirit. Asia was not ready to hear the gospel, at that time. If they had disobeyed Holy Spirit and had gone to Asia, they probably would have died there. The Holy Spirit told them not to go into Bithynia. Then they saw the Macedonia vision and went there.

In 1990, my husband Paul was going on a business trip. He was flying from the airport near us to the New York City Airport. From there he was flying to Texas. As usual, I took him to the local airport, but Holy Spirit warned me that if Paul got on the plane, he would die. An overwhelming feeling of grief came over me and I knew something was wrong with the plane. I begged him not to get on the plane. He said, " I have to. I'll miss my connecting flight." In tears, I walked away and prayed. " Father God, send an angel to open the eyes of whoever is checking out the plane. Let them see what is wrong with it and let it not leave the ground, in Jesus name, Amen." About five minutes before they were to board the plane, an announcement came over the intercom, " This flight is cancelled due to major mechanical failure." Limos arrived to drive the passengers to New York City. The plane that had major mechanical failure was a small 14 to 20 passenger plane. One man was screaming at the girl behind the desk, "I'll miss my connecting flight!" I yelled in a loud voice, " I thank God that plane didn't take off. You would all be dead." Then the man shut up. Paul was driven by limousine to the New York City Airport, upgraded to an earlier flight and arrived at the Texas Airport earlier than he would have arrived otherwise. God is good! After this plane incident, Paul received Jesus as his Savior and Lord that same year, 1990.

Usually, I didn't fast when leaving on a six-week-long preaching/mission trip to Africa. The Lord wanted me to be strong, not weakened in my body, from fasting. But one trip to Kenya was different. The week before I was to leave, the Lord had me fast for five days, eat for 2 days, and leave for Kenya. I only had liquids for 5 days, no solid food. Once I arrived in Kenya, I realized why.

The day after I arrived, my coordinator and I were walking down the street in Nairobi, to buy Some Bibles to take into the villages. People, in the distance, were running back and forth zigzagging all over the place trying to avoid someone or something. As we approached, we saw a 4 ft tall woman, full of demons, chasing people through the streets. She was out of her mind, in dirty rags, demanding money of them and climbing on them. She started toward me. I pointed my finger at her and said "In the name of Jesus," and she fell to the ground. The Lord said, "It is Legion." Legion means that she had thousands of demons in her. I said, " Legion, in the name of Jesus, come out of her." They began manifesting as long strands of mucus coming out of her nose and puke coming out of her mouth. They were running out of her. It took less than eight minutes and they were all gone. My coordinator Chris interpreted for me as I asked her some questions. She had been in the marketplace three years sleeping outside in the gutter. She was from a town miles away. I preached Jesus Christ to her and she received Jesus into her heart and life. People were amazed to see her in her right mind, walking with us. I took her to my hotel room, let her wash in the shower, and gave her a skirt and blouse to wear. Then I brought her some food and a bus ticket to go back home. I told her to get into a church where Jesus is preached and Holy Spirit is present she needed to read the Bible and press into God to keep the demons from trying to return.

After this incident, I realized that I had to fast that time because certain demons only come out by prayer and fasting. An entire Legion of demons had to bow before the Name of Jesus and had to leave her right away, when I commanded them to, in Jesus name. Every knee will bow to Jesus. Even Satan himself must bow to My Jesus. Satan is just a fallen angel. Jesus created the angels.

While in Rwanda and Burundi, a pastor interpreted for me into French. He told me that many Rwandan pastors had been killed in a plane crash. He was supposed to go with them, on this trip, but he got a check in his spirit, that something was wrong. Holy Spirit warned him not to go. He didn't go, and his life was spared. I am sure Holy Spirit warned the other pastors too, but they did not listen. A fog came up, the pilot couldn't see, and the plane hit the side of a mountain. All aboard were killed. Listening to Holy Spirit can save your life.

There were a few times when Holy Spirit told me I wasn't safe in a hotel. One time my interpreter Ben, coordinator Chris and I arrived in a town. The hotel was a separate building from the restaurant that was across the parking lot from the hotel. My coordinator, Chris was tired and went to his room. I went to my room. My interpreter, Ben, was hungry, so he went across to eat in the restaurant.

While in my room, I had no peace. I couldn't sleep and felt something was wrong. I rebuked the devil, thinking it was the enemy trying to rob my sleep. I still had no peace. When I asked the Lord why I had no peace, Holy Spirit said, " You are not safe here. In the morning, change hotels."

The next morning I bathed and got dressed. Then I knocked at the coordinator's door and said, " Pack up your things, we have to change hotels." He was annoyed because he had just unpacked for the week. I knocked at my interpreters door and told him we had to change hotels. He said, " It is good we are getting out of here. While at the restaurant, I overheard the owner of the place talking to another guy trying to figure out whether to call the police or not. His daughter had just been kidnapped by gangsters who were holding her for ransom." I would have been their next victim, had I stayed there. Most Africans have the idea that anyone with white skin has a lot of money or can get a lot of money. That is why it's important to listen to Holy Spirit's warnings. We changed hotels.

There were times Holy Spirit warned me not to cut across a field to get to the post office, to call home. Sometimes I would be in the villages for weeks. There were no phones, cell phones, computers, mailmen etc… When I got back to Kisumu, Kenya, I would eagerly head to the post office to phone Paul. I obeyed the Holy Spirit when he told me not to cut across the fields. There could have been a poisonous snake there or someone hiding in the tall grass to ambush me. I walked on the roadway instead. It took a few more minutes, but I was kept safe from harm.

Sometimes Holy Spirit can reveal to you the real heart of someone around you. One time, while preaching in a village church, a woman in the church came up to me and said "Sister Kathy, I am so glad you are here." When I looked into her eyes, I saw something demonic glaring at me and realized she was into witchcraft.

> Matthew 6:22 "The light of the body is the eye: If therefore your eye be single, your whole body shall be full of light. But if your eye be evil, your whole body shall be full of darkness. If therefore the light that is in you be darkness, how great is the darkness." I always Look into people's eyes to see if I see the Light of Christ in them.

This same woman came up to me with a package wrapped in newspapers. She said, "Sister Kathy, I got you a present." Immediately Holy Spirit warned me it was evil. Under my breath, I bound the demons in it. When I opened it, I saw two African heads made out of clay. She had made them with spells, incantations, witchcraft and demons attached. She figured I would carry them with me everywhere I went and the demons would attack me and prevent me from accomplishing anything. After she walked away, my coordinator took them to an outhouse and threw them down into the outhouse hole with the poop where they belonged.

Sometimes people's eyes can be full of false light. They can shine with some kind of weird illumination from attending New Age Movement, demonic festivals where strange music is played and some kind of crazy lights and demons are released. They believe the lie that they are going to "evolve into gods." It is the same lie Satan told Adam and Eve, in the garden, before they ate the forbidden fruit.

Genesis 3:4-5 " The snake said unto the woman, "You shall not surely die. For God knows that in the day you eat thereof, then your eyes shall be opened, and you shall be as Gods, knowing Good and Evil." The New Age Movement is Satan's old lie with a new packaging. Don't be deceived. The real light is Jesus Christ, the Word of God.

Paul, Brian, and I, met a man who conducts these demonic New Age light shows, when we attended a poetry reading event. When we tried to tell him about Jesus, he said a belief in God was ridiculous. He talked about some kind of weird four dimensions. After walking away from him, we prayed against Satan, his four dimensions of lies and occult practices and spiritual blindness. The man doesn't realize the darkness he is in and is promoting. Sadly, he is so intellectually wrong no one can get through to him with the Gospel of Jesus Christ. He said it is archaic to believe in God and he would not engage in such an unintelligent conversation. Some day he will stand before the God he refused. His fake light will not save his soul from hell. Jesus Saves. Without Jesus there is no Salvation.

Not all bad dreams come from the devil. Sometimes Holy Spirit warns people in dreams about what Satan is planning to do. If they pray against it, they can dismantled before it happens for example, a woman in Kenya, had a dream that her daughters car collided with a sugarcane truck. She saw the car destroyed in the dream, and knew her daughter was injured. She should have said " Satan, in Jesus name, your plans to destroy my daughter's car and injure my daughter in a collision with a sugar truck are canceled, null and void and will not happen in Jesus name. Amen." She didn't pray against it. A few weeks later, it happened.

In a Village, my coordinator had a dream that people jumped out of the bushes and were dragging us away somewhere, against our will. When he told me about the dream, I prayed, " in Jesus name, Satan your plans are cancelled, your plans to have people kidnap or attack us, or drag us off somewhere, or harm us, are canceled, null and void. This will not happen, in Jesus name. Amen." Because we prayed against it, it did not happen.

If you have a dream about an accident, an illness attacking a loved one, someone attacking a loved one or you, a bad thing happening… pray against it and dismantle it, in Jesus name. As a child of God, we can stop the enemy before his plans can manifest if we pray against them in Jesus name.

When Holy Spirit warns you about someone or tells you not to go somewhere, or about an object, Listen and Obey him. He is trying to protect your life. If it wasn't for Holy Spirit, I would have been wiped out by our enemy, the devil, many years ago.

The Holy Spirit can warn you not to purchase an object, a piece of jewelry, an item of clothing, a certain antique, etc. . if there is a demonic spirit or demonic anointing on it.

> Acts 19:11 "And God wrought special miracles by the hands of Paul; So that from his body were brought unto the sick handkerchiefs or aprons, and the diseases departed from them, and the evil spirits went out of them."

Paul would lay his hands on the handkerchiefs and aprons, and impart a Holy Spirit anointing into them. That anointing when brought to the sick, healed them. People would carry the Holy Spirit's anointed cloths to their sick family members and they would recover.

As the Holy Spirit Anointing can be imparted into objects by God's People, a demonic spirit and demonic anointing can be imparted into objects by Satan's people.

Years ago, my mother phoned me from another state to tell me that my sister was seeing things moving in her room. Her blood cells were all at crazy levels and she was in horrible pain.

When I heard that she was seeing things moving in her room, I knew she was under demonic attack. After packing my suitcase, I drove for four hours praying in tongues (Holy Spirit's Language), and arrived at the house. Tongues is one of the giftings given to the Body of Christ mentioned in 1 Corinthians Chapters 12 and 14.

When I don't know how to pray for someone, what to pray, what is really going on with them, what is attacking them, etc...I ask Holy Spirit to give me the right prayer that needs to be prayed. The Holy Spirit knows what the situation really is, what needs to be prayed, and how to help the person effectively. He is God the Holy Spirit. He knows it all and sees it all. I don't. I pray in my Holy Spirit Prayer Language until I have peace in my heart. Then I know it will be OK.

In the middle of the night, the Lord led me to go into my sister's room. There was a white spirit form moving at the foot of her bed. I said, "I bind you in the Name of Jesus and cast you out of this house never to return again." It vanished. Then I prayed, "Lord show me what is causing this attack on my sister."

My sister's boyfriend had purchased a piece of artwork from a local roadside stand and gave it to my sister. The painting was of a black panther with it's teeth barred waiting to bite someone. It was hanging on her bedroom wall.

When I asked the Lord to show me anything demonic that I needed to stand against, I was shocked to see a spirit form go over the face of the panther. It's green eyes began moving and its teeth began moving up and down as it's jaw opened and closed. I jumped back a few feet and said ,"Lord, what do you want me to do with this?" The Lord said, "Burn it." I said, "Lord, if I burn her painting and she gets angry, how am I to lead her to You?"

The Lord said , "Take it outside and put it under the tree." I went forward, grabbed the painting, turned the back of the frame toward me (the face away from me), marched it outside and threw it under the tree.

I went back into my sister's room and asked the Lord if there was anything else. He said, "No." Then the Lord had me anoint my sister with oil and pray for the healing of her body and her Salvation, in Jesus Name. The next day, she was no longer in pain and I was able to lead her in a Salvation Prayer to receive Jesus.

I told her the painting was demonic and to burn it. Instead, she gave it back to her boyfriend. He put it on his wall above his tropical fish tank. In the morning, the fish were all dead floating belly up in the water. He got frightened and threw the painting in the back seat of his car.

Unknown to my sister, she borrowed the car to drive my nephew to pick up a cat someone had promised him. She told my nephew what I said about the painting. The car ran out of gas and they had to walk several miles to get a gas can. The car gauge said they had gas in it. While driving, a dog came out of no where and ran into the side of the car. My nephew noticed the painting in the back seat . Needless to say, they lit a fire and burnt it up.

> Deuteronomy 7:25-26 says, "The graven images of their gods shall you burn with fire: you shall not desire the silver or gold that is on them, not take it unto you, lest you be snared, for it is an abomination to the Lord your God, Neither shall you

bring an abomination into your house, lest you be a cursed thing like it: but you shall utterly detest it, and you shall utterly abhor it: for it is a cursed thing."

In 1Corinthians 2:11-14, we see that the Holy Spirit compares spiritual things with spiritual. Someone who doe not have the Holy Spirit, does not see what things really are. With my natural eyes, in my flesh, I couldn't see what was wrong with my sister's painting. When I asked Holy Spirit to show me, He opened up my spiritual vision to see what was really there. Holy Spirit reveals what is really of God and what is not of God.

The world promotes Ouija boards. People ignorantly buy them and allow their children to play with them. They don't realize that a demonic spirit moves and answers their questions. It's object is to destroy your children. There was a college honor student who began playing with a Ouija board. She became depressed, her grades dropped, and she had a total mental breakdown.

People allow their children to have witchcraft books, watch wizard movies, read wizard books, watch demonic murderous horror films, practice witchcraft, enchantments, tarot card reading, seances (necromance), etc... All these things are listed in Deuteronomy 18:9-12 as "Abominations to God."

When you bring objects that are connected with these things into your house, you are welcoming Satan and his demons to come in and attack you, your family, your marriage, your finances, your health, etc...

Years ago, there were silver statues of wizards and dragons sold in local stores. People were buying them, not realizing that they were bringing Abominations into their homes.

In Revelation12:9, Satan himself is described as "the great dragon, that old serpent."The Chinese people worship the red dragon. They don't realize they are actually worshipping Satan.

Karl Marx who invented the "Communist" and "Socialist" ideologies was a Satanist. These Wicked Ideologies are designed to deny God, deny Christ, deny the Bible, deny God Given Freedoms ,liberty, justice, kindness, goodness, decency, righteousness, truth, self-will, etc... Marx was possessed by Satan.

These Wicked Marxist ideologies are used by Satanists to control entire populations of people with intimidation, oppression, threats of death, persecutions , beatings, imprisonments, murders, tyranny, misery. Anyone who opposes these Satanists is tortured, imprisoned, and put to death. Communism shows no mercy, no genuine love, no compassion, no tolerance for any opposition etc… Under Socialism, the Government owns Everything. It owns the people it rules over,. body, soul ,and spirit, and demands total obedience to it or death. It demands that People worship IT, instead of God. Government demands the Worship of Everyone it Governs. No one can own a house, pick the job they want, get rewards and raises for working hard, enjoy the fruits of their labor, etc. They control the entire brain washing of the children into their demonic mindsets and sick ideologies.

If you are a Christian and agree with any of these demonic ideologies, you have been deceived by Satan. Our freedoms, liberties, talents, abilities, giftings, free-will and our very lives are all gifts from God. They do not come from government at all. Read the Bible and discover God's Truth. If you know God's Truth, you won't be deceived by Satan's lies.

The Holy Spirit is God The Holy Spirit. He knows what Satan is up to and can warn you, ahead of time, of any and all danger. If you obey Him, He can save your life.

I had a cousin who had been addicted to alcohol and drugs. He came to faith in Jesus, was attending a Salvation Army Church, and was doing well.

One day, an old friend approached him and convinced him to go off with him. The old friend was still addicted to drugs and had purchased some. I'm sure the Holy Spirit tried to warn my cousin not to go with that old friend. He didn't listen.

My cousin was found dead a few days later from a drug overdose. Satan will always tempt you in the thing God delivered you from. If it is lust, he will tempt you to watch lustful TV programs, soaps, porn, computer sex sites etc…

If it is alcohol, drugs, gambling, etc…, he will tempt you, using people to try to lure you back to them.

We are to flee temptation. If you try to resist it by being exposed to it, you will be snared by it. Get away from it. Don't be around it.

Flee Temptation and resist the devil and he will flee from you. First draw near to God. He will give you all the strength and power you need to fight the devil. Listen to and obey Holy Spirit when He warns you. It may save your life.

CHAPTER SIX
THE FIVE FOLDS OF MINISTRY

Ephesians 4:10-15 "He that descended is the same also that ascended up far above the heavens, that he might fill all things. And he gave some, apostles, and some, prophets; and some, evangelists; and some, pastors and teachers; For the perfecting of the saints, for the work of the ministry, for the edifying of the body of Christ: Till we all come in the unity of the faith, and of the knowledge of the Son of God,, unto a perfect man, unto the measure of the stature of the fulness of Christ; That we henceforth be no more children tossed to and fro, and carried about with every wind of doctrine, by the slight of men, and cunning craftiness, whereby they lie in wait to deceive; But speaking the truth in love, may grow up unto him in all things, which is the head, even Christ; From whom the whole body fitly joined together and compacted by that which every joint supplies, according to the effectual working in the measure of every part, makes increase of the body unto the edifying of itself in love."

Notice here that the Lord has given FIVE FOLDS OF MINISTRY THAT SHOULD BE IMPARTING AND PREPARING THE BODY OF CHRIST FOR THE WORK OF MINISTRY. They are all supposed to be functioning in the Church and Preaching from the Pulpit to impart their fold to Grow the Body of Christ.

IF a Church only has one fold- The Pastor, functioning, the sheep are under nourished, under fed, and ill equipped to be able to continue on in the faith. Many sheep have been stolen, by the enemy of our souls, because of a lack of the knowledge and instruction the other four folds would have imparted to them. IF the other four folds were denied the pulpit and the access to the sheep to impart their God-given knowledge, understanding, witness, testimonies, and encouragement; the sheep are not being fed the way God ordained. Their spiritual growth is being stunted, deliberately, by unfaithful pastors who want to keep them babies, fully dependent upon them, so they are not free to be led by the Spirit of God into Father God's Will and purpose for their lives.

Many sheep will not hear Jesus say, "Well done My good and faithful servant," because pastors stole their gifts, stole their God given talents, stole the call of God on their lives and made them subject to serve them and their churches over the Will of God Himself. Many Pastors have the illusion that they are God and that everyone should serve them above even God the Holy Ghost/Holy Spirit. Many Pastors have kept the Holy Ghost/Holy Spirit out of their churches because they do not want Him to take His Rightful Place as God. Like the scribes and Pharisees who wanted to be worshipped and refused to let Jesus Christ be God, these pastors refuse to let the Holy Ghost/Holy Spirit be God as He should be. They demand that everyone in their church submit to them over God the Holy Spirit. They want to take the place of God the Holy Spirit and rule their own wills over the sheep, even over the mature believers who know the voice of God. This is why many mature believers have LEFT THE CHURCHES. They see the witchcraft and controlling Pharisee Spirits in these wicked pastors and cannot sit under them.

These Pastors who refuse to let the other four folds of ministry operate have a spirit of Diotrephes mentioned in 3 John verses 9-11. That spirit is a demonic spirit that refused to allow the Apostles to minister to the sheep, prated against the apostles with evil words, threatened to throw out the people, in the Church, if they housed the Apostles etc… That Pastor wanted the preeminence. HE Wanted to be the one in charge and refused even the Apostles of God who knew more and could have taught more to the sheep. It is a jealous ,selfish, WITCHCRAFT, CONTROLLING, DOMINATING, FEAR INDUCING SPIRIT. It is NOT OF GOD. Sadly, it has infiltrated many Churches here in the Northeast and kept the brethren from spiritually growing in their faith. It keeps people totally dependent on the Pastor as the only one who they can receive instruction, guidance, and direction from. It even denies the Holy Spirit from operating in the Church and refuses to allow any Holy Spirit filled people to minister from the pulpit.

As a result, there are many people sitting in the pews who remain baby Christians year after year. They can only grow spiritually to the extent that their pastor grows them. They are stunted in their spiritual growth, never hear messages that can change their lives, change their hearts, teach them how to pray effectively, walk the walk, live for Jesus in a way that honors Him, spiritual warfare, how to proclaim the Word of God into their situations, to put sin out of their lives, how to have Victory over the devil etc…They will never develop into the strong believers that will be able to stand firm, fight the devil, and fulfill the call of God on their lives, unless these WICKED PASTORS ARE THROW OUT AND HOLY GHOST PASTORS REPLACE THEM.

In order for the Lord to really use you, you have to spiritually grow up. Unless you grow, the Lord will not choose you to do much of anything. In the natural realm, a baby knows very little. In the spiritual realm, a spiritual, baby Christian, knows very little. They live a life of the milk of the Word of God, but cannot endure strong meat.

> Hebrews 5:12-14 "For when for the time you ought to be teachers, you have need that one teach you again which be the first principles of the oracles of God, and are become such as have need of milk, and not of strong meat. For every one that uses milk is unskillful in the word of righteousness: for he is a babe. But strong meat belongs to them that are of full age, even those who by reason of use have their senses exercised to discern both good and evil." WE see here, that the disciple Paul was rebuking the Hebrews for not growing in their faith. They should have been able to teach God's Word, but instead they were baby Christians who weren't growing in their faith.

The Disciples of Jesus Christ were only with him three years. They were Baptized in the Holy Ghost and were able to preach the Word with Power, raise the dead, heal the sick, cast out demons, etc.. Why are people sitting in Church year after year after year; not growing in their faith, not witnessing the Gospel of Jesus Christ to lost souls, not doing anything to advance the Kingdom of God on planet earth? Why are they living useless lives when they could be living Amazing Lives Filled With God's Holy Spirit and God's Glory?

Isn't It Time These Pastors Get Out OF The Way and Stop Trying To Cover And Control Everyone and Everything that Goes on? Isn't It Time the Holy Spirit is welcomed Back Into the Churches and Holy Spirit Filled People Are Welcomed to Preach In The Pulpits of America Again? Isn't It Time For All Of The Five Folds OF Ministry to Minister to God's Sheep as God Ordained? Isn't It Time To Put Away The Physical Building Projects and BUILD THE BODY OF CHRIST? Isn't it time that Bible Seminaries and Bible Colleges really get Pastors Ready to be Pastors instead of hirelings? Isn't it time they STOP TEACHING FUTURE PASTORS TO WALK IN INTELLECTUALISM, LED BY THEIR FLESH, AND NOT The HOLY SPIRIT?

> Isaiah 30:1 "Woe to the rebellious children, saith the Lord, that take counsel but not of me; and that cover with a covering, but not of my spirit, that they may add sin to sin." The Only Covering a Mature Believer should have is God the Holy Spirit. IF the believer is a woman, she also should have her husband's covering. When the Lord called me to Africa 23 times, six weeks at a time over a period of seven years, I had God's Covering and my Husband Paul's Covering. No Pastor or Church covered me, paid for the trips, sponsored me, chose me, or even agreed to pray for me. Man did not choose me, teach me, anoint me, appoint me, sponsor me, agree to keep me in prayer, or send me. God the Holy Spirit and my Husband Paul sent me. There were a few women, friends of mine, who said they would keep me in prayer and a group of boys at the Highland Residential Youth Prison that also agreed to keep me in prayer, along with several family members. If I had to depend on any church, any pastor, any board of elders, any human beings to send me, I would still be waiting and wouldn't have accomplished anything. The Lord sees the hearts of people. Many say, "Here I am send me," but would refuse to go if He tries to send them. Many sing, "I surrender All," but refuse to give Him their whole lives. When I sang these things and spoke these things to God, I meant them. To say and sing things to God and not mean them, is to lie to Almighty God. Fear God and depart from evil.

When the Prophet Samuel went to Jesse to anoint one of his sons to be King, Samuel thought Eliab must be the one. God told Samuel that man sees the outward appearance, but God sees the hearts of people. If a Church were to try to find an Evangelist to Africa, they would have chosen a black man. They would never have considered a "White Woman." For one thing, I am a woman. Many Pastors are VERY PREJUDICED AGAINST WOMEN PREACHERS. Many won't even give a woman the pulpit to preach or teach anything. God Chose ME. Man did Not. I went with God My Father, The Son of God Jesus Christ, and God the Holy Spirit, two angels Jesus chose to accompany me, God's Covering and My Husband Paul's Covering. God kept me safe 23 trips into villages, slums, towns, cities, mountains and deserts. To Him Be The Glory and Honor Forever. Amen!

The Witchcraft spirit of Diotrephes (3 John verses 9-11) entered the Churches and Bible Colleges and Bible Seminaries through a lie that began in the 1970's called "The Shepherding Movement." The Lie goes like this "EVERYONE MUST BE UNDER A PASTOR." This demonic lie put the other four folds of ministry under the one fold of "Pastor" and made them unable to function , if the "Pastor" refused to let them function. IT has done much to cripple the Body of Christ. There is No Biblical Scripture that puts the Office of Evangelist, Prophet, Apostle, and Teacher "Under the Office of Pastor." They are all callings of God Himself and these Other Four Folds of Ministry Are all Accountable to God himself.

Of course I am not saying that a pastor cannot remove a false teacher, a false apostle that is preaching un-Biblical lies, a false prophet, or an evangelist that is teaching and preaching nonsense. But I am saying that genuine believers that have been Called by God, Chosen by God, Trained by God and operating in these folds of ministry for years, are living Godly lives, and have learned many things by God the Holy Spirit's Leading and Direction, should be able to share what the Lord has given to them to impart to the Body of Christ. Why Should Everything the Lord has for His Body be denied His Sheep? Because of one man called a "Pastor"?

If a pastor is an intellectual pastor who does not have the Baptism of the Holy Spirit, he needs to step down from the pulpit and let someone who is Holy Ghost/Holy Spirit Filled, minister to the sheep. Without the anointing of God, the pastor is ill equipped to pastor anyone.

Isaiah 10:27 "And it shall come to pass in that day, that his burden shall be taken away from off thy neck, and the yoke shall be destroyed because of the anointing." Notice the yoke of bondage will be taken away because of the anointing. Without the Anointing of God the Holy Spirit/Holy Ghost, the pastor cannot set anyone free of any bondage they are entangled in. Without the Holy Ghost anointing, the flesh has no ability to do anything.

Jeremiah10:19-21 "Woe is me for my hurt, my wound is grievous; but I said, Truly this is a grief, and I must bear it. My tabernacle is spoiled and all my cords are broken; my children are gone forth of me, and they are not; there is none to stretch forth my tent any more, and to set up my curtains. For the Pastors are become brutish, and have not sought the Lord, therefore they shall not prosper, and all their flocks shall be scattered." This is why many Churches are shrinking and closing. The Lord is not going to draw more sheep into dead churches where they cannot grow spiritually. Unfaithful pastors refuse to recognize the giftings in the flock. They rob the giftings and callings of God from the sheep and insist the sheep "Obey Them" over God the Holy Ghost/Holy Spirit. They refuse to encourage the sheep to hear the voice of Jesus and obey Him.

Jeremiah 23:1-3 "Woe be to the pastors that destroy and scatter the sheep of my pasture! Saith the Lord. Therefore thus says the Lord God of Israel against the pastors that feed my people; You have scattered my flock, and driven them away, and have not visited them; behold, I will visit upon you the evil of your doing, says the Lord."

THE EVIL THAT PASTORS DO TO THE LORD'S SHEEP, FROM MY OWN PERSONAL EXPERIENCES

For ten years, my husband Paul and I attended a New Covenant Christian Church. I taught Sunday School to five year olds, three months a year, made cakes for the coffee hour, cleaned the church building, tithed, and continued to study the Word of God 6,7, or 8 hours a night while on security posts. On a twelve hour shift from 6 P.M. to 6 A.M., we could read to stay awake and alert, so I read and studied the Thompson Chain Reference King James Bible, with God the Holy Spirit teaching me for 9 years. It was not man who taught me the Word of God. IT was God Himself.

The Pastor of the New Covenant Christian Church kept teaching that "Women Can't Teach Men." "Women can't teach or preach", "Women Can't, Women Can't, Women Can't."

One day the Holy Spirit had me turn on TBN. I saw the Evangelist T.L. Osborne who was Preaching. He was looking at me through the T.V. pointing his finger and saying, "You Women out there, don't let any man rob you from your gifts and calling of God. My wife Daisy was given the same giftings that God the Holy Spirit gave to me. Who am I to tell Daisy that she cannot use the gifts that God the Holy Spirit has given to her. You are accountable to use the gifts He has given to you, for the Glory of God and the Advancement of His Kingdom."

When I heard his message I was set free of the ten years of "Women Can't, Women can't, women can't." Needless to say, I had to leave that Church. IF I stayed, and obeyed the Lord by traveling to preach and teach His Word, the Pastor would have accused me of being a "rebel." IF the Pastor came against me, and I stopped preaching and teaching God's Word, I would have been in rebellion against God Himself. It was a no win situation. I was not a rebel against the Lord or what He was calling me to do. For the sake of the calling of God on my life and peace, I had to leave.

My job required fire watch checks in buildings. WE were made to wear steel toed shoes and walk 1700 stairs (concrete and metal) doing fire watches in various buildings. The men were supposed to rotate that post, but always put the women on it. My knees began to hurt and after a while, I couldn't stand up for five minutes without pain. I could no longer do the job. I had surgery on one knee and the pain in my knees kept me up in the night with heating pads on my legs. I saw on T.V. a Messianic Jewish Pastor who was welcoming the Gentile believers in Yeshua (Jesus) to come to his Congregation. I began attending Shabbat Chaim in Kingston, N.Y. They shared a Building with Fountain of Life Church. The Presence of God the Holy Spirit was there . I began driving people to these services and spent many hours, for years on the floor, in the Presence of God the Holy Spirit. I was set free of "fear of Man," "fear of what people would think," "Fear of witnessing to large groups of people", etc… Another time, the Holy Spirit showed me I had resentment in my heart toward someone. I repented of it and was set free. Another time, in a vision, I saw my Jesus dancing with me in a beautiful garden. I was wearing a shining, white, wedding gown. Another time, I had a vision of my Jesus hanging on the cross. His blood was flowing down over me and washing me clean.

Holy Spirit set me free of a lot of pain and hurt of my childhood as He ministered to me , brought it to the surface, and removed it through my tears. God the Holy Spirit can do more in a person's heart, soul, and spirit, and body than any psychiatrist, psychologist, or doctor could ever do. He knows each person, individually and knows all they have been through in their lives. He knows their pains, their hurts, their wounded spirits, their hurt emotions, their broken hearts, and everything about them. The meetings were amazing. People were set free of fear, depression, grief, un-forgiveness, hatred, bitterness, hidden sins, addictions, bondages, etc…

> II Corinthians 3:17-18 "Now the Lord is that Spirit; and where the Spirit of the Lord is, there is liberty. But we all, with open face, beholding as in a glass the glory of the Lord, are changed into the same image from glory to glory, even as by the Spirit of the Lord."

Why are Pastors Denying the Liberty the Holy Spirit Wants to Bring To His Sheep? Why are the Pastors Refusing TO Allow The Holy Spirit to Come Into The Churches to Change the Sheep From Glory To Glory To Be More Like Jesus? These Pastors will be ashamed when they stand before Jesus and have to give an account for what they have done to God's Sheep. They have been hirelings and not faithful to the Lord or His Sheep.

THE DEMONIC LIE OF TOLERATION THAT HAS ENTERED THE CHURCHES

Proverbs 29:27 "An unjust man is an abomination to the just; and he that is upright in the way is abomination to the wicked." We, as Christians cannot afford to TOLERATE THE WICKED. WE MUST STAND FOR JESUS CHRIST AND THE WORD OF GOD. WE MUST HATE THE WICKEDNESS THAT GOD HATES AND SPEAK THE TRUTH ABOUT THE ISSUES THAT FACE OUR NATION. Either we Stand for the Lord, or we will be destroyed with the wicked. IF we remain silent and allow the wickedness to continue in our families, our churches, our government, our military, our businesses, our schools, our colleges, our media, and our entertainment, God Will Hold Us Accountable For It. GOD DOES NOT TOLERATE EVIL AND WICKEDNESS AND NEITHER SHOULD WE.

Proverbs 6:16-19 "There are six things the Lord hates; yes, even seven are abominations unto him. A proud look, a lying tongue, and hands that shed innocent blood, A heart that devises wicked imaginations, feet that are swift to run to do mischief, A false witness that speaks lies, and he that sows discord among the brethren."

IF the Lord hates these things, we should also hate these things. The media has continually lied to the American People about many issues.

Anyone who listens to the lying media, the atheist lies of evolution, Greek myths, vain philosophies, and other nonsense, gets deceived in their hearts, their souls, and their minds. The wicked media attacks anyone who is upright, wants truth, wants God and prayer back in our schools, wants America to prosper, wants Our Constitution to be upheld as written (not distorted), wants freedom of speech, religious freedom, wants to live out their Biblical Views, wants to refuse the sin that they want to promote, and wants to do what is right in the sight of God. The media spews lies to cover up wicked crime families within our own government. The media accuses innocent people of crimes they didn't commit and covers up for those who are really doing the crimes.

IF we agree with the lying media, Hollywood's lies, the lies of talk show hosts, the lies of so called "stars" that promote darkness and wickedness, the lies of the secular worldly people, we are no better or different than them.

Isn't it time we preach the TRUTH OF GOD'S WORD FROM THE PULPITS. If our youth heard in church that sex outside of marriage is sin against God and against their own bodies, many would repent and be saved from hurtful, lustful, wicked relationships that destroy them body, soul, and spirit. Christian girls would no longer be getting pregnant and aborting (murdering) their babies. The abortion rate among so called Christians is just as high as the world. As many Christians are murdering their babies as people who don't claim to be Christian. This should not be.

If Christian youth were taught that God designed them to be the gender they are, the devil wouldn't be able to lie to them and say that God made a mistake when He made them a boy or a girl. IF they knew the love of God and understood that everyone is created, by God, to be a one of a kind individual with unique giftings and talents God has given only to them, it would help them to accept who they are in Christ. If they were taught to press into the Lord Jesus, read the Word of God, grow in their faith and become the strong Men and Women of God that He created them to be, they could advance God's Kingdom on this earth and reach their generations with God's Truth. We must train up the next generations to know Jesus, to love Jesus, to obey Jesus, to walk with Jesus, to live for Jesus, to reach others for Jesus, and to serve Jesus with all their hearts, souls, minds, and strength. Otherwise, the question that Jesus asked, "When I return will I find faith on earth? Is in jeopardy of a no answer.

> Romans 1:18-32 (KJV) "For the wrath of God is revealed from heaven against all ungodliness of men, who hold the truth in unrighteousness; Because that which may be known of God is manifest in them; for God has shewed it unto them. For the invisible things of him from the creation of the world are clearly seen, being understood by the things that are made, even his eternal power and Godhead; so they are without excuse: Because that, when they knew God, they glorified him not as God, neither were thankful; but became vain in their imaginations, and their foolish heart was darkened. Professing themselves to be wise, they became fools. And changed the glory of the uncorruptible God into an image made like to corruptible man, and to birds, and four footed beasts, and creeping things. Wherefore God also gave them up to uncleanness through the lusts of their own hearts, to dishonor their own bodies between themselves: Who changed the truth of God into a lie, and worshipped and served the creature more than the Creator, who is blessed for ever. Amen. For this cause God gave them up unto vile affection; for even their women did change the natural use into that which is against nature: And likewise also the men, leaving the natural use of the woman, burned in their lust one toward another; men with men working that which is unseemly, and receiving in themselves that recompense of their error which was meet. And even as they did not like to retain God in their knowledge, God gave

them over to a reprobate mind, to do those things which are not convenient; being filled with all unrighteousness, fornication, wickedness, covetousness, maliciousness; full of envy, murder, debate, deceit malignity; whisperer, Backbiters, haters of God, despiteful, proud, boasters, inventors of evil things, disobedient to parents, Without understanding, covenant breakers, without natural affection, implacable, unmerciful: Who knowing the judgment of God, that they which commit such things are worthy of death, not only do the same, but have pleasure in them that do them."

THERE IS NO SUCH THING AS A GAY CHRISTIAN OR A GAY CHRISTIAN CHURCH. GOD GAVE THEM OVER TO REPROBATE MINDS. ANY CHURCH ORDAINING GAY PEOPLE IS A CHURCH OF SATAN AND NOT OF GOD. ANY BIBLE COLLEGE PROMOTING GAYNESS IS A DEMONIC COLLEGE. God is the Same Yesterday, Today, and Forever.

> Jude verses 4-8 "For there are certain men crept in unawares, who were before of old ordained to this condemnation, ungodly men, turning the grace of God into lasciviousness, and denying the only Lord God, and our Lord Jesus Christ. I will therefore put you in remembrance, though you once knew this, how that the Lord, having saved the people out of the land of Egypt, afterward destroyed them that believed not. And the angels which kept not their first estate, but left their own habitation, he has reserved in everlasting chains under darkness unto the judgment of the great day. Even as SODOM and GOMORRHA, and the cities about them in like manner, giving themselves over to fornication, and going after strange flesh, are set forth for an example, suffering the vengeance of eternal fire."

Even the children and teens of Sodom and Gomorrah were sexually perverted and wicked. God destroyed them also when His Wrath came on Sodom and Gomorrah. Is this wickedness something that we want taught to our children and grandchildren in our public schools and colleges? STAND UP AND FIGHT AGAINST IT AND DRIVE IT OUT OF OUR SCHOOLS AND COLLEGES before all our youth are CORRUPTED

BY THESE WICKED PEOPLE AND THEIR WICKEDNESS. Start Christian Charter Schools, home school your children, put them into a Christian School, or FIGHT THE WICKED BRAINWASHING AND LUST THAT IS GOING ON IN THE PUBLIC SCHOOLS.

Many colleges are not really schools of higher learning. Many have become indoctrination centers for Communism, Socialism, Marxism, Racism, Lust, Perversion, etc…Many Professors are traitors to our nation, condemn America, promote the sick Marxist agenda, liberal ideas that are against God, etc…

Gayness, lesbianism, bi-sexuality, homosexuality, bestiality, fornication, adultery, pornography, masturbation, group sex, orgies, wife swapping, transgender (trying to alter the sex of the person God designed in the womb to be someone God did not create), and other perversions are all sexual sins. THERE IS NO GAY MARRIAGE THAT GOD ACCEPTS. GAYNESS IS AN ABOMINATION TO GOD. People need to REPENT and GET DELIVERED FROM IT before it is too late to save their souls. GOD DID NOT CREATE THE PEOPLE OF SODOM AND GOMORRAH TO BE GAY AND THEN RAIN FIRE AND BRIMSTONE ON THEM BECAUSE THEY WERE GAY. They chose to be gay in rebellion against God. IT is not a minority. It is a sexual sin. To be into sexual sin and pridefully flaunt that sin, against God, will eventually incur the Wrath of God on those doing it.

Fornication SEX OUTSIDE OF MARRIAGE IS SIN. Despite the fact that T.V. Commercials, programs, the media and Hollywood says it is fine, IT IS SIN IN THE SIGHT OF GOD. REPENT AND STOP IT. ADULTERY IS SEXUAL SIN. It causes many marriages to break up, children to be hurt, and lives to be destroyed. The two biggest things that cause marriage break-ups are financial debt and ADULTERY. The soap operas promote adultery, fornication, other types of sexual sins, and many other things that God says are wicked.

Pornography is all over the internet. Many children and teens are being corrupted and sexually confused by it. Many Pastors and church leaders are addicted to it. They need to REPENT and be delivered from the spirits behind the pornography. Many have generational curses of porn watching. Their grandparents watched porn, their parents watched porn, and they watch porn. The filth is out there. We must guard our minds and hearts. The BIBLE says, "As a man thinks in his heart, so is he."

Deuteronomy 27:25 "Cursed be he that takes reward to slay an innocent person. And all the people shall say, Amen." The abortion industry's entire motive is to get paid to slay innocent, unborn babies and sell their body parts to wicked scientists, wicked college labs, and wicked makeup producers, wicked cannibals who eat their body parts, wicked witches that use their blood in demonic sacrifices, and others that are equally wicked.

THE WORDS "FETUS"< "PRODUCT OF CONCEPTION"< "BLOB OF PROTOPLASM" are NOT IN THE BIBLE. In the sight of God A BABY IS A BABY.

Jeremiah 1:4-5 "Then the word of the Lord came unto me, saying, "Before I (GOD) formed you in the belly I knew you; and before you came forth out of the womb I sanctified you, and I ordained you a prophet unto the nations." IT was God who formed Jeremiah in the womb. God had a plan for Jeremiah's life. God molded Jeremiah, sanctified Jeremiah, and Ordained Jeremiah to be a prophet to the nations while he was still in his mother's womb. GOD HAS A PLAN FOR EVERY BABY HE CREATES IN THE WOMB. Abortion is SATAN DESTROYING AN INNOCENT LIFE THAT GOD IS CREATING FOR A DIVINE PURPOSE AND PLAN. Abortion IS MURDER. "Thou shall not murder" is one of God's Commandments.

Psalm 139:13-17 (KJV) David is speaking to God. "For you have possessed my reins; you have covered me in my mother's womb. I will praise you; for I am fearfully and wonderfully made: marvelous are your works and that my soul knows right well. My substance was not hid from you, when I was made in the lowest parts of the earth. Your eyes did see my substance, yet being unperfect; and in your book all my members were written, which in continuance were fashioned, when as yet there was none of them. How precious also are your thoughts to me, O God! How great is the sum of them!"

First, David is praising God for his life. David is giving God the credit for covering him in his mother's womb and creating him. In God's book, David's parts were written; and God in continuance fashioned him the way God had planned him to be. God planned David's height, his eye color, his hair color, his strengths, his weaknesses, his talents, his abilities, his gender, etc…

There are only two genders that God creates. Genesis 1:27 "So God created man in his own image, in the image of God created he him; male and female created he them." All people are created by God to be either a male or a female. They are not created to be both sexes or to change the Gender God created them to be. GOD MAKES NO MISTAKES. Man in his foolishness rebels against God and against who God created them to be. Satan wants people to rebel, destroy their bodies with transgender drugs and transgender surgeries in order to keep them from fulfilling God's Divine Plan for their lives. Satan wants to destroy the reproductive organs of girls and boys so they cannot produce any babies or future generations of human beings made by God in God's own image. Because of abortion and now transgender, GENERATIONS OF HUMAN BEINGS WILL NEVER BE.

IF you are reading this and you have counseled people to abort their babies or have had an abortion yourself, there is forgiveness for you if you repent and believe Jesus Christ died on that cross for your sins, including your sin of murdering an innocent person. Repent and ask Jesus to come into your heart and life and be your Savior and Lord today. Today is the day of salvation for you.

MY PERSONAL TESTIMONY CONTINUED

Now, to go on with my personal testimony. In 1996, the Lord called me to go on a mission trip with Marilyn Hickey as part of her prayer team. In 1997, I went again with Marilyn Hickey Ministries to Kenya, Comoros, Zanzibar and Madagascar. After that, the Lord called me to do crusades in Kenya and my Africa Missions began. At the same time, the Jewish Pastor Eddy, was called by the Lord, to move to Israel with his family. Pastor Eddy, was the only real Pastor who never tried to rob my gifts, discourage me from the call of God on my life, or devalue what the Lord had done in my life. I was sorry to see him move away.

The Lord led me to another church. Even though the Pastor knew that I did Africa Missions, crusades, preached in Churches, taught the Word of God even on local T.V., and then on Jesus is Lord Radio, Nakuru, Kenya and Sayre Voice of Mercy T.V. and radio from Eldoret, Kenya, he would never give me the pulpit to impart to the Body of Christ what the Lord wanted them to have. My gifts were denied and I was discouraged there.

There was a witch in the church She would pretend to be of God, but clearly wasn't. I recognized her actions and deeds as Holy Spirit revealed them to me. She had a Jezebel Spirit. She refused to hear the Word of God. She would dance around during worship, and before the Pastor went up to preach, she would throw herself down on the floor between the Pastor and the Congregation blocking his message from getting to the people (Pretending That the Holy Ghost was upon her). She would lay there moaning, like she was having sex with someone. The Pastor never told her to get up. Other times she would sit in her seat praying in a demonic language (not Holy Ghost Tongues). The Holy Spirit of God, Holy Ghost, would never have someone chattering during the Word of God. That was not God's Spirit, but a demon. Other times, she would go to the back of the church pacing up and down chattering. She was Refusing to sit in her seat and hear the Word of God.

> In John 8:43-47 Jesus said, "Why do you not understand my speech? Even because you cannot hear my word. You are of your father the devil, and the lusts of your father you will do. HE was a murderer from the beginning, and abode not in the truth, because there is no truth in him. When he speaks a lie , he speaks of his own, for he is a liar, and the father of it. And because I tell you the truth, you believe me not. Which of you convinces me of sin? And if I say the truth, why do you not believe me? HE that is of God hears God's words. You therefore, hear them not , because you are not of God."

This witch would secretly pray over people in the bathroom or outside the church. Brethren were phoning me saying, "Kathy, I just want to die and be with Jesus. I'm so depressed, I just don't want to live any more." I asked her when she began to feel like that. Did anyone lay hands on you or pray over you at that time? She named the witch. The witch had also prayed over her daughter. Her daughter began rebelling against her , almost immediately. I prayed and broke the Spirit of Jezebel off of her and her daughter, and they were fine.

The witch would hand people pens with a demonic anointing on them to get the demons into their homes to attack their families. She was also doing voodoo. One day I felt like someone was sticking me with pins. I was going to a morning prayer meeting at the church. When I arrived in the parking lot, she drove her car in from another direction. She waltzed up to me and said, "Do you ever feel like someone is sticking you with pins? It's the witches, we must pray for them." The Lord showed me it was her.

After many incidences like those mentioned above, I went to the Pastor and told him what the witch was doing in the church. He said, "I'm not throwing anyone out of my church." The Lord sent someone else to tell the pastor the same thing I told him, and he would not listen. The WITCH remained in the Church, with the Pastor's Permission. The Lord led eighty people out of that church to keep them safe from what was being released there.

    One time I was away, in Africa, ministering, for two and a half months. When I got back, the Pastor totally snubbed me. Brethren would come up to me and say, "Even though the Pastor isn't glad you are back, we are happy to see you. When I was attacked from the pulpit as the pastor said, "Just Because Someone Isn't Going To Africa Doesn't Mean They Are Not Doing The Will Of God, " I decided it was time to leave that church.

I began attending a local Vineyard Church. When the Christian walk was being compared to a "Roadrunner Cartoon," and Father God was being compared to the "Wizard of Oz", I decided it was time to leave there.

After that, I tried a Faith Assembly of God Church. I knew that the Assembly of God Churches had begun as a result of the Azusa Street Revival, so I thought it would be a Holy Spirit filled Church. I thought I would be able to use my gifts there. I was wrong.

The Senior Pastor kept bashing the King James Version of the Bible and promoting Bible versions based on the Alexandrian Manuscripts that were heresy. My Husband Paul looked up on the internet the various Bible versions and had a printed out comparison of them and all the distortions the other versions left out. The other versions left out scriptures on the Blood of Jesus, the Diety of Christ, the Trinity, etc… Some even left out the Great Commission of Mark 16:15-20. They stopped at verse 13. Other versions had a blasphemous lie attached to them.

> Isaiah 14:12 K.J.V. says : How art thou fallen from heaven, O Lucifer, son of the morning!." IT makes it clear who rebelled from Father God and got thrown out of heaven. One fraudulent version says, "How art thou fallen from heaven O bright and Morning Star!"

> Revelation 22:16 "I Jesus have sent my angel to testify unto you these things in the churches. I am the root and the offspring of David,, and the BRIGHT AND MORNING STAR." Some false versions have Jesus Christ rebelling against Father God and being thrown out of heaven. Isn't it time we get back to the Real Word of God and not the corrupt words of unjust men.

The Senior Pastor admitted to me that many churches and organizations had invested heavily into the Alexandrian Versions of the Bible and he would not stop promoting them. I believe that the Alexandrian Manuscripts were on older paper because our forefathers refused them as heresy. They were placed into a safe and left there, unused, for many years. The other manuscripts (scrolls) were used and had to be re-written as they wore out from use. That is why the paper was newer on them. You can get the best Bible Scholars, the best Language Interpreters, the best theologians, etc… But if the Original Manuscript is Corrupt, you will have a corrupt finished product. The Alexandrian Manuscripts were corrupt. These newer Bibles based on them are corrupt. They distort the real Word of God, giving meanings that are over-amplified, twisted, distorted, changed, and left out. They will leave the believer confused as to what God really said. Just as in the garden of Eden, the devil will say to them," did God really say that?"

The Holy Spirit is under no obligation to perform any words that are just man's words and not God's Words by the holy men of God as they were moved by the Holy Ghost. Words without the inspiration of God the Holy Ghost, are just man's words. The Spirit of God will not accompany them at all. People who refuse the real word of God and study man's words instead, will have a jack knife to stand against the devil with, instead of the Double Two Edged Sword.

If you encourage people to read many Bible Versions, How much scripture will people know and memorize? IF you take the real Word of God and fake words, that are not of God, and you jumble them up in people's minds and hearts, you will have total confusion. People who try to stand on fake words will have no real Sword of The Spirit to fight the devil with. The Holy Spirit is under no obligation to perform fake words that God has not really spoken. This is why I will never preach from any other version but the King James Bible. My Sword of the Word of God has been powerful to defeat the enemy in Africa, Venezuela, Columbia, and everywhere the Lord sends me. I wouldn't trade it for a jack knife.

In 2011, the Lord told me to do Crusades in three parks in our area. I went to the senior pastor of Faith Assembly of God church and asked if he could put the outreaches into the Church bulletin so brethren could know about the outreaches and come out to the parks to minister. He said, "No." I had told him I was paying all the park fees so it wasn't about the money. I asked if I could borrow some equipment. HE Said, "No." So I went to Ballentine Communications and bought my own speaker system with huge speakers, a mixer, stands, microphones, a cd player, etc… I asked the Pastor if he could send some of the musicians to play some Christian Music in the parks. HE wouldn't release them to join us.

The Lord sent a Pastor from Westchester to come into Warriors Park with his rams horn at our first park meeting. We played Christian CDs on the CD Player, then I preached a salvation message, we put on more CDS, then the Pastor from Westchester preached a message, then we played more CDS and read the Father's Love Letter as the Holy Spirit directed. One day the Lord sent a woman from a Baptist Church to play a keyboard and sing. Another day, a woman at a birthday party, in the park, had background music from her Church and she sang. Another day the Salvation Army showed up and gave some testimonies of God's Faithfulness. Another day, three little girls from a birthday party came up and said, "Can we sing a song for Jesus?" Of course you can. During that summer we had 27 salvations in the park, ministered to many people, broke generational curses off of five men from the rehab center, handed out Bibles, and planted seeds of faith in many. WE obeyed the

Lord, even though we had no help from the pastor. We wondered why we were attending Faith of God Church, since all we got there was total discouragement. We decided to leave. There was no reason for us to remain there.

    We left and decided to try the Calvary Chapel Church and see what that was like. The Church had some huge screens way up in the air that they would put the words to the hymns on. We were standing up worshipping the Lord. I have a habit of lifting up my hands to the Lord, looking up to heaven where He is, and singing to Him. Also, at times I bow in respect to Him. As I was worshipping the Lord, staying in one place, the Pharisee police came up to me and told me that I could not dance in the sanctuary. IF I wanted to dance, I would have to go into a side room. I was shocked to think that I would have to hide my worship to God in a side room. Weren't we there to Worship God? Weren't we there to please God? After the service, I went up to the Pastor and said, "We cannot worship God in this Church?" He said, people have been reporting to me that you have been raising your hands and blocking the screen. The screen was WAY UP IN The air. They had a DEMONIC FEAR OF Man and what PEOPLE WOULD THINK. They were people pleasers and not God Pleasers. Needless to say, we were done with that church.

    We decided to try a Hudson Valley Christian Church in Newburgh. We attended there three years. The Pastor knew I was an Evangelist to the lost and to the Body of Christ, but he would never let me preach a message to the church. I helped make soup for the soup kitchen, knit hats and scarves for the homeless, teach women's Bible study, etc… The Lord spoke to me and told me He was changing the name of my ministry from "Fishers of Men Ministries" to "Pure Grace Ministries" and He was calling me to America. We went to the senior pastor and told him we were going to start doing Evangelism Outreaches in the city of Newburgh. He said, "Your ministry is not under this churches covering." We said, "That is fine. WE have God's Covering and that is all we need."

    The next Wednesday, when we were supposed to teach the men and women's Bible Studies, the pastor called us into his office. He said, "Your ministry has to come under our Board of Elders. Otherwise you cannot be members of this Church." I said, "Then we will not be members of this church. Where in the Bible does an Evangelist who God has Called, who God has Anointed, who God has Appointed, have to be under a board of lay people who God has not chosen into the five folds of Ministry? A Board of Elders is supposed to help the pastor run the church. They have nothing to do with the other four folds of ministry. What you are trying to do is NOT BIBLICAL." He screamed , "IF you are not members of this church, you cannot teach the Bible Studies. If I were you, I would run out of this church." Needless to say, we did. I could not deny God the Holy Spirit, His Call, and His Leading ; to submit to man's demonic witchcraft, controlling, manipulating, fear inducing spirit. NO HUMAN BEING WILL EVER BE My GOD.

Sadly, because of the attitude of the pastor, the Lord took us out of Newburgh and the great awakening He wanted to do there didn't happen. I inquired of the Lord if I should rent a building and continue to try to Evangelize Newburgh, but the Lord said, "No." Because of the pastor's attitude, I would have received no help from the church, no worship team, and no brethren as a prayer team. HE would have fought me and the entire work the Lord wanted to do there. The Lord had even sent a Christian woman, from another state, to be the mayor of Newburgh, so the meetings wouldn't have been objected to, by the city government. That Pastor is accountable to the Lord for his wickedness. Today, Newburgh is a city of high crime, poverty, homelessness, slums, and drive by shootings. It could have been different. I had to shake off the dust of my feet at that pastor and move on. I had said, "Lord, if this church does not work out, I am done with Church. We will worship you every day at home."

We have been worshipping the Lord at home for the last four years. We worship, dance, we study the Word of God, pray for each other, the nation, the awakening, the greatest move of Holy Spirit to happen on planet earth etc… Our tithe money does not go to anyone's physical building projects, parking lots, country clubs, etc… Our tithe goes to Evangelism Outreaches, Preachers who Preach the Gospel, our own ministry outreaches, and other outreaches for souls to be saved; not only in America but in other lands.

Many of the mature brethren, in Jesus Christ, have left the Churches and are worshipping at home. They are tired of having their gifts stolen by jealous pastors, tired of being discouraged by the pastors who only want the tithe money to pay off their huge debt for earthly buildings, tired of church building projects, tired of chauvinist pastors who refuse to let women use their gifts, tired of hearing dead messages by dead intellectuals who do not have God the Holy Spirit, tired of church as usual, tired of seeing no miracles, signs, or wonders, tired of looking for a church where God's Holy Spirit is moving mightily…Many brethren have been so wounded and abused by pastors, they will never enter a "CHURCH" again.

IF it wasn't for my strong faith in Jesus Christ Himself, I would have walked away from "Christianity" a long time ago. The pastors would have destroyed my faith, if my trust was in them, instead of in my Jesus. They have destroyed the faith of many. They have stolen and fleeced the sheep. They have preached nonsense from the pulpits and denied true preachers and teachers the ability to impart their wisdom, understanding, and discernment to the sheep. People come to Church to hear the Word of God, NOT YOUR PEDIGREE PAPERS, NOT WHERE You GOT YOUR DEGREES, NOT your VACATIONS, not cartoons, Greek Myths, Public events, or anything else. IF YOU ARE NOT GOING TO PREACH THE WORD OF GOD-THE ENTIRE WORD OF GOD-AGAINST SEXUAL Sins, AGAINST Abortion, AGAINST STEALING, AGAINST LYING, AGAINST IMMORALITY, etc…GET OUT OF THE PULPIT NOW. God will hold you accountable for the sheep you destroy, for the ridiculous messages you preach that are not His Word, for refusing to let His Holy Spirit Minister to His Sheep, for destroying ministries God has called into being, for robbing the gifts of the brethren, and for your own hidden wickedness that only He and you know about. How many souls have you destroyed? How many people have you wounded, hurt, and discouraged? How many brethren have walked away from Jesus because of you? How many cities have not been reached with the gospel because you refuse to release the Evangelists? How many brethren are suffering needlessly because you won't let the Holy Spirit into the church?

Father, I pray that the holy fear of God would come upon every pastor, elder, church leader, evangelist, prophet, teacher, apostle and lay person. That all would fear you and depart from evil. That they would all be teachable and willing to surrender everything to You. The head of the Church is supposed to be Jesus Christ because He purchased the Church with His Own Righteous Blood. Convict the pastors who demand that people worship them and obey them, over you Lord. Convict the pastors who refuse to obey you and remove them from the pulpits. Convict the pastors who refuse to preach against abortion, sexual sins, and other sins. Remove the Pastors who are telling people that "they don't have to repent anymore. IT is all under the Blood." They are deceiving the brethren into keeping unrepented of sin in their hearts and lives. Why in Revelation 2 and 3 are five churches told to "REPENT." Convict the pastors who want to be God, play God, rule over people and demand their allegiance over God, and refuse to release the mature believers into the ministries You Have for Them. Raise up pastors after your own heart who will preach the Whole Word of God and not just the parts that tickle peoples ears. Raise up pastors who will want the sheep to grow up spiritually. Pastors who will allow the Apostles, the Evangelists, the Teachers, the Prophets, and the Holy Spirit to minister to the People to change them to be more like Jesus. Raise up Pastors who will teach the Body of Christ the Word of God and not compromise with public opinion, the devil or Hollywood. Raise up Pastors who will pray over and release the Evangelists, Prophets, Teachers, and Apostles to stand in the pulpit and impart their folds to the sheep. Raise up pastors who will encourage the sheep to use their giftings to the Glory of God. Raise up pastors who will release the people into the ministries that You have ordained for such a time as this. Raise up pastors after Your Own Heart that really love and care for the sheep. Raise up pastors who desire Your Kingdom to come and Your Will to be Done Here on Earth as it is in Heaven. Raise up pastors who will **STOP BUILDING THEIR OWN KINGDOMS OF BUILDING PROJECTS AND BUILD The KINGDOM OF GOD.** Raise up pastors who will not schedule and pencil out God the Holy Spirit. Raise up **HOLY SPIRIT FILLED PASTORS, TOTALLY SURRENDERED TO YOU AND YOUR WILL AND YOUR KINGDOM's** Purposes. Raise up pastors who will follow the example of the early church in the Book of Acts. I ask this in Jesus name. Amen!

CREATIVE EVANGELISM

There is a way to share the Gospel of Jesus Christ with people without really confronting them face to face. I call it indirect evangelism. I'll give you some examples of this:

A youth group or people in the church can pair off two by two. The two agree to enter a store, a deli, a shop, a college campus, separately; then meet and one of you preaches Jesus Christ to your friend loud enough for people to hear the Gospel Message.

Youth group members pair off and enter a college campus separately. As you walk along two by two, one of you preaches the Gospel of Jesus Christ to the other, loud enough for students outside to hear the gospel. Every time you get near a group of students, you preach Jesus Christ to your friend nice and loud so the students you walk near can hear what you are saying. No one can accuse you of proselytizing because you are not approaching any of the students face to face. You can always say, "I was talking to my friend." You can always talk loud about how Jesus came into your heart and changed your life. Preach your testimony to your friend loud enough for students to hear you. You are planting seeds in people's hearts that the Holy Spirit can water.

Years ago I had a friend named Bea. Every time I ran into her, whether in a dollar store, a food store, or any other shop, she knew I would run up to her and say, "Hi Bea. Did you know that Jesus Christ loves you so much that he left heaven and came to this earth to die for your sins on the cross so you could be forgiven and go to heaven. Jesus is alive. He rose from the dead and is the living Savior and Lord of all who receive him. Jesus Loves You so much. Do you want to receive Jesus?" She would say, "Yes." I would lead her in a salvation prayer loud enough for people to hear. We were planting Gospel Seeds into the people who heard us.

Another friend, named Maureen, and I would walk around a college campus where most of the students were non practicing Jews. I would wear Star of David earrings and a cross necklace. We would get near a group of students and I would preach about Yeshua the Jewish Messiah and how the Old Testament Scriptures told of Jesus Christ, hundreds of years before He came. I would preach about how the angel of death passed over the children of Israel because of the Blood of the Lamb on their door posts and how the Blood of the Lamb of God, Jesus Christ, was shed on the cross for us and saves us from spiritual death now. We were planting Gospel Seeds in the hearts of the hearers. IF anyone approached us, we could always say we were talking to each other.

Another way to plant seeds is to get Bible tracts and put them in Christmas Cards, Birthday Cards, thanksgiving Cards, of unsaved relatives and friends, etc… Leave the tracts on benches, in public bathrooms, on the table in the post office, give them to waiters and waitresses along with their tips, hand them to UPS delivery people, cashiers, etc…

I take them in a large handbag every time I go to the VA for a physical and hand them out to whoever wants a "Love Story." The Lord has had me hand out Love Story tracts at the V.A in C.T., the V.A. in the Bronx, and the local Castle Point V.A. No one can fire me. I don't work there.

Parades are great places to hand out Bible tracts. People are gathered on both sides of the road. Some people, marching in the parade, are handing out fliers, candy, business cards, and other things, so you are not out of place to hand out Bible tracts to whoever will accept them. You can Bible tract the people watching the parade, or hand the tracts to the people marching in the parade, when they pause in front of you.

Bumper Stickers are another way your can plant seeds. I have heard some ignorant pastors bash people who put bumper stickers on their cars or insinuate that people who display bumper stickers aren't living right. Personally, THEY NEED TO SHUT UP AND STOP ATTACKING THE EVANGELISTS Called by God, and their attempts to reach souls for Christ. I have seen many people, at the red lights, reading my bumper stickers pointing them to faith in Jesus Christ, telling them their life matters, and telling them that a baby in the womb is a baby and not a blob of tissue. God's Truth is Truth and it needs to be told, whether on a bumper sticker, in a Bible tract, in person, or from a pulpit. Lost souls need to be reached in whatever way we can reach them. The time to reach them is NOW.

For a season, the Lord had me paint a piece of plywood white, attach it to the telephone pole in front of my house, put heavy cardboard with Bible Scripture verses written with heavy magic markers on it. Every week or every other week, I would change the verses. People walking by, riding bikes, pushing baby strollers, or driving by, would stop and read the sign with the scriptures on it. I was planting seeds of faith in people. Hopefully, the Lord watered those seeds and a harvest of souls came in.

IF you are trying to share the gospel and a person seems to want to argue, then immediately tell them how your life was before Jesus came into your heart and how Jesus Christ changed your life. They cannot argue with your personal testimony.

One time I was on an airplane flight to Africa for ministry. I was sharing the Gospel of Jesus Christ with the two people sitting next to me. All of a sudden someone in a seat behind me poked my elbow. I turned around and he said, "I see you are one of them." I said, "One of what?" He said, "You are one of those born-again Christians. My parents are born-again but I am an atheist. I don't believe in God." I said, "The fool says in his heart there is no God. All nature declares that God exists so you are without an excuse." He said, "why don't you come back here and tell me about God. There is an empty seat next to me." I said, "You already believe that God doesn't exist. I could speak to you forever and never be able to convince you of God's existence. What I will do is pray that God Himself will reveal Himself to you in such a way that you won't be able to deny his existence any more, in Jesus Name. Amen." I said, "God will show you who he is." Then I continued to witness to the original two people I was speaking to and led them to Jesus Christ in a sinners prayer.

It would have been a waste of my time and energy to go back and argue with this foolish man. I would have lost the opportunity to reach those two souls for Christ, had I changed seats. Sometimes the devil will try to interrupt you, distract you, or hinder you from reaching someone's soul for Christ. We need to be aware of the enemies tactics and avoid them.

Once when I was first born-again in 1984 a man, at my job, said to me, "Why are you reading that book. That book is for sinners." I said, "He who says he is without sin is a liar and the truth is not in him." He shut his mouth and never tried to get me to stop reading God's Word again. If you know and understand the scriptures, the Lord will give you His Answer to someone's foolish questions, ridiculous comments, or nonsense. You will easily silence them and the foolishness operating through them.

The Great Commission that Jesus spoke to the Body of Christ is listed in Mark 16:15-18 KJV. "Go ye into all the world, and preach the gospel to every creature. HE that believes and is baptized shall be saved; but he that believes not shall be damned. And these signs shall follow them that believe. In my name they shall cast out devils; they shall speak with new tongues; They shall take up serpents; and if they drink any deadly thing, it shall not hurt them; they shall lay hands on the sick and they shall recover." How many people, in the Body of Christ are willing to reach the lost souls by obeying Jesus' Great Commission?

Luke 9:26 "For whosoever shall be ashamed of me and of my words, of him shall the Son of man be ashamed, when he shall come in his own glory, and in his Father's, and of the holy angels."

Romans 1:16 "For I am not ashamed of the Gospel of Christ; for it is the power of God unto salvation to every one that believes; to the Jew first, and also to the Greek."

There are millions of lost souls in the valley of decision. Unless we, the Body of Christ, go outside the church buildings into the highways and byways to reach them, they will not be reached. Many have been taught the atheist lie of evolution (that God doesn't exist). They have been fed a demonic lie that attacks the first verse of the Bible, "In the beginning God created the heaven and the earth." Since they believe there is no God, there is no reason to read the Bible, enter a church building, or try to have a relationship with a non-existent God. We have to go out and worship in public, preach the Gospel of Jesus Christ in the parks, in the playgrounds, at the beach, in the stores, and where ever people gather in the summer months. We must obey Jesus and Preach the Gospel to the lost. Some will come to faith in Jesus when they hear the Truth of the Gospel.

THE MAIN ISSUE WITH GOD THE FATHER, IS THAT SOULS BE SAVED. God is not concerned with large, physical building projects, parking lots, or country clubs. He is coming back for souls, not buildings. STOP WASTING THE LORD's MONEY ON Yourself, personal airplanes, limos, mansions by the sea, AND DO EVANGELISM AND REACH THE LOST NOW, BEFORE THEY END UP IN HELL AND CAN'T BE SAVED. God will hold you accountable for what you do now. Reach your classmates for Jesus. Your teacher can't preach Jesus or they will lose their job, BUT YOU, AS A STUDENT CAN PREACH JESUS. TALK ABOUT JESUS TO YOUR CLASSMATES. INVITE THEM TO YOUR YOUTH GROUP. START A YOUTH GROUP AND TEACH THEM. GET OUT INTO THE PUBLIC ARENA AND BE SALT AND LIGHT AND TRUTH NOW. STAND UP AND PREACH THE ENTIRE BIBLE. STOP CONDONING SIN AND TICKLING PEOPLE'S EARS ON THEIR WAY TO HELL. WARN THEM BEFORE IT IS TOO LATE FOR THEM.

Dear Father, give every believer in Christ a revelation of hell so they will share the gospel with their family members, friends, neighbors, and people they meet. Lead them by your Holy Spirit into what scriptures to speak and how to witness to the lost. Make your people as bold as lions. Remove any fear of man, fear of what people will think, fear of rejection, and fear of speaking to people, in Jesus Name. Take the demonic vails, coverings, and scales off of unsaved people's eyes, ears, minds, and hearts. Give them hearts of flesh to believe. Make their hearts fertile ground so your Word can get planted deep into their hearts and souls and bear the fruit of Salvation, in Jesus Name. Amen.

Let the Greatest Holy Ghost/Holy Spirit Awakening come forth throughout America and throughout the entire earth. Raise up Pastors, Evangelists, Teachers, Apostles, and Prophets filled with Your Holy Spirit, Your Holy Word, Your Holy Fire, Holy Anointing, and Your Holy Presence. Let us see the Greater signs, wonders, and miracles that Jesus said we will do now that He is up with you. Give us boldness to stand for You, Proclaim the Gospel of Jesus Christ, and Reach the lost. Let billions of souls come to Jesus Christ and be saved, delivered, and healed, in Jesus Name. Make us vessels and give us your wisdom and creative ideas on how to reach these souls for you. In Jesus Name we pray. Amen.

CHAPTER SEVEN

OBEY GOD'S COMMANDMENTS, STAND ON HIS WORD, NO COMPROMISE

We are living in a time where "Good" is called evil and "Evil" is called good. People who do not know the Lord, do not have the Holy Spirit, and do not know what God's Word says about any issue, can easily be swayed by the media, Hollywood, Disney, CNN, NBC, MSNBC, ABC, wicked politicians, wicked talk show hosts, wicked groups of people, wicked books about witchcraft, wizardry, and other occult practices, occult video games, occult toys, occult mind meditations such as yoga, seances, spell casting, enchantments, , etc…The list seems to be endless.

Sadly, many Pastors, elders, deacons, and Christian Churches are as spiritually blind as the world around them. Many have compromised with the world to the point that there is no difference between them and the world. Many Pastors are into pornography, are cheating on their wives, are not living right, not preaching the whole Word of God, and are lukewarm. IF the Lord came into their churches, He would SPEW Them OUT OF HIS MOUTH.

The spirts of sexual lust, perversion, pornography, fornication, adultery, gayness, homosexuality, lesbianism, bi-sexuality, bestiality, transgender, self mutilation, self destruction, suicide, depression, woks, filth, addictions, fears, materialism, witchcraft, wizardry, occultism, the love of money (which is the root of all evil), etc… seem to be everywhere.

People don't understand that God gave us the ten commandments to live by, because HE Loves US. Can you imagine a world where there were no laws to protect anyone's private property. No one would be able to leave their home to shop, to get a haircut, to go to work, to enjoy their life, if they couldn't leave their possessions safely at home. No one would have any peace of mind, heart or soul, if everyone was a thief and no one was honest. Can you imagine a world where anyone could murder anyone else without any consequences. No one's life would be safe. Can you imagine a world where no one would listen to the wisdom, instruction, and advice of their parents or anyone who would help them to make wise decisions. Can you imagine a world where marriage was just a word but everyone was unfaithful, unloving, uncaring, selfish, irresponsible, lewd and filthy in mind, heart, and soul and actions. There would be no stable, normal, loving, whole families on planet earth. Can you imagine a world where everyone lied about every topic and no one could hear any truth about any real issue that was effecting everyone's lives. Can you imagine a world where no news media ever told the truth about anything. All they did was brain-wash the public into their wicked agendas and schemes. Can you imagine a country where it's leaders hated the people and wanted to destroy them through Abortion, moving covid19 into nursing rooms to murder the elderly, destroy morality, destroy unity, legalize drugs so more youth get addicted, lace marijuana with fentanyl, steal their freedoms, force them into submission to them and government over God Himself. Can you imagine a country that wanted to brainwash the children into hating their Christian heritage and roots, into lust, perversion, rotten Satanic ideologies of Communism and Socialism, CRT, BLM, Atheism, false Greek god worship, child sacrifices to Baal, and other forms of WICKEDNESS. Imagine what it would be like if AI Computers take over our children's schools, their minds, hearts, souls, emotions, feelings, and self-wills. They will no longer be free to think, make wise decisions, reason, or choose to follow Jesus. They will be like unfeeling, unloving, computers. WE MUST STOP THIS FROM COMING INTO OUR SCHOOLS AND HOMES. WE must protect our children and future generations of human beings on planet earth.

BEWARE, WE HAVE TO FIGHT THIS WICKEDNESS OR THIS HORRIBLE WORLD I HAVE JUST SPOKEN OF WILL BE OUR NATION. MANY OF OUR SO CALLED LEADERS ARE WICKED IN THE SIGHT OF GOD. UNLESS WE FIGHT THIS WICKEDNESS, OUR CHILDREN WILL BE

OPPRESSED, DEPRESSED, CONTROLLED BY COMPUTERS AND WICKED DEMONIC GOVERNMENT OFFICIALS.

No where in the Bible are we instructed to give up, quit fighting, throw in the towel, roll over and be silent, while the enemy of our souls runs rampant devouring people.

> II Corinthians 5:14-21 "For the love of Christ constrains us; because we thus judge, that if one died for all, then were all dead; And that he died for all, that they which live should not henceforth live unto themselves, but unto him which died for them, and rose again. Therefore if any man be in Christ, he is a new creature; old things are passed away; behold, all things are become new. And all things are of God, who has reconciled us to himself by Jesus Christ, and has given to us the ministry of reconciliation; To wit, that God was in Christ, reconciling the world unto himself,, not imputing their trespasses unto them, and has committed unto us the word of reconciliation. Now then we are ambassadors for Christ, as though God did beseech you by us; we pray you in Christ's stead, be reconciled to God. For he has made him to be sin for us, who knew no sin; that we might be made the righteousness of God in him."

The Church should be preaching the Gospel of Christ to the lost of this world. We should be agents of Christ/Ambassadors to reach people for Christ so they can be reconciled to Father God.

> II Timothy :1-4 "You therefore, my son, be strong in the grace that is in Christ Jesus. And the things that you have heard of me among many witnesses, the same commit to faithful men, who shall be able to teach others also. You therefore endure hardness, as a good soldier of Jesus Christ. No man that wars entangles himself with the affairs of this life; that he may please him who has chosen him to be a soldier." Disciple and teach new believers the Word of God.

> I Peter 2:11 "Dearly beloved, I plead with you as strangers and pilgrims, abstain from fleshly lusts, which war against the soul; having your conversation honest among the Gentiles." Stay away from sexual sins.

II Timothy 4:7-8 the disciple Paul said, "I have fought a good fight. I have finished my course, I have kept the faith: Henceforth there is laid up for me a crown of righteousness, which the Lord, the righteous judge, shall give me at that day; and not to me only, but unto all them also that love his appearing."

WE are soldiers in the army of the Lord. WE must stand and fight the good fight of faith and lay hold of the promises that await us in heaven. In an army, each person needs to know their position and how to march. Otherwise there is confusion, descension, disorder, and stagnancy. Many people in the Body of Christ have not surrendered their entire lives and wills to Jesus. They do not know the WILL OF GOD FOR THEIR LIVES. They are very busy doing all kinds of things the Lord has not called them to do and they are missing out on what He really has for them.

When someone in the Body of Christ asks you to do something, pray about it first and ask the Lord if it is HIS WILL for you to get involved in it. Don't just agree to occupy your efforts, your time, your energy, and your funds without asking the Lord first.

After I fully surrendered my entire life and will to the Lord, I received two phone calls. The crisis pregnancy center asked me if I wanted to be a pregnancy counselor and offered to train me. TBN phoned and asked me if I wanted to answer their phone lines when people wanted prayer. My answer to both was, "Let me pray about this and see if this is what the Lord has for me." When I asked the Lord, HE SAID NO. Both things are nice, Christian Ministries, but they were not what the Lord had for me. There were other people the Lord had in mind for those positions.

A few days later, I saw Marilyn Hickey Ministries on the T.V. looking for people to travel to China, the Philippines, and Hong Kong as part of her prayer team. The Lord told me to go with her. A few months later, the Lord sent me with her again to Kenya, Comoros, Zanzibar, and Madagascar as part of her pray team again. After that, He sent me back into Africa 23 trips six weeks at a time to grow the Body of Christ there.

IF I had taken the positions in the crisis pregnancy center or at TBN, I wouldn't have been free to go with Marilyn Hickey and I wouldn't have been used by God as Fishers of Men Ministries in Africa. Many souls were won to the Lord, villages were set free of demonic witchdoctors, false prophets, unforgiveness, tribal hatred, fear, rejection, depression, the shame of being raped, the spirit of rejection, etc…Many people were healed of baroness, back pain, broken bones, malaria, alcoholism, diseases, etc…Many were grown spiritually as I preached the Word of God in Churches, seminars, giant camp meetings, Pastor's Conferences, on Jesus is Lord Radio (Nakuru, Kenya) and Sayre Voice of Mercy T.V. And radio out of Eldoret, Kenya, etc…A demoniac with a legion of demons was totally delivered and came to Jesus, a dead boy was raised, babies almost dead of malaria were healed, etc…

If I had taken the position at the Crisis Pregnancy Center, I would have been out of the will of God and I would have prevented God's person from taking their rightful position in His Army.

IF I had taken the position answering prayer lines for TBN, I would have been out of the will of God, and I would have prevented God's person from taking their rightful position in His Army.

Always pray and ask the Lord to show you HIS WILL. Surrender your entire life and will to the Holy Spirit and ask Him what He would have you do. Line up with God and see the amazing things HE will do in you and through you. WE, as soldiers in the Lord's Army, need to get into the right positions to WAR A GOOD WARFARE AND FINISH THE RACE WELL.

THE MISTAKE OF TRYING TO UNITE WITH FALSE RELIGIONS

No where, in the Bible, is the Body of Christ told to join ourselves with people of other religions who pray to other gods. Biblical Unity involves the people of God, (believers in Jesus Christ as Savior and Lord), uniting with each other to combat our real enemy, Satan, and not each other.

Trying to blend the real God and prayer and worship to Him with false god worshippers, is not pleasing to God. "Thou shall have no other Gods beside me." God is not pleased when we try to have joint prayer meetings with Hindus, Muslims, Islamic believers, Buddhists, JWs, because the god they worship is another god. "How can two walk together unless they agree." WE can have no agreement with false gods and those promoting them. Some pastors have compromised and encourage people to attend joint prayer meetings with other religions, BUT THIS IS NOT BIBLICAL UNITY. THIS IS WICKEDNESS IN THE SIGHT OF GOD.

> John 14:6 Jesus said, "I am the way, the truth, and the life; no man comes unto the Father but by me. IF you had known me, you should have known my Father also; and from henceforth you know him, and have seen him." The mansions that Jesus speaks of in John 14:1-4, in his Father's house, are ONLY FOR THOSE WHO BELIEVE ON JESUS. THERE WILL BE NO FALSE GOD WORSHIPPERS UP IN HEAVEN. Unless people repent of their sins and receive Jesus Christ as their Savior and Lord, they will not be in heaven.

A lie has been taught by many denominational pastors. The lie is this: In my Father's house are many mansions. WE believe there will be separate mansions for the Muslims, for the Islamic People, for the Hindus for the Buddhists, etc… That is NOT BIBLICAL. NO ONE BUT BELIEVERS IN JESUS CHRIST WILL HAVE THESE MANSIONS IN HEAVEN. NO ONE CAN COME TO THE FATHER BUT By ME (Jesus).

> Revelation 7:9-17 Speaks about a multitude, which no man could number standing in heaven before Father God and the Lamb . They were people from every nation, kindred, and tongue. In verse 14, the Bible says, "These are they which came out of great tribulation, and have washed their robes,, and made them white in the blood of the Lamb." Another words. They were all people who had repented of their sins and believed Jesus Christ died on the cross for them, personally, and rose again. Their sins had been washed clean in the Blood of Jesus and their garments were white as snow. They believed that Jesus paid for their sins on the cross and they received Jesus as Savior and Lord. God so loved the world that He gave Jesus BUT ONLY THOSE WHO RECEIVE JESUS WILL BE SAVED. THOSE WHO REJECT JESUS WILL NOT GO TO HEAVEN. No false God worshippers were there in heaven. Only believers in Jesus Christ were there.

Read the Bible and weight everything that anyone tells you by the Word of God. Rightly Divide the Word of Truth. Read the entire chapter and context. Who is being spoken to? What is being said? What is going on- what are the circumstances? What is Jesus actually saying? IS He speaking to believers, or to the scribes, or to the lost souls?

There are many fake pastors, fake preachers, fake reverends, fake ministers, fake apostles, fake prophets, fake Christs, lying doctrines of devils and seducing spirits, etc…IF you don't study the Bible, you can easily be deceived by Satan's lies. IF you know what God says about everything, you won't believe the lies of the devil. Satan is out there as a roaring lion seeking to destroy people's bodies, souls, minds, and spirits.

If you know the truth – Jesus Christ Himself, and the Word of God, you won't believe the lie that truth is relative. God's Word is TRUTH. Jesus Christ is THE WORD OF GOD WHO BECAME FLESH AND DWELT AMONG US. He is the way, the truth and the life. Jesus said, "I am the light of the world. He who follows me shall not walk in darkness but will have the light of life." Read, study and memorize God's Holy Bible and apply its teachings to your life. Renew your mind with the Word of God. Replace the devil's lies and demonic mindsets with God's Truth and with the Mind of Christ. Weigh carefully what your preacher says to see if it lines up with what God says. If it doesn't, change Churches. God hasn't changed His Mind about anything. What was sin in the Old Testament is still sin in the New Testament. The devil wants you to think God has changed His Mind about sexual sin, gayness, fornication, adultery, pornography, lesbianism, homosexuality, bisexuality, bestiality, sodomy, and transgender.

God creates a person, in the womb of their mother, to be either male or female according to His Plan and Purpose for their life. When a person believes the lie that God Made a Mistake when He created them, they are open to the devil's plans to destroy them physically, emotionally, mentally, and spiritually. Sadly, many have fallen victim to the devil's lies of transgender surgeries, mutilation of their physical bodies, destruction of their emotions and feelings, and destruction of God's Plan and God's Purpose for their lives. As the opposite sex, they are outside of the will of God, will never really be who they are trying to be, and will never fully accomplish God's Plan and Purpose for their lives. A woman will never grow a penis.

She will never be a "REAL MAN." A man will never grow a uterus, Fallopian tubes, and the reproductive organs needed to have a child. HE will never be a "REAL WOMAN." Aspiring to be someone they can never really be will leave a person emotionally and spiritually bankrupt. Sadly, many of these people have committed suicide due to depression that results from transgender surgeries. John Hopkins Medical Center has stopped doing transgender surgeries due to the horrible depression that it causes and the tendency for suicide.

Read God's Word. Study Ephesians Chapters one and two. God Loves you. God has forgiven you. God has adopted you into His Family. God has chosen you. God has a good plan for your life. Get to know Jesus, Father God and His Holy Spirit. Read the Gospels. Read the Book of Acts. Read Romans. Read the entire Word of God. Begin in the New Testament and then read the Old Testament. He has given us over 8,800 promises that are real, yes, and Amen. See what the God, who cannot lie, has promised you. Apply His promises to your life.

CHAPTER EIGHT
SATAN'S PLAN TO DESTROY AMERICA'S YOUTH

    Back in 1948, wicked Supreme Court Judges began the lie of "Separation of Church and State" and put it into our law books, preparing the way to remove Christianity and replace God with the no God atheist lie of evolution. Prior to 1948, our laws lined up with God's Laws. For example, when a pornographer tried to bring porn onto a college campus, the courts ruled that he could not destroy the morals of our youth. When a Mormon wanted to marry more than one wife, the courts ruled he couldn't as per I Timothy 3:12 "Let the deacon be the husband of one wife, ruling their children and their own house well." 1 Timothy 3:2 "A bishop then must be blameless, the husband of one wife,"

    Once the lie of "Separation of Church and State" was put in place, school prayer to the real God, was taken out of our schools in 1968. The atheist, Godless religion , OF EVOLUTION, was deliberately put into our schools, under the guise of "science."

    The King James Bible makes it clear in 1 Timothy 6:20 "O Timothy, keep that which is committed to your trust avoiding profane and vain babblings, and oppositions of science falsely so called. Which some professing have erred concerning the faith."

    Evolution has been taught as a science falsely so called. IT is man's attempt to explain how he came to exist without believing in a Creator God. The RELIGION OF ATHEISM denies that God created everything seen and unseen. IT is a Godless, Christless Religion and belief that everything came about by chance, by a chemical soup that "evolved into apes and evolved into human beings, over millions of years." IT denies that there is a God given Plan and a God given purpose for every life God molds in the womb of their mother. It teaches the youth that there is no God and no Divine Purpose for their life or the life of anyone else. Evolution theory is directly responsible for the disregard of human life through school shootings, suicides, abortion murders of innocent human beings, rapes, murder, stealing, and every other assault on other human beings by people who deny there is a God, deny God's Commandments, and deny God's Word.

IF you view yourself as a monkey, What is your life worth? IF you view other people as just evolved apes, it is no big deal to lie to them, steal from them, rape them, murder them, attack them,….After All, they are just evolved monkeys.

IF you believe the lie that there is no God, there is nothing to hinder you from doing everything and anything you accept as right in your own eyes. If you believe you don't have to answer to anyone for what you do, how you live, and how you treat or mistreat others, you will become a very selfish person who has no regard for anyone else but yourself. The denial that God exists does not negate the Fact that God Does Exist. You can deny that you breathe the air, but the air does exist.

Stephen Hawkins has physically died. HE denied God, refused the Blood of Jesus that would have cleansed him of his sins, and chose to be an atheist to the end. He is in the nether most parts of the earth, Hell, and is paying for his own sins, himself. He rejected God the Father, God the Son (Jesus Christ), and God the Holy Ghost/Holy Spirit. He rejected the Loving Savior who went to the cross, to pay for his sins, so that he, Stephen Hawkins, could go to heaven. Stephen Hawkins refused the Blood Sacrifice that Jesus Christ gave on the cross and chose hell; rather than heaven. No person goes to hell because God wants them there. They reject God and choose to go to hell with Satan and the fallen angels.

> John 3:16-21 "For God so loved the world, that he gave his only begotten Son, that whosoever believes in him should not perish, but have everlasting life. For God sent his Son into the world not to condemn the world; but that the world through him might be saved. HE that believes on him (Jesus) is not condemned; but he that believes not is condemned already, because he has not believed in the name of the only begotten Son of God. And this is the condemnation, that light is come into the world, and men

loved darkness rather than light; because their deeds were evil. For every one that does evil hates the light, neither comes to the light, lest his deeds should be reproved. But he that does truth comes to the light, that his deeds may be made manifest, that they are wrought in God."

As we can see here, people who don't want to be reproved (corrected), hate Jesus Christ and will not repent and come to Christ. They hate Jesus the light and choose to walk in the darkness, do works of darkness, continue in evil and wickedness, and refuse the salvation that God has offered them through Jesus Christ. As a result, they die in their sins, separated from God forever and spend an eternity in hell and are eventually thrown into the lake of fire; (after the Great White Throne Judgment listed in Revelation 20:10-15). By their own choice and free will, they have refused the Savior and Lord Jesus Christ. They have refused heaven and chosen hell. They have made a fatal error that has destroyed their own soul. IF they remain an atheist, they will end up with Stephen Hawkins in hell.

IF you think there is no hell, I would advise you to read Ezekiel Chapter 31 verses 16-18. Pharaoh and his multitude went to hell after they drowned in the Red Sea. They are down in the pit, the nether parts of the earth, the center of the earth, etc…

> Mark 9:37 Jesus said, "Whosoever shall receive one of such children in my name, receives me; and whosoever shall receive me, receives not me, but him that sent me." When a person receives Jesus Christ as their Savior and Lord, they receive Father God also. You cannot refuse Jesus Christ without refusing Father God who sent him.

> I John 5:9-13 "If we receive the witness of men, the witness of God is greater; for this is the witness of God which he has testified of his Son. HE that believes on the Son of God has the witness in himself; he that believes not God has made him a liar; because he believes not the record that God gave of his Son. And this is the record, that God has given to us eternal life, and this life is in his Son. He that has the Son has life; and he that has not the Son of God has

not life. These things have I written unto you that believe on the name of the Son of God; that you may know that you have eternal life, and that you may believe on the name of the Son of God.

AS we see here, God isn't interested in what sect of Christianity, what denomination you were or what church you attended. He will look at you and see if you received Jesus into your heart as your personal Savior and Lord or if you rejected Jesus. Were your sins washed clean under the blood of Jesus, or did you die in your sins without Jesus? If you died without Jesus, you will pay for your own sins yourself, in hell.

Evolution is contrary to the Bible that states in Genesis 1:1 "In the beginning God created the heaven and the earth." Evolution is Satan's attack on the entire Bible. IF people do not believe there is a God, then they will not believe His Words or anything HE is trying to say to them. IF people do not believe there is a God, they do what is right in their own eyes; no matter how wicked God says it is.

Generations of Americans have been brain-washed by our public school system to believe that God doesn't exist and that their ancestors were nothing but "EVOLVED APES." As a result, they are living lives of bondage to alcohol and drugs, sexual immorality, violence, stealing, lying, falsely accusing others of the things they have done, refusing anything that is right in the sight of God, etc…Many have committed suicide because they believe the lie that there is no God, no purpose for their lives, no reason for their existence, etc…The divorce rates, violent crime rates, sex trafficking of children, abortion (murders of innocent unborn BABIES), mutilation of children through transgender surgeries, rapes in schools by boys and men that say they are transgender so they can enter locker rooms and rape women, the rapes of women in our women's prisons by transgender men, etc…is all a result of removing God and Prayer from our schools and from our seven pillars of society: OUR FAMILIES, OUR CHURCHES, OUR SCHOOLS AND COLLEGES, OUR GOVERNMENT AND MILITARY, OUR MEDIA, OUR BUSINESSES, CORPORATIONS, AND ORGANIZATIONS, and OUR ENTERTAINMENT.

The only "Religion" that the lie of separation of church and state has kept out of our schools is real Christianity rooted and grounded in Jesus Christ Himself.

IF a student believes that he is nothing more that an evolved ape, then there is no reason for his existence, no Divine Purpose for his life, and no Divine Purpose for anyone else's life. Because of the lie of Evolution, many of our youth have shot up our classrooms and killed other students, committed suicide, gotten on drugs, filled themselves with alcohol, dropped out of school., turned to lives of crime and prostitution, got pregnant and murdered their babies,(believing the lie that a baby is not a baby in the womb), etc....They have no hope, do not know there is a real God who loves them, A God who molded them in their mother's womb according to His Divine Purpose for their lives, etc... If they have parents who never heard about God or experienced His Love for them, their children don't experience God either.

We have generations of people, in America, who do not know God. Many don't even believe He Exists. Many have been taught the lie of Evolution and believe they are just evolved apes. IF you are an evolved ape, WHAT IS YOUR LIFE WORTH? NOTHING> IF you believe YOUR BABY IS JUST AN EVOLVED APE, WHAT IS YOUR BABIES LIFE WORTH? Nothing. IF YOU BELIEVE YOUR CLASSMATES ARE JUST EVOLVED APES, WHAT ARE THEIR LIVES WORTH? NOTHING. IF YOU BELIEVE THAT ALL PEOPLE ARE JUST EVOLVED APES, KILLING THEM IS NOTHING. ROBBING THEM IS NOTHING. RAPING THEM IS NOTHING. The Lie of Evolution is Responsible For All of Societies Woes. We are reaping a harvest of our own Godlessness.

There is an interesting book called, "AMERICA: TO PRAY OR NOT TO PRAY?" by David Barton. IT is a statistical look at what has happened since 39 million students were ordered to stop praying in public schools. This book was copyrighted in 1988. This book shows charts, tables, and graphs of the negative effects of removing God from our schools. Corporate, verbal prayer was completely removed in a limited manner on June 25, 1962. In a second far-reaching decision on June 17, 1963, it was completely removed from our schools. Academics began to decline in 1963. The normal school prayer went like this, "Almighty God, we acknowledge our dependence upon Thee, and we beg Thy blessings upon us, our parents, and our teachers and our Country." David Barton searched the statistical information from governmental agencies and Depts of Health and human Services, Dept. of Agriculture, Dept. of Labor, Dept. of Education, Dept. of Commerce, etc...

Our State Constitutions, our money, our National Anthem, our Pledge of Allegiance, reflect our dependence on God. We are a Christian Nation founded upon God, His Commandments, His Laws, and His Constitution. In June 1962, God was taken out of our daily lives. The Supreme Court in Engel v. Vitale, Murray v. Curlett, and Abington v. Schempp, forbade the free exercise of voluntary public prayer in our nation's schools. IT was the Supreme Court who did this wickedness.

In a single year 39 million students and over 2 million teachers were barred from doing what had been done since our nations founding- praying in school. To make a long story short, the SAT Scores went down, premarital sexual activity went up, sexually transmitted diseases went up, widespread immorality occurred, pregnancies to unwed women escalated, youth suicides zoomed, divorce rates escalated, single parent homes increased in number, fornication, adultery, pornography, school violence, corrupt teachers, corrupt curriculum, child abuse, drug use, alcoholism, etc… are all a result of taking God and prayer out of our schools and out of our seven pillars of society.

Isn't it time we welcome God back into our Nation and into every pillar of our society? Isn't it time we preach against fornication, adultery, pornography, gayness, lust, homosexuality, lesbianism, drag queens, transgender surgeries, abortion, stealing, lying, bearing false witness against your neighbor, etc…Isn't it time we preach the Gospel of Jesus Christ unto Salvation (a real Heart to Heart Relationship With Jesus Christ) instead of Religion that doesn't save anyone from hell? Isn't it Time WE REPENT OF ALL THIS WICKEDNESS OUR NATION IIAS DONE AGAINST The GOD OF HEAVEN? Isn't IT Time?

The main insult and rejection of the God of Heaven was done in a place called Bethel, New York. This total REBELLION AGAINST THE GOD OF HEAVEN opened the door to all of the drug addictions, alcoholism, idol temples, false god worship, witchcraft, wizardry, murders, the ritualistic sex-trafficking of children, pornography, fornication, lusts, adultery, gayness, homosexuality, orgies, self-mutilation, body piercings, tattoos, and now the mutilation of children's bodies to change them from who God created them to be, into Satan's destructive plan for their lives. Even John Hopkins Medical Center has refused to do transgender surgeries on children and teens because these surgeries leave the people in a state of depression.

Kathleen Hollop
THE NATIONAL SIN OF WOODSTOCK

For years, most of the Body of Christ has been ignorant of the worst Spiritual Wickedness that took place against our God, here, in Bethel, New York at a Demonic Festival called, "WOODSTOCK," in 1969. The wickedness was planned and orchestrated by witches and Satanists to rebel against, reject, insult, and grieve the real God of Heaven and Earth. The entire purpose of this event was to gather together young people from every state in the United States to worship other gods; using stocks of wood, stones, nature, every type of paganism possible, mid Eastern gods, the sun, moon, and stars, and every form of nature worship over the Creator God who created it all. They erected stone altars, made offerings, burnt incense to false gods and performed the sexual acts that are part of false god worship. Fornication, adultery, orgies, witchcraft, wizardry, sorcery, Baal Worship, drugs, alcoholism, and other lusts were everywhere. Their so called "Peace Symbol" is really an upside down cross. IF you take the lower points that hang down, on the right side and the left side, and put them straight across, you have an upside down demonic cross of Satan.

> In 1 Samuel 15:23, the Bible says, "For rebellion is as the sin of witchcraft, and stubbornness is as iniquity and idolatry." The people were rebelling against God, His Commandments, the government, the war, their parents, morality, decency, any laws, any rules, any restrictions, any values, etc…They did not want any instruction, any correction, any rules, anyone telling them what to do, including God Himself.

The demonic music of Santana's "Black Magic Woman", the voodoo music of Jimmy Hendricks "Voodoo Child", and other songs he played and sang released demons into the crowd. People were bouncing their children on their shoulders to this occult music and dancing to it, while a portal to hell was opened there and demons were coming up and entering the crowd. As the music played and the singers sang songs to glorify Satan and the occult, people were getting infested with demonic spirits. When they left, they carried all the demonic spirits into their states and drug addictions, lusts, alcoholism, perversions, false god temples, and all other types of bondages and wickedness seemed to break out everywhere all at once, right after WOODSTOCK 1969. There were even some deaths on the property due to drug overdoses.

In 2011, my Husband Paul, Son Brian, and I were on vacation at Villa Roma Resort near where the Woodstock Museum and Bethel Woods were. We saw signs advertising the Bethel Woods Woodstock Museum and the Holy Spirit told me to take a tour of the place to see what happened there.

In 1969, I was only sixteen years old, when the Woodstock event happened. I liked Elvis Presley. All I could remember, of that time, was seeing people on T.V. dressed in tie-dyed tee shirts, burning draft cards, wearing flowers in their unkept hair and yelling "PEACE NOT WAR." Somehow some musicians were thrown into the mix, but I really didn't know what took place there.

The Holy Spirit led us to see the museum and gave us understanding as to what happened back then, in the spiritual realm. As we entered the Bethel Woods Museum, we saw a video clip of people sitting all over the ground in the pouring rain, shaking their fists up at God and screaming, "NO RAIN.""NO RAIN.""NO RAIN." Our Son Brian said, "The reason it rained all three days is that God the Father was weeping in heaven because these people did not want Him." God was hurt and rejected.

As we walked through the museum, there were zodiac symbols, Buddha Statues, hippie buses with flowers on them, pictures of a mid-Eastern guru and his followers, photos of naked people swimming in a pond, stone altars to false gods all over the grounds, the so-called peace symbol which is an upside-down cross everywhere, people strung out on drugs and alcohol, etc… But the worst thing we saw was a video music clip of Jimmy Hendricks singing "VOODOO CHILD," and people dancing to it, while bouncing their small children up and down to the demonic music.

We could feel the demons jumping off the video screen and had to plead the Blood of Jesus over ourselves. The school system takes BUS LOADS OF SCHOOL CHILDREN INTO THAT MUSEUM EVERY YEAR AND EXPOSES THEM TO THE DEMONIC MUSIC OF JIMMY HENDERICKS and the demonic spirits that jump at them from the video clip. Children are exposed to all the demonic rebellion and witchcraft that took place there and it is presented as a "GOOD THING."

IF you take the two sides of the peace symbol that hang down, and put them up straight across, you have an upside-down cross. IT is a demonic symbol. People buy purses, tee shirts, children's clothes, and other items with a "peace Symbol" on them and they have no idea what it really is. Ignorance is not bliss. It is very destructive. Wearing an upside down cross can open people up, in the spiritual realm, to demonic activity, lies, and Satan's destruction. IT is like giving the devil permission to attack your children.

AS Christians, we cannot be ignorant of Satan's devices. The Bible says a witch, a wizard, a necromancer (one who contacts spirits of the dead), an enchanter, a sorcerer, etc…are ABOMINATIONS TO GOD. Read Deuteronomy 18:9-14. Burn up your Harry Potter movies and books, put away your witchcraft movies, witchcraft items, spell casting, demonic video games, Ouija boards, Dungeon and Dragons occult games, occults items, etc…and get serious about the Lord. Ask the Lord to show you what does not please Him and get rid of those demonic things.

SCRIPTURES THAT SHOW WHAT HAPPENED IN THE SPIRITUAL REALM AT WOODSTOCK

The very night after we went to the Woodstock Museum, in Bethel, New York, the Holy Spirit began showing me what these foolish people did, in the spiritual realm, and all of the devastation it has caused in America. My Bible fell open to Jeremiah Chapter 2 and I began to read as the Holy Spirit led me.

> Jeremiah 2:11 "Has a nation changed their gods, which are yet no gods? But my people have changed their glory for that which does not profit."

> Jeremiah 2:26-28 "As the thief is ashamed when he is found, so is the house of Israel ashamed; they, their kings, their princes, and their priests and prophets, Saying to a stock (of wood), You are my father; and to a stone, You have brought me forth; for they have turned their back unto me, and not their face: but in the time of their trouble they will say, Arise, and save us. But where are your gods that you have made

you? Let them arise,, if they can save you in the time of your trouble; for according to the number of your cities are your gods, O Judah."

We see here that God's people were worshipping stocks of wood (Woodstock) and stones. They rejected the real God of Heaven, who created everything. They were praising and worshipping nature, as their god, instead of worshipping the real God who created nature. God made the sun, the moon, the stars, the solar system, the trees, the flowers, the birds, the stones, the seas, …HE is not pleased when people turn from him to worship objects that cannot help them, save them, deliver them, or answer their prayers. At the WOODSTOCK EVENT IN BETHEL, N.Y. the same sins Israel did in Jeremiah 2:26-28 were done by one million Americans from many different states of the United States. They worshipped pagan gods and goddesses and turned their backs on the real God who made us a great nation.

> In Jeremiah Chapter 7:8-11 "Behold, you trust in lying words, that cannot profit you. Will you steal, murder, and commit adultery, and swear falsely, and burn incense unto Baal, and walk after other gods whom you know not; And come and stand before me in this house, which is called by my name, and say, We are delivered to do all these abominations? Is this house, which is called by my name, become a den of robbers in your eyes? Behold, even I have seen it, says the Lord."

I wept as I thought about people who would go into God's house and worship other gods in his house. HE said to me, "Now look up the meaning of Bethel. BETHEL MEANS HOUSE OF GOD. In the spiritual realm, these people went into a place called HOUSE OF GOD and worshipped other gods in His House, to defile it. WOODSTOCK WAS HELD THE EIGHTH MONTH THE FIFTEENTH DAY.

> In I KINGS 12:26-33, King Jeroboam made two golden calves so that the people would not go up to Jerusalem to worship God. In verse 28 Jeroboam said, "IT is too much for you to go up to Jerusalem; behold your gods, O Israel, which

brought you up out of Egypt." HE set up the two golden calves in Bethel and set up false priests (not the sons of Levi). HE sacrificed to the golden calves in BETHEL, ISRAEL THE EIGHTH MONTH THE FIFTEENTH DAY.

IT is no coincidence that WOODSTOCK WAS DONE TO DEFILE BETHEL,N.Y. ON THE EIGHTH MONTH THE FIFTEENTH DAY AND JEROBOAM DEFILED BETHEL, ISRAEL THE EIGHTH MONTH THE FIFTEENTH DAY. This was all planned by satanists and witches to defile GOD'S HOUSE.

IF we look at Genesis 28:10-19, we see the account of Jacob, who fell asleep and saw a ladder ascending up into heaven and angels going up with prayer requests and other angels coming down with answers. In verse 16, Jacob says, "Surely the Lord is in this place; and I knew it not". And he was afraid,, and said, "How dreadful is this place! This is none other but the house of God, and this is the gate of heaven." And Jacob rose up early in the morning and took the stone that he had put for his pillow, and poured oil upon the top of it. And he called the name of that place BETHEL"

We see here that BETHEL was a portal to heaven. Jacob called Bethel the gate of heaven. HE saw the angels ascending up to heaven and returning. When WOODSTOCK happened in BETHEL, N.Y., the portal to heaven was closed and a portal to hell was opened up, in the spiritual realm. BETHEL in N.Y. was defiled by the false god worship that took place there in the house of God. The voodoo, witchcraft, false god religions, lust, depravity, adultery, fornications, orgies, drugs alcoholism, etc…were carried back to every state represented in Woodstock, by the people who attended. They were used as pack mules to bring the demons along with them back home to their states. Addictions, lusts, false god temples, witchcraft, wizardry, tarot card reading, enchantments, spell casting, contacting spirits of the dead, self-mutilation, suicides, fornication, abortions, adultery, gayness, lesbianism, tattoos, piercing every body part, etc… are the result of the wickedness of false god worship and the spirits of self destruction. There are generations of people caught up in the false god worship, lusts, addictions, occult practices, etc…here in the Northeast. The darkness must be broken off of the churches, the brethren, and the people in these states.

Church God's Way

    The people of God must REPENT OF WOODSTOCK AND ASK GOD'S FORGIVENESS AND MERCY ON Our NATION. Right now, America is reaping a harvest of its false god worship, its rejection of the real God of Heaven and Earth, its refusal to REPENT, its Pride and Rebellion, its wickedness, its idols, its paganism, its insanity, and its filth in the sight of God.

    Our nation began as a nation under God. Our fore-fathers left Europe to be able to have the freedom to Worship God. They were tired of being beaten, thrown in prison, and possibly murdered for their faith in Jesus Christ. They came here for the freedom to practice their Christian Faith. The Pilgrims, Separatists, Ana-Baptists, Huguenots, and other groups WERE ALL CHRISTIANS. God led them here to begin a new nation that would be a nation of salt, light, and truth. David Hunt in Cape Henry in the 1600's dedicated this nation to be a Nation that would serve the God of Heaven and bring the Gospel of Jesus Christ to all the nations of the world. He made a Holy Covenant with God, put up a Cross, and dedicated this Nation to God. We were to be a city on a hill, proclaiming the Gospel of Jesus Christ to the entire world. Our Constitution and our laws and our freedoms were given to us by the God of Heaven and Earth.

    It was God who gave us the Victory over the British. We were a rag tag group of colonists, not a well trained army. The men were farmers, barrel makers, black smiths, ranchers, etc…They were not a well trained militia with fancy guns, cannons, and military experience. The British had the greatest, most well-equipped army on planet earth, Yet we defeated them and won our Independence. Why? IF the God of Heaven and Earth didn't help our fore-fathers, we would have never become a nation in the first place. Read these books and let your children read them. See the REAL HISTORY OF OUR NATION, HOW IT BEGAN, AND WHAT GOD DID TO HELP US:

    "THE LIGHT AND THE GLORY" by Peter Marshall and David Manuel

    "FROM SEA TO SHINING SEA" by Peter Marshall and David Manuel

    "MIRACLES IN AMERICAN HISTORY" 32 Amazing Stories of Answered Prayer by Susie Federer

    Adapted from William J. Federer's American Minute

Kathleen Hollop

"MIRACLES IN AMERICAN HISTORY VOLUME 2"
Amazing Faith that Shaped the Nation by Susie
Federer Adapted from William J. Federer's American Minute

The above books are true stories about Our Nation and how our nation began as a Christian Nation. Whoever says that America is not a Christian Nation is lying. Teach your children the true history of our Nation. Don't let the public school system indoctrinate them into Karl Marx's demonic communism and socialism lies.

America is a Nation chosen by God to bring forth the truth of the Gospel of Jesus Christ to a lost and dying world. IT was chosen by God to give people their God Given rights and freedoms and liberties that Jesus Christ purchased for us on the Cross. Our laws used to be based on God's Holy Bible. Why is it wrong to steal, lie, commit adultery, bear false witness against your neighbor, have other Gods, take God's Name in vain, worship idols, etc…because God says these things are wrong.

Prior to 1948, our laws were in line with God's Laws. The Bible was taught in school. The first text book for reading, in our Nation, was the Bible. Prior to 1968, Teachers and children could pray a short prayer asking God's Blessing on their families, their teachers, their school work, etc… When the lie of separation of Church and State was put on the law books by wicked judges, our laws became tainted. Our courts no longer stood for God, His Laws and His Commandments. We have gotten to a point where teachers cannot mention the Name of Jesus in a public school classroom without loosing their jobs, or being sued by the ACLU. JESUS CANNOT BE MENTIONED IN SOME WORK PLACES WITHOUT SEVERE CONSEQUENCES. The ONLY RELIGION THAT THE LIE OF SEPERATION OF CHURCH AND STATE HAS KEPT OUT OF OUR SCHOOLS AND OUT OF OUR PILLARS OF SOCIETY IS CHRISTIANITY. A witch, a Muslim, a Hindu, a Buddhist, Yoga (Mid-eastern religious mind meditation), Harry Potter (a wizard-an ABOMINATION TO GOD Deuteronomy 18:9-12), a Satanist, a drag queen, AN ATHEIST THROUGH THE LIE OF EVOLUTION, GREEK MYTHS AND FALSE GODS, all can enter our schools , BUT JESUS CHRIST CANNOT EVEN BE MENTIONED. WHY? BECAUSE SATANIC JUDGES PUT THE LIE OF SEPERATION OF CHURCH AND STATE IN OUR

LAW BOOKS. THIS WICKED LIE MUST BE REMOVED AND JESUS CHRIST MUST BE PREACHED IN OUR SCHOOLS AND COLLEGES AGAIN.

Haven't enough children and teens committed suicide because they do not know God and His Love For Them? Haven't enough young people died of drug overdoses, alcoholism, diseases due to sexual perversion and lusts? Haven't enough people gone through their entire lives believing they are nothing more than an evolved monkey? Hasn't the devil destroyed enough human beings? Isn't it time that our youth are told they are valuable, that God loves them, that God created them, that God has a good plan for their lives. Isn't it time that brotherly love, kindness, goodness, values, morality, decency, genuine love, respect, patriotism, the true history of our nation, and Faith in Jesus Christ come back into our Nation and into society?

THE SPIRITS OF SELF DESTRUCTION/SELF MUTILATION/AND SELF HATRED

In Africa, many deceived mothers have taken their children to witch doctors who did cuttings on their children's bodies claiming that the cuttings would offer them some kind of protection against evil spirits. In reality, these cuttings were blood sacrifices to Satan and left permanent scars on their children's arms, legs, and bodies.

1 Kings 18:17-28 states that the prophets of Baal called upon their false god Baal from morning to evening but he didn't answer them. In verse 28, "And they cried aloud, and cut themselves after their manner with knives and lancets till the blood gushed out upon them." They mutilated their own skin with knives and lancets to give their false god Baal blood sacrifices, but he never answered them. Whenever human blood is shed, people are murdered, blood sacrifices are made to false gods through cuttings, abortions, transgender surgeries, the raping of innocent children, etc…It is a Satanic Ritualistic Sacrifice to the devil.

The Real God, Jesus Christ, came to earth to become the Perfect Lamb OF God who would take away the sins of the world. Adam sinned but Jesus Christ did no sin neither was guile found in His mouth. He was always God. HE came out of love for us. We are all sinners and needed the Savior to die in our place on a cross so that we could be forgiven. Jesus Christ, God Himself, came to redeem fallen mankind back to Himself by paying for our sins on that cross with His Own Sinless Blood. His Righteous Holy Blood is the only sacrifice for sin that Father God will accept as payment.

We cannot earn our way to heaven. WE don't deserve to go to heaven. We cannot do enough good works to compensate for even one sin we have done. Jesus Paid IT All. All TO Him I Owe. Sin Had Left A Crimson Stain, He Washed IT White As Snow. The Real God of Heaven does not require human blood sacrifices. He Sacrificed Himself for us so that we could be forgiven. We all need to know Jesus Christ in our hearts. We all need to repent of our sins and believe Jesus died on that cross for us personally and rose again on the third day. If our children and grandchildren could be taught that God exists, that God Created them for God's Divine Purpose, that they are loved, that they are valuable, that their lives matter, that they are important, that all human life is precious and important, that all races are loved by God, that their gifts, talents, and abilities come from God, etc…they will not be so quick to throw their lives away on drugs, alcohol, and ungodly lusts.

> Romans 5:8-9 "But God commended his love toward us, in that, while we were yet sinners, Christ died for us. Much more then, being now justified by his blood; we shall be saved from wrath by him."

THE SPIRIT OF TATOOS AND PIERCINGS

Leviticus 19:28 You shall not make any cuttings in your flesh for the dead; nor print any marks upon you: I am the Lord." People used to mourn for the dead and cut their own skin open to show sadness. People in Kenya were in the Churches one minute and in December running out into the brush to do sacrifices to their dead ancestors, according to their tribal customs.

I Corinthians 10:19-21 "What shall I say then? That the idol is anything or that which is offered in sacrifice to idols is any thing? But I say, that the things which the Gentiles sacrifice,, they sacrifice to devils, and not to God, and I would not that you should have fellowship with devils. You cannot drink the cup of the Lord, and the cup of devils: you cannot be partakers of the Lord's table, and of the table of devils. Do we provoke the Lord to jealousy? Are we stronger than he?"

They needed to Repent of their demonic sacrifices because they were telling Jesus Christ that His Holy Blood Sacrifice to take away their sins was not enough. They were sacrificing to devils in the bush. You cannot serve God and Satan and expect to go to heaven. Choose you this day who you will serve. IF it is Jesus, serve Him Only. Love Him enough to obey Him. Obey His Commandments, seek Him, and follow Him. IF it is your dead ancestors and devils and demons, get out of the Church of God and stop pretending to be a Christian. The entire village REPENTED AND GOT RIGHT WITH JESUS.

How many Pastors, Prophets, Apostles, Teachers, Evangelists, and lay people here in America need to REPENT of having Harry Potter Wizard books and movies in their homes, witch craft items, the "Good Witch" movies, tarot cards, Ouija boards, false god books, fortune telling crystal balls, pornography books and magazines, occult video games, etc…that they know are not pleasing to God? Isn't it time you burn up the occult items and get serious in your walk with Christ? You CANNOT SERVE GOD AND SATAN. CHOOSE YOU THIS DAY WHO YOU WILL SERVE.

There is a spirit behind all of the body piercings. The bulls of Bashan pierced Jesus Christ's hands and feet. No where in the Bible does it approve of puncturing many parts of your body to insert rings and jewelry through your skin. The only thing the Bible mentions is that if a servant wants to belong to their master, he can put an aul through his ear and he will serve his master forever. (Exodus 21:6, and Deuteronomy 15:17).

I have one hole in each ear for an ear ring. The clip on earrings made my ears hurt so I got my ears pierced to be able to wear one ear ring in each ear. That is the only holes I have on my body.

People get tattoos all over their skin and never check to see what is in the tattoo dye that is being injected into their skin. Google " tattoo dye" and see what is being injected into your body; -car paint, plastics, arsenic, metals, lead, and all kinds of foreign substances are in the tattoo dye. The European Union has outlawed certain ingredients in tattoo dye because there is a strong possibility they can travel through the body and cause lymph node cancer and other types of cancer. The FDA here in America has no requirements for tattoo dye and no standards for tattoo artists to keep. They don't even have to disclose what is in the dye they are putting into your body.

Many tattoos have spiritual side effects. For example, people get dragon tattoos. Satan is described in Revelation 12:7-9 as a great dragon. Getting something that represents Satan tattooed on your skin is like a welcome mat to the devil. People get chains tattooed around their necks. Chains symbolize bondage. Most people do not even know that the Bible says we are not to print any images on our skin. (Leviticus 19:28) The worst thing of all is that once you get a tattoo, you cannot get rid of it. You are stuck with it your entire life. Hitler forced tattoos on the arms of the Jews. Every time they look at the tattoos, they remember the horrors they endured in the prison camps at the hands of DEMONIC PEOPLE.

> I Corinthians 19 "Know you not that your body is the temple of the Holy Ghost which is in you, which you have of God, and you are not your own? For you are bought with a price (the blood of Jesus); therefore glorify God in your body, and your spirit, which are God's." WE owe it to God to take care of our bodies because we are the temple of the Holy Ghost.

There is no need for you to pierce every part of your body, cover yourself with tattoos, dye your hair all kinds of strange colors, transgender yourself, etc…to get attention. God sees you and loves you, for you. He created you in His Own Image to be beautiful in His Sight. He created you to be either a man or a woman. You are a beautiful, one of a kind, unique person that God designed you to be. Accept who you are in Christ, seek Him, follow Him, and receive His Divine Direction for your life. He has a good plan for your life. You will never know His Plan if you don't surrender your own puny plan for your life and allow Him to show you His Big Plan.

There is a demonic spirit of self loathing. IT tells you that you are a nothing, a no body, a useless excuse for a human being. You may look into the mirror and hate the person you see in it. You may hate what you are doing but have no power to stop. You may be filled with shame, emotional pain, spiritual pain, and self hatred. You may believe Satan's lie that God could never love you, that God could never accept you, that God wouldn't ever forgive you, that you sinned too much, that you blew it, that there is no hope for you. SATAN IS A LIAR AND THE FATHER OF LIES.

At one point in my life, before I came to Jesus, these were the lies Satan was telling me. I hated myself, hated what I was doing but couldn't stop, hated my life, knew I was a sinner separated from God, but didn't know what I could do to get right with God. I thought of suicide but thoughts of my children came into my mind as I was about to run my car into a tree, and I couldn't have my children asking themselves "What did we do to cause mommy to kill herself." The next day, I cried, "God if you really exist help me." I went to work and the Lord sent two men to my security booth that really knew Jesus Christ in their hearts and lives. They said, "Do you want forgiveness for every sin you have ever done?" I wept and cried and said, "God could never love me. God could never forgive me. I have blown it. I have sinned too much." They showed me John 3:16-17 "For God so loved the world that HE gave his only begotten Son, that, whosoever believes in him should not perish, but have everlasting life. For God sent His Son into the world not to condemn the world; but that the world through him might be saved." They said, "You are a part of this world, aren't you." I said, "Yes." They said, "If you were the only person on planet earth, Jesus would have came here to save you." "Would you like to receive Jesus as your Savior and Lord." I said, "Yes."

They led me in the following sinners prayer. I prayed, "Father God, I am a sinner. I am sorry for my sins. I believe that Jesus Christ died on that cross to save me and rose from the dead on the third day. Lord Jesus, come into my heart and life. Make me a new person. Help me to know You more and to live for You, in your Holy Name. Amen.

After I prayed that prayer, it felt like a cement block of guilt, depression, self hatred, hopelessness, fear, and misery got lifted off of my heart and I felt the love of God pour into me. I felt clean for the first time in years. I knew that the God, who created heaven and earth, really loved me. After that, I began reading the Gospels – John first and then Matthew, Mark, and Luke. I grew in my faith in Jesus as I learned about believers water baptism and the Holy Ghost Baptism and wanted both. The Holy Spirit taught me the Bible 6,7, and 8 hours a day for the nine years I still worked on the night shift. I never realized then, that the Lord would use me to reach souls for Him, heal the sick, raise the dead, and write books to share the spiritual teachings and things He taught me, with others. Jesus renewed my mind with His Holy Bible, continued to pour His Love into me, continued to teach me and grow me up spiritually, filled me with His Holy Spirit, and anointed me for His service. He made me a new creature/a new person on the inside. I was no longer the depressed, hopeless, discouraged, fearful, angry person that I once was. He changed me, cleansed me, restored me, healed me, and gave me a brand new life. What He did for me, He can do for you if you willingly repent of your sins and receive Him into your heart and life, as your personal Savior and Lord. HE Loves You. He Suffered on that cross for you. His Holy Blood was shed as payment for your sins so you can be forgiven. HE can Save You, Deliver You, and Heal You. Come to Him today. HE will accept you as you are. Trust Him.

I was never sorry that I received Him back in 1984 as my personal Savior and Lord. I hear His Voice, I know Him, I follow Him, and He leads me into Father God's Will and purpose for my life. He is my Savior, my Comforter, my Best Friend, the lover of my soul, the lifter of my head, the strength of my life, my healer, my teacher, my God, my King, my Lord, and so much more.

Religion didn't save my soul from hell. My Jesus Saved me, Delivered me from self-destruction, and healed my marriage and my life. Jesus Paid For ME when He died on that cross. I sinned. He did no sin. He took my punishment, my pain, and my shame upon Himself on that tree so that I could be forgiven and become an adopted daughter of God. I am a child of God through my faith in Jesus Christ. Read Romans Chapter 8. You can be a child of God too if you repent and receive Jesus into your heart and life.

Whatever gender God has Created you to be was no accident. God makes no mistakes. You may feel unloved, insecure, confused, or depressed. You may be going through puberty where your body has begun to mature and your hormones are beginning to change from a child to a teen to an adult. These years bring about many developmental changes, emotional changes, and hormonal changes. Trans gendering yourself will not help you to feel loved, accepted, secure, and satisfied.

The devil wants you scarred and marred and destroyed. Satan's plan is to keep you from achieving God's Plan and Purpose for your life. If he can get you to change your gender, destroy your reproductive organs with transgender drugs, and mar your body forever with scars from transgender surgeries; he can destroy the person God created you to be, destroy your future, destroy any children you would have, and destroy God's Plans and God's Purposes for your life. Don't believe Satan's lies that you would be happier if you became the opposite gender. Satan is the father of lies and a murderer from the beginning. He hates human beings because we were Created In The Image of God. Satan hates God. Satan hates us. Don't believe his lies. Trust in the Lord with all your heart and don't lean on your own understanding. In all your ways acknowledge God and He will direct your paths. God would never want you to transgender yourself. Repent of your sins, receive Jesus Christ into your heart and life as your Personal Savior and Lord, get to know Him, read the Gospels, walk with Jesus, let Him heal you, let Him pour out His Love into you, and make you clean from the inside out. He can restore to you what the devil has stolen.

Sexual promiscuity is destroying many young people today. When you link yourself with someone else sexually, you become one flesh with them. You not only join your bodies together, but your souls (emotions, wills, feelings), and your spirits. You leave pieces of yourself with every one you have sex with and take into yourself pieces of them. IF you have sex with a demonized person, those spirits enter you when you have sex with them. You become one with them in every area of your life. That is why broken relationships that involved sex are so destructive. They cause a lot of heartbreak, emotional pain, spiritual pain, distress, and hurt. This is why God's Word says that fornication (sex outside of marriage is a sin). God has tried to spare people from the destruction that sexual lusts cause in a person's mind, heart, body, emotions, and feelings.

To be used, abused, and thrown away by another person is hurtful, painful, degrading, and very destructive. To be left with an unwanted pregnancy, to do away with your child in your womb, to suffer with venereal diseases (some of which are incurable), to suffer with physical ailments due to sexual abuse, to suffer emotional pain, to suffer with a wounded spirit when you opened your heart to someone and loved them but they just used you, is horrible.

Many people try to change their outward appearance and become someone else due to the pain and hurt they have suffered as themself. Trying to change your outward appearance is not the answer. It is your heart, your mind and your spirit that need to change. The one that can change you from the inside out is Jesus Christ. He can save your soul, wash your sins clean, make you a new person, heal your broken heart and life, take away your sin, take away your shame, your pain, your hurtful memories, etc…and give you a brand new life and a brand new start. If you are willing to ask God's forgiveness for your sins and ask Jesus Christ to come into your heart and life and be your Savior and Lord, He will come in and do a deep work in you. He will accept you as you are. The Blood of Jesus is Powerful Enough to cleanse you of all sin and all unrighteousness. There is no sin that the Blood of Jesus cannot cleanse. All who come to him, he will in no wise cast out. Don't Wait. Repent and Receive Him Today. Today is the day of Salvation. None of us know if we have tomorrow.

Just because our wicked government has legalized marijuana doesn't mean that God wants you to smoke it, get addicted to it, and try other drugs. You need to get high on God, not on drugs and alcohol. Satan plans to get the youth of America all strung out on drugs so they won't be able to think clearly, reason clearly, make wise decisions, and fulfill the call of God on their lives.

Do you remember the Boston Bomber who made bombs out of pressure cookers? He had two roommates who were on pot and playing demonic video games. They knew he was making bombs and intended to blow up innocent joggers, but they didn't care. They didn't report him to the police. As a result, many people were injured, were maimed for life, were killed, others were emotionally traumatized, fearful, and lost loved ones , due to their refusal to see what was happening around them and stop it. The pot made them unaware of their surroundings, unaware of the danger, unaware of what their roommate was doing, and selfish and uncaring about other people. They didn't care who would get killed, hurt, or maimed. All they cared about is their next pot cigarette.

Many people who get addicted to drugs end up dying of drug overdoses. Drugs are pouring into Our Nation through the open southern boarder. The lying media and others won't admit the truth about anything. Anyone telling the truth is labeled a "Conspiracy Theorist." These drugs have already killed thousands of teens and young adults, in our southern states. The parents of these young people and their brothers and sisters have to live their whole lives without them. They are dead. Even the pot is being laced with stronger drugs to get the children, teens and young adults of America hooked. No one becomes a drug addict, who refuses to try drugs. Don't try it. Keep your brain, your mind, and your body free from the destruction that drugs will cause you. IT is another trap of the devil to rob you of God's Plan and God's Purpose for your life.

Many people get addicted to drugs and commit violent crimes in order to get money for their next fix. They shake, go through horrible withdrawal symptoms, see demonic images, hallucinate, scream, get paranoid, depressed, and feel hopeless.

When a child is asked "What do you want to be when you grow up," none of them say, "I want to be an alcoholic." Or "I want to be a drug dealer." OR "*I want to be a drug addict." Protect your life and your future. Don't let Satan ruin your childhood dreams of having a good life. Reject the things that Satan would try to use to destroy your future. Draw near to God, Resist the devil and he will flee from you.*

Receive Jesus, read the Bible, renew your mind with the Word of God, get water baptized as a believer, ask Jesus to baptize you in the Holy Ghost, grow in your faith, memorize the scriptures that will help you in your daily walk with Jesus. Here is a challenge for you:

> Philippians 4:13 "I can do all things through Christ who strengthens me." Write this scripture verse on paper and put it on your refrigerator door, or your wall, or somewhere you will see it several times a day. Every time you look at it, read it out laud so your ears hear you speaking it. Speak it over and over again out laud several times a day for four weeks. Speak it until it gets from your mind into your heart and you believe it. Then, nothing Godly will be impossible for you. This was the scripture I stood on when God called me to preach in Africa when I had never preached before in my life. Satan kept telling me that no one would meet me at the airport. Then he said, "What if you get on that crusade platform and get tongue tied?" I said, "Shut up Satan. I can do all things through Christ who strengthens me." I went, preached and saw many people come to faith in Jesus, saw people healed of ailments, and saw God move in me and through me.

Believe what God says about you. IT doesn't matter what other people say or think about you. When I was a child I was teased, made fun of, bullied, etc…It didn't destroy me. I became a stronger person. God delivered me from "the fear of man," "the fear of what people will think of me," the fear of speaking to people," "the fear of rejection," etc.. and gave me Holy Spirit Boldness. Some people will love me. Others will hate me for preaching the Gospel of Jesus Christ. IT doesn't matter to me what anyone thinks as long as God Himself Loves Me and I stay right with him.

My identity is found in Jesus Christ. I am a child of God, bought by the precious blood of Jesus Christ. I am loved, redeemed, restored, valuable, accepted, forgiven, approved of, cleansed, and a new person in Christ. The old me is gone forever, Praise God. HE has made all things new, in me and in my life. What He did for me, He can do for you, if you let Him. God will not go against your self-will. God forgave me. God will forgive you if you want Him to. You can become a child of God today and be born into God's Holy Spirit family by repenting of your sins and believing in your heart that Jesus died on that cross for you personally. Accept Jesus Christ today as your Savior and Lord. You will have a brand new God Breathed Identity and life; as a child of Almighty God. May the Lord help you to see yourself through His Eyes as precious and special and loved, in Jesus Name. Amen.

CHAPTER NINE
SPIRITUAL WARFARE AND CHRIST'S VICTORY OVER SATAN AND PRINCIPALITIES

Jesus Himself gave us some examples to follow when we consider spiritual warfare against the temptations of the devil. Lets look at Matthew 3:13-17 "Then came Jesus from Galilee to Jordan unto John, to be baptized of him. But John forbad him, saying, I have need to be baptized of you, and you come to me? And Jesus answering said to John, Suffer it to be so now for it becomes us to fulfill all righteousness." Then John baptized Jesus. And Jesus, when he was baptized, went up straightway out of the water: and, the heavens were opened unto him, and he saw the Spirit of God descending like a dove, and lighting upon him: And a voice from heaven saying, This is my beloved Son, in whom I am well pleased." We see here that Jesus was first baptized in water by John and then the Holy Spirit came upon Him. HE was baptized in water and in the Holy Spirit.

> Matthew 4: 1-4 "Then was Jesus led up of the Holy Spirit into the wilderness to be tempted of the devil." Notice that the Spirit of God led Jesus to be tempted of the devil. Jesus didn't lead himself. The Spirit of God led Him. "And when he had fasted forty days and forty nights, he was afterward hungry. And when the tempter came to him, he said, If you be the Son of God, command that these stones be made bread." But Jesus answered and said, "IT is written, Man shall not live by bread alone, but by every word that proceeds out of the mouth of God." Where is it written? IN THE HOLY BIBLE SCRIPTURES. Jesus spoke the Word of God against the devil's temptation.

> Matthew 4:5-7 "Then the devil took Jesus up into the holy city, and sat him on a pinnacle of the temple. And said unto him, "If you be the Son of God, cast yourself down; for it is written, He shall give his angels charge, concerning you: and in their hands they shall bear you up, lest at any time you dash your foot against a stone." Jesus said, "IT is written again, You shall not tempt the Lord thy God." Where is it written? IN THE HOLY BIBLE. JESUS QUOTED THE BIBLE SCRIPTURES EVERY TIME HE WAS TEMPTED.

Pinnacle A pointed formation as at the top of a mountain peak, the highest point. The devil was tempting Jesus to jump off the highest point of the temple and kill himself. The devil even twisted scripture about the angels keeping Jesus from dashing his foot against a stone, out of context, to further tempt Jesus into sinning against Father God. IF Jesus had done even one sin, he would not have been able to redeem fallen mankind back to Father God. Jesus was sinless. HE never sinned.

> Matthew 4:8-10 Again, the devil took Jesus up into a high mountain, and shewed him all the kingdoms of the world, and the glory of them; And said unto Him, All these things will I give you, if you will fall down and worship me." Then, Jesus said unto him, "Get thee behind me Satan: for it is written, You shall worship the Lord your God, and him only shall you serve." Where is it written? IT IS WRITTEN IN THE HOLY BIBLE SCRIPTURES. Then, the devil left him, and angels came and ministered unto him. People wonder how the devil could claim to have all the kingdoms of the world. When Adam sinned, he gave away his dominion over the earth to Satan. At the time Satan offered Jesus these things, they were in Satan's hands.

After Jesus bled and died on the cross for the sins of mankind, and rose again, the dominion of planet earth was taken away from Satan and given back to us. The Second Adam, (Jesus Christ) did no sin but redeemed fallen mankind back to God by His Holy, Sinless Blood Sacrifice, as the Lamb of God who would take away the sin of the world. (I Corinthians

15:21-27) Because of Adam's sin, the sin nature fell on all mankind. "All have sinned and fallen short of the Glory of God. But God commended His love toward us, in that, while we were yet sinners, Christ died for us. Much more then, being now justified by his blood, we shall be saved from wrath through him." (Romans 5:8-9)

IF the Son of God, Jesus Christ, used scripture against the devil when he was tempted, how much more should we know the scriptures and be able to use them against the devil, as children of God. IF the Son of God had the Holy Spirit come down and rest upon Him, how much more do we need the Holy Spirit to rest upon us. If Jesus Christ was led by the Holy Spirit, how much more should we be led by the Holy Spirit, and not our flesh.

I hear people say, "The devil made me do this or that." They are trying to blame the devil for things that they themselves thought about and did. The devil can put thoughts into our minds, but we have the power to refuse them and cast them out in Jesus Name. IT is when we entertain the wicked thoughts that Satan puts in our heads that we give place to the devil. WE cannot stop the bird (Satan) from putting a thought into our mind, BUT WE CAN STOP THE BIRD FROM MAKING A NEST IN OUR HAIR. WE can refuse that thought right away, in Jesus Name, so it gets no hold over us.

WE can stop watching evil, wicked programs, stop listening to music that promotes physical lusts, and stop playing demonic video games, reading Harry Potter wizard books, watching the "Good Witch", on T.V. etc… WE can rid our houses of anything that is an offense to Jesus Christ and get serious about our faith and our walk with Christ.

When the Lord confronted Adam and Eve in the garden about their sin, Adam said in Genesis 3:12 "The woman whom you gave to be with me, she gave me of the tree, and I did eat." The woman said, "The serpent beguiled me, and I did eat." They wanted to blame their sin on someone else. Many people on planet earth today try to blame their sin on someone else. "I had a bad childhood." "My mother, or my dad said this or that to me." It is my parent's fault. IT is my teacher's fault. It is my friend's fault."

Every evil thing, that we do, begins as a thought in our own mind area. First a person thinks, "I would like to have that cell phone, car, house, piece of jewelry, watch etc… They think and think about that object. The devil will give them a chance to steal that object. IF they have thought about it over and over, they have given the devil a place (a strong hold) in their soul area. They will eventually do whatever has been flooding their mind and heart over and over again.

If a person fills their mind and heart with pornography, watches soap operas (where everyone is fornicating, committing adultery) , listens to lustful music, reads steamy, lustful, sexually explicit romance novels, EVENTUALLY THEY WILL ACT ON WHAT THEY OPEN THEIR MIND AND HEART TO. The devil will put someone into their life to lure them into what they have already been thinking about and imagining. He will make it all available to them.

"As a man thinks in his heart, so is he." IF you allow sexual lusts to penetrate your mind and heart, you will become a lustful person. The Bible says that if a man looks upon a woman to lust after her, he has already committed adultery with her in his heart. IT also means that if a woman looks at a man to lust after him, she has committed adultery with him in her heart. The scriptures go both ways.

The Bible says, "Flee youthful lusts that war against your soul." The lust of the flesh, the lust of the eye, and the pride of life are not of the Father, but of the world.

That is why in Philippians 4:8 warns us, "Finally, brethren, whatsoever things are true, whatsoever things are honest, whatsoever things are just, whatsoever things are pure, whatsoever things are lovely, whatsoever things are of good report; if there be any virtue, and if there be any praise, think on these things."

> Romans 12:1-2 "Present your bodies a living sacrifice, holy, acceptable to God, which is your reasonable service. And be not conformed to this world: but be transformed by the renewing of your mind, that you may prove what is that good, and acceptable, and perfect, will of God." WE ARE NOT TO AGREE WITH THE WICKEDNESS OF THIS WORLD. WE MUST RENEW OUR MINDS WITH GOD'S WORD AND LIVE DIFFERENT FROM THE WORLD. Otherwise, we will be no heavenly good at all.
>
> Ephesians 4:17-25 "This I say and testify in the Lord, that you walk not as other Gentiles walk, in the vanity of their mind. Having their understanding darkened, being alienated

> from the life of God through the ignorance that is in them, because of the blindness of their heart. Who being past feeling have given themselves over unto lasciviousness, to work all uncleanness with greediness. But you have not so learned Christ: IF so be that you have heard him, and have been taught by him, as the truth is in Jesus; that you put off concerning the former conversation the old man, which is corrupt according to deceitful lusts; And be renewed in the spirit of your mind; And that you put on the new man, which after God is created in righteousness and true holiness. Wherefore putting away lying, speak every man truth with his neighbor: for we are members one of another."

Lasciviousness according to Websters Dictionary fourth edition means: characterized by or expressing lust or lewdness, wanton. Tending to incite lustful desires. WE are to avoid these things.

> Ephesians 4:26-32 "Be angry, and sin not: let not the sun go down upon your wrath: Neither give place to the devil. Let him that stole, steal no more; but rather let him labor, working with his hands that thing which is good that he may have to give to him that needs. Let no corrupt communication proceed out of your mouth, but that which is good to the use of edifying, that it may minister grace unto the hearers.

And grieve not the Holy Spirit of God, whereby you are sealed unto the day of redemption. Let all bitterness, and wrath, and anger, and clamor, and evil speaking, be put away from you, with all malice; And be kind one to another, tender hearted, forgiving one another, even as God for Christ's sake has forgiven you."

The world is full of lust, sin, wickedness, lies, stealing, false accusations, laziness, false god worship, anger, hate, unforgiveness, perversions, etc…WE are to be different from the world.

> I John 2:15-17 "Love not the world; neither the things that are in the world. IF any man love the world, the love of the Father is not in him.

For all that is in the world, the lust of the flesh , and the lust of the eyes, and the pride of life, is not of the Father, but is of the world.

And the world passes away, and the lust thereof: but he that does the will of God abides for ever."

The world is passing away. Only those who do the will of God will abide for ever. People who do their own will, do not have God's Promise that they will abide for ever.

Jesus said in Matthew 16:24-25 "If any man will come after me, let him deny himself, and take up his cross, and follow me. For whosoever will save his life shall lose it; and whosoever will lose his life for my sake shall find it."

Mark 8:34-38 says, "Whosoever will come after me, let him deny himself, and take up his cross, and follow me, For whosoever will save his life shall lose it; but whosoever shall lose his life for my sake and the gospel's, the same shall save it. For what shall it profit a man, if he shall gain the whole world, and lose his soul? OR what shall a man give in exchange for his soul? Whosoever is ashamed of me and of my words in this adulterous and sinful generation; of him also shall the Son of Man be ashamed, when he comes in the glory of his Father with the holy angels."

Galatians 2:20 The Disciple Paul said, "I am crucified with Christ, nevertheless I live; yet not I, but Christ lives in me, and the life which I now live in the flesh I live by faith of the Son of God, who loved me, and gave himself for me."

Paul was saying, I am dead to myself. I am dead to my own will, my own plans, my own purposes, and my own agendas. It is Jesus Christ who is living in and through me to do the Father's Will and the Father's Purposes. Jesus Christ is alive in me. Jesus Christ is the Lord of My Life. I have given Jesus Christ my entire life and will. I have "SURRENDERED ALL TO JESUS." This life belongs to Jesus, not me.

In order to overcome the devil, there are three things a person must do. If we look at Revelation 12:7-11 the dragon, the devil, Satan was cast out of heaven onto the earth. He is the accuser of the brethren. Verse 11 "And they overcame (Satan) by the blood of the Lamb, and by the word of their testimony; and they loved not their lives unto the death." We overcome Satan by repenting of our sins and receiving Jesus Christ into our heart and lives as Savior and Lord. Then, we share our testimony of our faith with other people. For many, in the body of Christ, they stop there. IF WE REFUSE TO SURRENDER OUR ENTIRE LIVES AND WILLS TO JESUS CHRIST AND LET HIM BE OUR LORD, WE WILL NEVER GET FULL VICTORY OVER THE DEVIL. We HAVE TO DIE TO OURSELVES, OUR OWN AGENDAS, OUR OWN WILLS, AND TRUST JESUS WITH OUR ENTIRE LIVES. We must say to the Father what Jesus said in the garden, "NOT MY WILL BUT YOUR WILL BE DONE." IF JESUS IS NOT THE LORD OVER EVERY AREA OF YOUR LIFE, the areas you refuse to surrender are under the control of SELF AND SATAN. You will never get full victory with yourself and Satan in control of parts of your life. It all must be given over to Jesus Christ in prayer. He must be Lord over your entire life and will. Give Everything to Jesus Today. Surrender All To Jesus Christ And see what God will do with the life He has given you. Trust Him Completely. You will never fulfill His Divine Purpose and Plan for your life Until You Surrender Your Life And Your Will Fully to Him.

> Ephesians 6:12 "For we wrestle not against flesh and blood, but against principalities, against powers, against the rulers of the darkness of this world, against spiritual wickedness in high places." Our flesh is no weapon against this spiritual wickedness and darkness in high places. WE NEED THE HOLY GHOST/HOLY SPIRIT BAPTISM IN ORDER TO HAVE SPIRITUAL POWER TO FIGHT AGAINST THE WICKEDNESS IN HIGH PLACES. Our warfare is not against human beings. IT is against spirits.

> In Matthew 12:22-30 there is an account that we need to see. "Then was brought to Jesus one possessed with a devil, blind and dumb; and he healed him, insomuch that the blind and dumb both spoke and saw. And all the people were

amazed, and said, Is not this the son of David? But when the Pharisees heard it, they said, This fellow does not cast out devils, but by Beelzebub the prince of the devils. And Jesus knew their thoughts, and said unto them, "Every kingdom divided against itself is brought to desolation; and every city or house divided against itself shall not stand: And if Satan cast out Satan, he is divided against himself; how shall then his kingdom stand? And if I by Beelzebub cast out devils, by whom do your children cast them out? Therefore they shall be your judges. But if I cast out devils by the Spirit of God, then the Kingdom of God is come unto you. Or else how can one enter into a strong man's house, and spoil his goods, except he first bind the strongman? And then he will spoil his house."

WE see here that it is by the Spirit of God that we can cast out devils. We, without the Spirit of God, cannot do anything. Here, Jesus speaks of binding the strong man (the dominant spirit) that is operating in someone and then we can bind the others and see the person fully delivered. The man in this example had a deaf and dumb spirit that was keeping him from being able to hear and speak. By the Power of the Spirit of God, the man was delivered.

Matthew 16:15-19 Jesus said, But whom do you say I am? And Simon Peter answered and said, You are the Christ, the Son of the living God. Father God had revealed that to Peter. Upon the revelation that Jesus Christ is the Son of God, Jesus built his church and the gates of hell could not prevail against it. God gave his church the keys of the kingdom of heaven; and whatsoever we bind on earth shall be bound in heaven and whatsoever we shall loose on earth shall be loosed in heaven." I'll give you some practical examples of this.

I was preaching in Tanzania. I had to stay at a hotel that was full of drugs, prostitutes, alcoholism, etc…IT was the only hotel down the street from the church. During the night, I heard three drunk men outside my window talking about a mzungu. The word means white person. I said, "In the name of Jesus I bind the demons in these men that they cannot manifest against me, in any form. They cannot rape me, rob me, or harm me in any way, in Jesus Name." After I bound the demons, the men went away.

I was in a village in Uganda, staying in a pastor's home. Homes were being robbed in that area. The robbers would throw some chemical in the fan units, make it impossible to breathe, drive the people out of their houses and rob them in the middle of the night. I heard the heavy chains and padlocks rattling at the main gate in the middle of the night, and realized that someone was trying to get into the compound. I said, "In the Name of Jesus, I bind the demons in whoever is at the gate that they must go away. They cannot manifest here on this compound, in Jesus Name." The people went away.

Just speaking the Name of Jesus, if you are in danger, will chase the demons away. They cannot go against the Name of Jesus. They have to bow and submit to Jesus. Through Jesus, we have power over all the power of the enemy so nothing can harm us. IF you are in danger, say Jesus. When you call upon the Name of the Lord, He will save you.

> Ephesians 6:10-11 "Finally, my brethren, be strong in the Lord, and in the power of his might. Put on the full armor of God, that you may be able to stand against the wiles of the devil."

> Ephesians 6:13-18 "Take unto you the whole armor of God, that you may be able to withstand in the evil day, and having done all, to stand. Stand therefore, having your loins girt about with truth, and having on the breastplate of righteousness; And your feet shod with the preparation of the gospel of peace; Above all, taking the shield of faith wherewith you shall be able to quench all the fiery darts of the wicked. And take the helmet of salvation, and the sword of the Spirit, which is the Word of God: Praying always with all prayer and supplication in the Spirit, and watching thereunto with all perseverance and supplication for all saints"

The Sword of the Holy Spirit is The Word of God. AS we speak God's Word, the Holy Spirit goes into action. WE are instructed to pray in the Holy Spirit (pray in tongues). Without the Holy Spirit, we have no sword and no power. He is The Power of the Godhead. When we deny Him, we deny the third part of the Trinity and grieve Him. Our battle with the enemy is spiritual. We cannot war against the devil in our flesh which profits nothing. We must war in the Holy Ghost/Holy Spirit with His Power operating in us and through us. We must be led by Him into the spiritual battles we must fight to take back our nation for Jesus.

> We Must Ask For More OF The Holy Spirit. Luke 11:9-13 "And I say unto you, Ask, and it shall be given you; seek, and you shall find; knock and it shall be opened unto you. For every one that asks receives; and he that seeks finds; and to him that knocks it shall be opened. IF a son shall ask bread of any of you that is a father, will he give him a stone? Or if he asks a fish, will he for a fish give him a serpent? Or if he shall ask an egg, will he offer him a scorpion? IF you then, being evil, know how to give good gifts to your children: how much more shall your heavenly Father give the Holy Spirit to them that ask him?"

We can ask for more of God's Holy Spirit and God will give us more of His Holy Spirit. God will not give us any other spirit, but His Holy Spirit. Elisha asked for a double portion of the spirit that was on Elijah. He received a double portion. WE CAN RECEIVE AN UNLIMITED PORTION OF GOD'S HOLY SPIRIT. ALL WE NEED TO DO IS ASK HIM. IT is not wrong or greedy to ask God for More of His Holy Spirit. There is enough of God to go around. WE can keep asking for more, and HE will give us more.

> Luke 10:19(KJV) Jesus said, "Behold I give unto you power to tread on serpents and scorpions, and over all the power of the enemy, and nothing shall by any means hurt you."

Through the Holy Spirit, we have Power over all the power of the devil. IT is ours. Jesus gave the Holy Spirit/Holy Ghost the Power of The Godhead, To US. We have power over demonic spirits, principalities, spirits of wickedness, demonic activity, and over all the power of the devil. Read this scripture over and over until you believe you have power over all the power of the enemy. Get this truth from your mind into the depths of your heart and believe it and receive it. God did not leave us powerless. We have God's Power Available TO US. All we have to do is ask for Him.

> Psalm 103:20 "Bless the Lord, ye his angels, that excel in strength, that do his commandments, hearkening unto the voice of his word." The angels of God listen to us when we speak the Word of God, by faith, into our situations. They perform His Word. If we whine, complain, speak doubt and negative words Satan's fallen angels hear and bring the negativity about. For example: Proverbs 18:21 says, "Death and life are in the power of the tongue, and they that love it shall eat the fruit thereof." Our words we speak with our tongues either bring death or life. Our words have power in the spiritual realm. Instead of speaking your illness, try speaking Isaiah 53:5 "With Jesus Christ's stripes I am healed. Thank you Jesus for bearing stripes on your back for my healing. I receive the healing you purchased for me now, in Jesus Name. Amen. Rebuke the pain in Jesus' Name, and command it to leave your body, in Jesus Name. Rebuke any sickness, disease or infirmity in the Name of Jesus and speak the healing scriptures over your body, in Jesus Name, until you fully believe them and receive them. Amen.

About twenty years ago, I was passing giant blood clots. My doctor said I had fibroid tumors and needed a hysterectomy. I left his office and said, "In the Name of Jesus I will never need a hysterectomy. Any generational curses of hysterectomy are broken off of my family trees by the blood of Jesus. I curse these fibroid tumors and command them to shrink down to nothing and be gone, in Jesus's Name. Amen." The tumors disappeared. It has been twenty years and I have not passed a blood clot, been in any pain, or had any fibroid tumors, or surgery.

If your doctor tells you that you need surgery ask the Lord to show you whether or not you should have it. I did have surgery on one knee because the Lord wanted me to go through physical therapy and speak to the therapists about Jesus Christ. I was able to speak to three young therapists about faith in Jesus Christ. I never would have met them if I didn't have knee surgery.

There was a man who attended a home group that we attended. He said his MRI tests showed cancer in most of his eternal organs and that his surgeon refused to do surgery on him saying he would surely die on the operating table. He showed us his x-ray pictures. Another surgeon had agreed to do the surgery but said, "You better call your sons and say bye to your family members because it will be a twelve hour surgery and you will probably die on the operating table." The Holy Spirit led me to curse the cancer in his x-rays and command it to get out of his liver, his lungs, his pancreas, his kidneys, etc… I cursed the cancer in Jesus Name, commanded it to shrink down to a small thing that would be able to be removed with no chemo or radiation treatments, and the surgery would only take two hours, in Jesus Name. Amen. The man was taken to the operating room but was wheeled out after only two hours. His wife thought he must have died. The doctor only removed a small part of his stomach, got all the cancer out, and he didn't need radiation or chemo therapy. The Name of Jesus spoken into your situation changes everything. The Holy Ghost/Holy Spirit is the Power of God. He is available to move in us and through us if we let Him.

IF you are not obeying the Lord and living a Godly life, your prayers will be hindered. Obedience to the Word of God is vital.

> Job 22:21-30 "Acquaint now yourself with him, and be at peace; thereby good shall come unto you. Receive the law from his mouth, and lay up his words in your heart. If you return to the Almighty, you shall be built up, you shall put away iniquity far from your tabernacle (your person). Then shall you lay up gold as dust, and the gold of O'phir as the stones of the brooks. Yes, the Almighty shall be your defense, and you shall have plenty of silver. For then shall you have your delight in the Almighty, and shall lift up your face unto God. You shall make your prayer unto him, and he shall hear you, and you shall pay your vows. You shall also decree a thing; and it shall be established unto you; and the light shall shine upon your ways.

There are many promises in this scripture. Get to know the Lord. Receive His Commandments, His precepts, His Word, His Instruction, His Will, His Holy Spirit. Lay up His Words in your heart. Then He will build you up and you will put sin away. IF your delight is in the Lord, He promises to bless your finances, defend you and protect you, hear you, answer your prayers, and allow your decrees to be established.

I was in Butere, Kenya back in 1999 in a Richard Ungudi's Church, teaching on the Power of Decrees. After the teaching, I was in a side room having tea with the pastor and his wife. We heard a woman outside screaming, "MY BOY'S DEAD. MY BOY'S DEAD." We went outside and saw a small five year old boy laying dead on the ground. The Holy Spirit manifested in me, and I said, "You spirit of death leave this boy now, in Jesus Name. And In Jesus Name you will live and not die and fulfill all your days and they will not be shortened, in the Name of Jesus." With that, life came back into the dead boy. He opened his eyes and sat up and stood. He was totally healed of the malaria and alive and well. The mother said that he had been suffering with malaria for two weeks. In faith she had carried him many kilometers to the church, believing that God would heal her son. She got onto the church property and her son died. But now he was alive again. Praise the Lord!

There is great power available to those who surrender their entire lives to the will of Father God and walk led by the Holy Spirit of God. The Baptism of the Holy Spirit is available to everyone who has repented of their sins and received Jesus Christ into their heart and life as their personal Savior and Lord. Ask Jesus Christ to give you the Holy Ghost Baptism. Keep asking until you see God's Holy Spirit gifts operating in you and through you. Without the Holy Spirit, there would have been no power to raise that dead boy. Intellectualism and the flesh could not have put life back into the dead boy. God the Holy Spirit brought the boy back to life.

> Ezekiel Chapter 37:1-3 "The hand of the Lord was upon me, and carried me out in the Spirit of the Lord, and set me down in the midst of the valley which was full of bones, And caused me to pass by them round about; and behold, there were very many in the open valley; and they were very dry. And he said unto me, Son of man, can these bones live? And I answered, O Lord God, you know."

> Ezekiel 37:4-6 "Again he said to me, prophesy upon these bones, and say unto them, "O you dry bones, hear the word of the Lord. Thus says the Lord God unto these bones;

Behold I will cause breath to enter unto you, and you shall live; And I will lay sinews upon you, and will bring up flesh upon you, and cover you with skin, and put breath in you, and you shall live, and you shall know that I am the Lord."

Ezekiel 37:7-8 "So I prophesied as I was commanded and as I prophesied, there was a noise, and behold a shaking, and the bones came together; bone to his bone. And when I looked, the sinews and the flesh came up upon them, and the skin covered them above; but there was no life in them."

Ezekiel 37:9-10 "Then he said, Prophesy unto the wind, prophesy, son of man, and say to the wind, Thus says the Lord God; Come from the four winds, O breath, and breathe upon these slain, that they may live. So I prophesied as he commanded me, and the breath came into them, and they lived, and stood up upon their feet, an exceeding great army."

WE see here that God can put life into dead bones. The Lord spoke to me and said, "DAUGHTER, DO YOU NOT SEE HOW MANY MIRACLES I DID IN THAT VALLEY OF DRY BONES? I GAVE DRY BONES HEARTS, KIDNEYS, LIVERS, DIGESTIVE SYSTEMS, BLOOD, FACES, LIMBS, NERVES, MUSCLES, SINEW, SKIN, EYES, EARS, NOSES, THROATS, IMMUNE SYSTEMS, CELLS, INTESTINES, SPINAL COLUMNS, BRAINS, SINUSES, ETC… I sat in my prayer room stunned when the Lord showed me all the AMAZING MIRACLES HE DID IN THE VALLEY OF DRY BONES. IF THE LORD COULD DO THAT THEN, THE LORD CAN DO THAT NOW. NOTHING IS IMPOSSIBLE FOR THE LORD.

I have been believing the Lord for the greater signs, wonders, and miracles that Jesus said we will do now that he has gone to be with the Father in heaven. I believe I will lay hands on people missing limbs and watch them grow back. I believe for many other creative miracles to happen now…

John 14:12-14 "He that believes in me, the works that I do shall he do also, and greater works than these shall he do; because I go unto my Father. And whatsoever you shall ask in my name, that will I do, that the Father may be glorified in the Son. If you shall ask any thing in my name, I will do it."

We are saved by our faith (our belief in our hearts) that Jesus died for us personally on the cross and rose again. Everything in the Kingdom of God is received through faith. Healings are received through faith. Deliverance is received through faith. The gifts of the Holy Spirit are received through faith. All the promises of God are received through faith. Nothing comes from doubt and unbelief.

All of the promises of God through Jesus Christ are yes and amen. We need to speak the promises into our situations believing we have what we decree, proclaim, and stand on. Even the Old Testament Promises are for us. That is why it is important to study the Old Testament after you study the New Testament. Whoever says that the Old Testament is not important, is deceived. The New Testament is the Old Testament Revealed. Many Old Testament Prophesies were fulfilled by Jesus Christ thousands of years after they were spoken. Some Old Testament Prophesies have not been fulfilled yet, but will come to pass as written.

> Isaiah 19: 24-25 There is a prophesy about Egypt, Syria, and Israel being a blessing in the midst of the land. Whom the Lord of hosts shall bless, saying, Blessed be Egypt my people, and Assyria (Syria) the work of my hands, and Israel my inheritance." There has never been an alliance between Egypt, Syria and Israel to this extent yet. It will happen some day.

One day a piece of clothing got stuck in the back of my clothes dryer. I reached in to free it and burnt three of my fingers on the hot dryer. I quickly ran them under cold water. My skin turned red, large blisters appeared that were filled up with fluid on all three fingers and the pain was intense. The Holy Spirit brought to my remembrance a scripture in Isaiah 43:2 which I immediately claimed. I said, "IT is written I shall not be burned, in Jesus Name. I stand on the Word of God and command these burns to be gone. I shall not be burned. These burns have no right to form on my skin in Jesus Name. Leave Now, in Jesus Name. Skin return to normal, in Jesus Name." I watched the blisters flatten out, the fluid in them disappear, my skin turn back to normal color, the redness go away, and the pain stop. The Word of God is Powerful. Speak it.

Proclaim IT. Stand on It and See God Do The Miraculous.

Who is Satan? How much power does he really have?

If we look at Ezekiel Chapter 28, we can see some facts about the devil. He goes by many names, Satan, Lucifer, the Dragon, Lord of the Flies, son of the morning, prince of Tyrus, and other names. Satan, in Ezekiel 28:14 was an anointed cherub in the holy mountain of God . He walked up and down in the midst of the stones of fire. He wanted to be God. He rose up against God, rebelled, and led a rebellion in heaven against God. Ezekiel 28:15 "You were perfect in your ways from the day that you were created, till iniquity was found in you. By the multitude of your merchandise they have filled the midst of you with violence, and you have sinned: therefore I will cast you as profane out of the mountain of God: and I will destroy you, O covering cherub, from the midst of the stones of fire. Your heart was lifted up because of your beauty, you corrupted your wisdom by reason of your brightness: I will cast you to the ground, I will lay you before kings that they may behold you. You have defiled your sanctuaries by the multitude of your iniquities, by the iniquity of your traffic; therefore I will bring forth a fire from the midst of you, it shall devour you"

WE see here that Satan was a created being. God made the angels. Satan is described as an anointed cherub. If we look back at Ezekiel 28:13 "You have been in Eden, the garden of God, every precious stone was your covering, the workmanship of your tabrets and of your pipes was prepared in you in the day you were created."

Satan was a musical angel. He is responsible for all of the witchcraft music, the voodoo music of Jimmy Hendricks, , and other forms of demonic music with back masked messages, murder messages, rebellious messages, lust, perversion, etc…found in our music today. Any music that promotes anything contrary to God, is demonic music. We also see, in Ezekiel 28:13, that Satan is a created being. God is the Creator. Satan is not the opposite of God. God has no opposite. Satan is only a fallen angel. His power is limited, while God's Power is Unlimited.

> Isaiah 14:12-15 (KJV) It is important that you read the KJV and not some of the deceived Bible versions. The King James Version says:

"How art thou fallen from heaven, O Lucifer, son of the morning! How art thou cut down to the ground, which did weaken the nations!

For you have said in your heart, I will ascend into heaven, I will exalt my throne above the stars of God, I will sit also upon the mount of the congregation, in the sides of the north; I will ascend above the heights of the clouds: I will be like the most High. Yet you shall be brought down to hell, to the sides of the pit."

The sins of Satan were pride, rebellion, and self will. When we operate in pride, rebellion, or self-will, we are serving Satan and not God. Some of the deceived, blasphemous Bible versions have Jesus Christ (the bright and morning star), rebelling against Father God. The King James Bible makes it clear that it was Lucifer who rebelled against Father God, not anyone else.

> I Peter 3:21-22 Jesus Christ is gone into heaven, and is on the right hand of God; angels, and authorities and powers being made subject unto him." Notice here that all the angels and powers are subject to Jesus. Even Satan has to bow before Jesus. Satan is just a fallen angel.

> Philippians 2:5-11"Let this mind be in you, which was also in Christ Jesus: Who, being in the form of God, thought it not robbery to be equal with God: But made himself of no reputation, and took upon him the form of a servant and was made in the likeness of men: And being found in fashion as a man, he humbled himself, and became obedient unto death, even the death of the cross. Wherefore God also has highly exalted him, and given him a name which is above every name: That at the name of Jesus every knee should bow, of things in heaven, and things in earth, and things under the earth; And that every tongue should confess that Jesus Christ is Lord, to the glory of the Father."

Every demon, every dictator, every angel, every principality, every power, every person, everyone will bow their knees to Jesus Christ. Even SATAN MUST BOW TO JESUS.

The Bible says that the Power that raised Christ from the dead dwells in us. The Bible says that he who is in us is greater than he who is in the world. God the Holy Ghost/ Holy Spirit, Jesus Christ and Father God are greater than any fallen angel, demon, principality, power, ruler of darkness, or spiritual wickedness in high places. IF God be for us who can be against us. No Weapon formed against us will prosper.

One time, when I was in a hotel room in Kisumu, Kenya, I was awakened by someone stomping, huffing and puffing, and growling around my bed. The Holy Spirit said, "It is Satan." I said, "Satan in the Name of Jesus, get out of this hotel room and don't you come back, in Jesus Name." I got out of bed, turned on the light and saw he was gone. Then I shut the light and went back to sleep.

I realized that my Fishers of Men Ministries was effective in destroying the devil's hold on people. Satan is not omni-present, omni-potent, or omniscient. He can only be in one place on planet earth at a time. For him to be in my hotel room, I had no doubt that the advancement of God's Kingdom was breaking the darkness off of many regions and people groups through my ministry. PRAISE THE LORD!

We have a GREAT BIG GOD and an Itty Bitty Devil. You need to understand the authority you have in the Name of Jesus, and the Power you have in the Holy Ghost/Holy Spirit. The baptism of the Holy Spirit releases the Power of God to flow in you and through you. You have the Trinity, two thirds of the angels of heaven, the leading of God the Holy Spirit, and heaven's witnesses standing with you and for you. Be Strong in the Lord and in the Power of His Might. We are on the Winning Side.

CHAPTER 10

SATAN'S LIES AND FALSE THEOLOGIES THAT HAVE ENTERED THE BODY OF CHRIST

John 8: 42-47 "Jesus said unto them, If God were your Father, you would love me: for I proceeded forth and came from God; neither came I of myself, but he sent me. Why do you not understand my speech? Even because you cannot hear my word. You are of your father the devil, and the lusts of your father you will do. He was a murderer from the beginning and abode not in the truth, because there is no truth in him. When he speaks a lie, he speaks of his own: for he is a liar, and the father of it. And because I tell you the truth, you believe me not. Which of you convinces me of sin? And if I say the truth, why do you not believe me? He that is of God hears God's Words: you hear them not because you are not of God." All lies and half-truths come from the devil.

LIE NUMBER I-THAT IT WAS ONLY THE JEWS THAT CRUCIFIED JESUS. The Jews yelled, "Crucify Him, Crucify Him." But it was the Romans, the Gentiles, the non-Jews who beat Jesus, slammed a crown of thorns into his head, and drove the nails into his hands and feet. The TRUTH IS THAT WE ALL CRUCIFIED JESUS. If Jesus Christ did not die on the cross to pay for the sins of fallen mankind, we would all be destined to spend eternity separated from God, in hell. We would all have to pay for our sins ourselves in hell for all eternity. There is none of us that haven't sinned. When Adam sinned, sin fell on all mankind. We inherited the sin nature of Adam and Eve.

Matthew 26:52-53 Peter had drawn a sword and struck a servant of the high priest's ear. Jesus said, "Put up again your sword into his place: for all they that take the sword shall perish with the sword. Do you think that I cannot pray to my Father, and he shall presently give me more than twelve legions of angels? But how then shall the scriptures be fulfilled, that thus it must be?" WE see here, that Jesus could have prayed to God the Father to send angels to rescue him from all of the suffering, pain, shame, rejection, persecution, beatings, and the death on the cross. But Jesus Christ chose to submit himself to the Father's Will.

Philippians 2:5-11 Let this mind be in you, which was also in Christ Jesus: Who, being in the form of God, thought it not robbery to be equal with God: But made himself of no reputation, and took upon him the form of a servant, and was made in the likeness of men: And being found in fashion as a man, he humbled himself, and became obedient unto death, even the death of the cross. Wherefore God also has highly exalted him, and given him a name which is above every name: That at the name of Jesus every knee should bow, of things in heaven, and things in earth, and things under the earth: And that every tongue should confess that Jesus Christ is Lord, to the glory of God the Father."

John 10:17-18 Jesus said, "Therefore does my Father love me, because I lay down my life, that I might take it again. No man takes it from me, but I lay it down of myself. I have power to lay it down, and I have power to take it again. This commandment have I received of my Father."

Jesus came to fulfill the scriptures concerning his death for the sins of his creation. Isaiah 53, Psalm 22, and other Old Testament Scriptures told what Jesus would suffer as the sacrificial Lamb of God who would take away the sin of the world. Jesus loved us enough to come anyway. He died for the sins of the world. We have all sinned. We all nailed him to the cross. We all are the guilty ones.

LIE NUMBER 2 REPLACEMENT THEOLOGY

That the Church has replaced Israel, in God's sight. Romans Chapter 11 makes it very clear that the church has not replaced Israel. Romans 11 speaks of the nation of Israel and the gentile church. Verse 25 "blindness in part is happened to Israel, until the fulness of the Gentiles come in." The Natural branches were cut off (Israel) and the wild olive tree (the Gentile believers), were grafted into the tree (Jesus Christ).

> Romans 11:17-23 "And if some of the branches be broken off, and you, being a wild olive tree, were grafted in among them, and with them partaker of the root and the fatness of the olive tree; Boast not against the branches. But if you boast, you bear not the root, but the root thee, You will say then, The branches were broken off, that I might be grafted in. Well because of unbelief they were broken off, and you stand by faith. Be not high minded, but fear: For if God spared not the natural branches, take heed lest he also spare not thee. Behold therefore the goodness and severity of God: on them which fell, severity; but toward you goodness, if you continue in his goodness: otherwise you also shall be cut off. And they also, if they abide not still in unbelief, shall be grafted in: for God is able to graft them in again."

WE owe a lot to the Jewish People. The Bible was written by holy men of God as they were moved by the Holy Ghost. The Apostles were all Jews. The first disciples were Jewish men and women. The Jewish People wrote God's Words on scrolls and preserved them in caves. The Jewish Disciples were faithful in preaching the Gospel of Jesus Christ. WE would have no Christianity on planet earth right now if it wasn't for these faithful Jewish people. Jesus (Yeshua) came into the lineage of King David (a Jew). Mary and Joseph were Jews. They were not Gentiles.

Kathleen Hollop

LIE NUMBER 3 THAT ISRAEL SHOULD NOT BE A NATION

> Ezekiel 37:21-28 "And say unto them, Thus says the Lord God; Behold, I will take the children of Israel from among the heathen, whither they be gone, and will gather them on every side, and bring them into their own land; And I will make them one nation in the land upon the mountains of Israel ; and one king shall be king to them all; and they shall be no more two nations, neither shall they be divided into two kingdoms any more at all; Neither shall they defile themselves any more with their idols, nor with their detestable things, nor with any of their transgressions; but I will save them out of all their dwelling places, wherein they have sinned, and will cleanse them: so shall they be my people, and I will be their God.

And David my servant shall be king over them; and they all shall have one shepherd: they shall also walk in my judgment, and observe my statutes, and do them.

And they shall dwell in the land that I have given unto Jacob my servant, wherein your fathers have dwelt; and they shall dwell therein, even they, and their children, and their children's children for ever; and my servant David shall be their prince for ever.

Moreover I will make a covenant of peace with them; it shall be an everlasting covenant with them; and I will place them, and multiply them, and will set my sanctuary in the midst of them for evermore. My tabernacle also shall be with them; yes, I will be their God, and they shall be my people.

And the heathen shall know that I the Lord do sanctify Israel, when my sanctuary shall be in the midst of them for ever."

> Jeremiah 23:7-8 "Therefore, behold, the days come, saith the Lord, that they shall no more say, The Lord lives, which brought up the children out of the land of Egypt. But, The Lord lives, which brought up and which led the seed of the house of Israel out of the north country and from all the countries where I had driven them; and they shall dwell in their own land." Many Jews have left Russia and other nations to go back into Israel. This scripture is being fulfilled now.

Jeremiah 24:4-7 "Again the word of the Lord came unto me saying, Thus saith the Lord, the God of Israel; Like these good figs, so will I acknowledge them that are carried away captive of Judah, whom I have sent out of this place into the land of the Chaldeans for their good. For I will set my eyes upon them for good, and I will bring them again to this land; and I will build them, and not pull them down; and I will plant them, and not pluck them up. And I will give them an heart to know me, that I am the Lord; and they shall return unto me with their whole heart."

Zechariah 12:10 "And I will pour upon the house of David, and upon the inhabitants of Jerusalem, the spirit of grace and supplications; and they shall look upon me whom they have pierced, and they shall mourn for him, as one mourns for his only son, and shall be in bitterness for him, as one that is in bitterness for his firstborn."

The Nation of Israel was scattered throughout all of the nations and ceased to exist anymore. But God brought the Jews back to their own land and re-made them a Nation in 1948. No other nation has ever left planet earth and come back into existence, but the Nation of Israel. The Hebrew language was almost extinct, but God restored it to the Nation of Israel. ISRAEL EXISTS BECAUSE GOD HAS CAUSED IT TO EXIST. He that keeps Israel neither slumbers nor sleeps.

LIE NUMBER 4 WE DON'T HAVE TO OBEY GOD'S COMMANDMENTS ANY MORE BECAUSE WE ARE NOT UNDER THE LAW BUT UNDER GRACE.

No where, in the Bible, did Jesus take away the ten commandments. Jesus didn't come to take them away. He came to fulfill them. We don't have to do animal sacrifices any more because Jesus (God the Son) shed his own sinless blood for us on the cross. He is the perfect sacrifice. Jesus paid it all. Jesus said, "It is finished." Everything that was needed to redeem fallen mankind back to Father God was done on the cross.

John 14:21 Jesus said, "He that has my commandments, and keeps them, he it is that loves me; and he that loves me shall be loved of my Father, and I will love him, and will manifest myself to him. John 14:24 He that loves me not keeps not my sayings: and the word which you have is not mine, but the Father's which sent me." The test of whether or not you love Jesus is obedience to Him.

Gods Commandments are located in Exodus 20:3-17

1. Thou Shall Have No Other Gods Before Me
2. Thou shall not make any graven image, or any likeness of any thing that is in heaven above, or that is in earth beneath and bow down yourself to them nor serve them. Leviticus 26:1 no standing images
3. Thou shall not take the name of the Lord thy God in vain (use his name in a curse)
4. Remember the sabbath day to keep it holy.
5. Honor your father and your mother that your days may be long upon the land which the Lord your God gives you.
6. Thou shall not kill (murder) This includes unborn BABIES. Psalm 139:13-17
7. Thou shall not commit adultery (sexual sin)
8. Thou shall not steal.
9. Thou shall not bear false witness against your neighbor. Wok mentality, lying against others, calling people who don't agree with you names, throwing temper tantrums
10. Thou shall not covet. Never thanking God for what you have. Always wanting a bigger house, an expensive car, more jewelry, more, more, more, being jealous of what someone else has, never satisfied. When you go on a mission trip and see people having to haul water long distances, live in cows dung huts, have no electricity, no running water, etc…you thank God for a toilet seat to sit your rear end on. You will leave this world with nothing. The Spirit of greed and the love of money are behind every evil thing going on. These spirits came into our nation with the monopoly game which has you buy everything, get all the money, get all the properties, get all the railroads, etc…IT teaches greed, the love of money and material things, and the destruction of other players to get it all, obtain it all. Have it all.

Revelation 22:14 "Blessed are they that do his commandments, that they may have the right to the tree of life, and may enter in through the gates into the city. For outside are dogs, and sorcerers, and whoremongers, and murderers, and idolaters, and whosoever loves and makes a lie." Only those who obey God's Commandments will enter in. The foolish virgins will not be able to enter the city.

LIE NUMBER 5 THAT CONVICTION COMES FROM THE DEVIL

I have heard deceived preachers say that condemnation and conviction come from the devil. This is not true. CONDEMNATION COMES FROM THE DEVIL. CONVICTION OF SIN COMES FROM GOD THE HOLY SPIRIT.

John 16:7-11 Jesus said, "IT is expedient for you that I go away: for if I go not away, the Comforter will not come unto you: but if I depart, I will send him unto you. And when he is come, he will reprove (convict) the world of sin, and of righteousness, and of judgment, Of sin, because they believe not on me; OF righteousness, because I go to my Father, and you see me no more; Of judgment, because the prince of this world is judged." The word REPROVE means to speak to in disapproval, rebuke, to refute, to convict.

The Comforter who does these things is God the Holy Ghost/Holy Spirit. He convicts people of sin so they will repent and get their hearts and lives right with Father God. IT is the Holy Spirit who shows us when we speak something wrong, do something wrong, sin in some way, and we need to repent. IT is the Holy Spirit who helps us to keep short accounts with Father God so our relationship with Him will stay strong and healthy.

False preachers tell people, "It is all under the blood. You don't have to repent any more." They have even gone so far as to tell believers that I John Chapter I is not for them. IF the saved believers don't have to repent any more, then why does the Spirit of God tell five of the Seven Churches in Revelation 2 and 3 to REPENT.

IF Holy Spirit shows us we have sinned, we must REPENT right away and stop it. IF we don't, the sin will mount up and eventually the Holy Spirit will be grieved, wounded, and stop trying to convict us. The devil will tell you that you weren't really saved and pull you into more and more wickedness, as you ignore the Holy Spirit and keep sinning. You will wind up totally backslidden. Don't believe the fake preachers. Believe God the Holy Spirit, be led by Him, listen to Him, and repent when HE convicts you of something.

LIE NUMBER 6 THE LIE THAT CHRISTIANS SHOULD ALWAYS BE PEACEFUL AND NEVER CONFRONT ANYONE.

There is a lie that we are judging someone by telling them what God's Word says about what they are doing. If we stay silent and allow them to perish in sin when the Lord is telling us to speak to them, they may perish in their corruption, but the Lord will hold us accountable for not telling them the truth.

If we consider the story of Jonah; when God spoke to him to go to Nineveh to warn the people that God's Judgment was coming on them, Jonah went the other way. He hated the people of Nineveh and wanted God to destroy them. He did not want them to repent so that God would show them mercy. He wanted them dead. God had a whale swallow Jonah. When Jonah repented, the whale spat him out onto dry ground. Then he warned Nineveh , "Yet forty days, and Nineveh shall be overthrown." The king of Nineveh and all the people repented of their sins, fasted and prayed, and God had mercy on them. Jonah sat and waited to see Nineveh destroyed and when it didn't happen, he was angry at God.

Not warning people of God's Judgments, is actually hating them and wanting them to be destroyed. If you love people, you warn them to put the sin out of their lives and get right with God. To refuse to preach the entire truth to people, is to deny some of them from repenting and going to heaven. By not saying anything, we are condoning the wickedness they are doing. They will continue in their wickedness and eventually die and go to hell. If we love them, we will want them to repent and get to heaven, not hell.

In Matthew 27-28 Jesus said, "Woe unto you scribes and Pharisees, hypocrites! For you are like unto whited sepulchers, which indeed appear beautiful outward, but are within full of dead men's bones, and of all uncleanness. Even so you also outwardly appear righteous unto men, but within you are full of hypocrisy and iniquity." Jesus rebuked the scribes and Pharisees and tried to get them to see the evil of their ways. Jesus didn't tickle their ears and make them feel good.

If we look at Acts 6:8-15 and Acts 7:1-60 the disciple Stephen was speaking to a group of the synagogue people of Libertines and Sirenians and Alexandrians and Asians trying to preach the truth to them. In Acts 7:51 Stephen said "You stiff necked and uncircumcised in heart and ears, you do always resist the Holy Ghost; as your fathers did so do you." Stephen didn't tickle their ears and make them "FEEL GOOD." He told them the truth, even though they didn't want to hear it.

Matthew 3:7-8 John the Baptist saw many of the Pharisees and Sadducees, come to his baptism, he said unto them, "O generation of vipers who has warned you to flee from the wrath to come? Bring forth therefore fruits meet for repentance." Notice John called them a generation of vipers (snakes). He told them to repent of their sins first. I could go on and on with many more examples. We must tell people what God's Word says about the issues. Otherwise, we are allowing them to die in their sins and go to hell.

LIE NUMBER 7 THE LIE THERE IS NO HELL

Ezekiel 31:15-18 speaks of hell, the pit, the nether parts of the earth. "Thus says the Lord God; In the day when he went down to the grave I caused a mourning: I covered the deep for him, and I restrained the floods thereof, and the great waters were stayed; and I caused Lebanon to mourn

> for him, and all the trees of the field fainted for him. I made the nations to shake at the sound of his fall, when I cast him down to hell with them that descend into the pit: and all the trees of Eden, the choice and best of Lebanon, all that drink water, shall be comforted in the nether parts of the earth. They also went down into hell with him unto them that be slain with the sword, and they that were his arm, that dwelt under his shadow in the midst of the heathen. To whom are you like in glory and in greatness among the trees of Eden? Yet shall you be brought down with the trees of Eden unto the nether parts of the earth: you shall lie in the midst of the uncircumcised with them that be slain by the sword. This is Pharaoh and all his multitude, says the Lord God."

We see here, that after the Lord broke the chariot wheels and drowned Pharaoh and the Egyptian army in the sea, they went down to hell, the pit, the nether parts of the earth. They are still there, in hell, today.

Hollywood would like you to believe the lie that the center of the earth has birds, plush green gardens, flowers, etc…There is no beauty in hell. The people there will never see a flower, a bird, a sunset, or anything of beauty because they rejected God. Every good and perfect gift comes from God. There is nothing good or perfect in hell. It is a place of everlasting torment.

> Luke 16:19-31 Describes a rich man who went to hell and a beggar named Lazarus who went to heaven. At that time, heaven and hell were side by side with a huge gulf between them. No one could pass from hell into heaven and no one could pass from heaven into hell. The rich man, before he died, saw Lazarus at his gate and went right by him. He never helped the beggar with any crumbs from his table or any medicine for his sores. The rich man ate well, was selfish, and didn't care about anyone else.

In hell, the rich man could see across the gulf, he could speak, he could hear, he could feel the torment of the flames, and I believe he could smell. Lazarus was with Abraham in heaven. The rich man wanted Abraham to send Lazarus with water to cool his tongue because he was tormented in the flame. No one could go over. The rich man begged Abraham to send Lazarus to warn his five brothers so they wouldn't end up in hell. Abrahams reply was , "If they don't hear Moses and the prophets, nether will they be persuaded though one rose from the dead."

At that time, heaven and hell were side by side. The people who believed in Father God and obeyed Him could not go up to heaven (above), because none of them were without sin. They had to wait in a holding place until Jesus Christ died on the cross for their sins too and rose again. They could not enter heaven (above), with the filthy stains of their sins upon them. They also needed the Blood of Jesus Christ to wash them clean. IF they had tried to enter heaven, above, without the Blood of Jesus, Father God would have had to throw them into hell to pay for their own sins themselves. None of them would have been able to approach Father God.

When we look at I Samuel 28, Samuel had died. King Saul had tried to find a woman with a familiar spirit to inquire of her at Endor. In verse 11 Saul requested that the witch bring up the prophet, Samuel. In verse 12 "And when the woman saw Samuel, she cried with a loud voice : and the woman said to Saul, "I saw gods ascending out of the earth. Saul said, "What form is he of? And she said, "An old man comes up; and he is covered with a mantle." And Saul perceived that it was Samuel, and he stooped with his face to the ground, and bowed himself. And Samuel said to Saul, Why have you disquieted me, to bring me up? And Saul answered; I am sore distressed; for the Philistines make war against me, and God is departed from me and answers me no more, neither by prophets, nor by dreams; therefore, I have called you, that you may make known to me what I shall do. Then said Samuel, Wherefore then do you ask of me, seeing the Lord is departed from you, and is become your enemy?" Notice here that Samuel came up from the holding place in the earth and appeared. HE did not come down from heaven above. HE came up from the holding place where heaven and hell were side by side with the gulf between them. The witch cried with a loud voice because she expected to see a demon appear. When the real Prophet Samuel appeared, she screamed out.

IF we look at John 20:17 After Jesus rose from the dead; Jesus said to Mary, "Touch me not; for I am not yet ascended to my Father; but go to my brethren, and say unto them, I ascend unto my Father, and your

Father, and to my God and your God." Jesus needed to go up to heaven and put his blood on the names of the people in the book of life, so their sins could be washed clean. Many Old Testament and New Testament saints, past, present, and future, had their names sprinkled with the Blood of Jesus. John 20:19 "Then the same day at evening, being the first day of the week, when the doors were shut where the disciples were assembled for fear of the Jews, Jesus came and stood in the midst, and said, "Peace be unto you."

Notice here that Jesus could go up to heaven and return to earth on the same day. IT wasn't days later that he appeared. IT was the same day.

> Matthew 27:52-53 "And the graves were opened; and many bodies of the saints which slept arose. And came out of the graves after his resurrection, and went into the holy city, and appeared unto many." I believe that after Jesus Ascended up into Heaven, to remain there, these saints went up. He had washed their names in the Book of Life With His Blood. They were able to go up. There was no need for the holding place for the saints any more, in the earth. When they died, they could now enter heaven above. The Blood of Jesus had washed them clean. That entire area in the center of the earth became hell enlarging itself.

LIE NUMBER 8 EVERYONE IS A CHILD OF GOD AND GOES TO HEAVEN

Matthew 13:24-30 Jesus said, "The kingdom of heaven is likened unto a man which sowed good seed in his field; But while the man slept, his enemy came and sowed tares among the wheat and went his way. But when the blade was sprung up, and brought forth fruit, then appeared the tares also. So the servants of the householder came and said unto him, Sir, didn't you sow good seed in your field? From whence then has it tares? He said unto them, An enemy has done this. The servants said unto him, do you want us to gather up the tares? But he said, No; lest while you gather up the tares, you root up also the wheat with them. Let both grow together until the harvest: and in the time of harvest I will say to the reapers, Gather together first the tares, and bind them in bundles to burn them; but gather the wheat into my barn."

Matthew 13:37-43 Jesus explained this parable more fully. "He that sowed the good seed is the Son of Man; the field is the world; the good seed are the children of the kingdom but the tares are the children of the wicked one; The enemy that sowed them is the devil; the harvest is the end of the world; and the reapers are the angels. As therefore the tares are gathered and burned in the fire; so shall it be in the end of this world. The Son of Man shall send forth his angels, and they shall gather out of his kingdom all things that offend, and them which do iniquity; And shall cast them into a furnace of fire; there shall be wailing and gnashing of teeth. Then shall the righteous shine forth as the sun in the kingdom of their Father, Who has ears to hear, let him hear."

LIE NUMBER 9 GOD HAS NO WRATH

Hollywood would like you to believe that you can reject God, serve witchcraft and wizardry, live any way you want, and God will let you into heaven because God has no wrath. They are lying to you. The Bible makes it clear that God must judge wickedness because He is Holy.

Ephesians 2:1-6 "And you has he quickened, who were dead in trespasses and sins; Wherein in time past you walked according to the course of this world, according to the prince of the power of the air, the spirit that now works in the children of disobedience: Among whom also we all had our conversation in times past in the lusts of our flesh, fulfilling the desires of the flesh and of the mind; and were by nature the children of wrath, even as others. But God, who is rich in mercy, for his great love wherewith he loved us, Even when we were dead in sins, has quickened us together with Christ, by grace we are saved: And has raised us up together and made us sit together in heavenly places in Christ Jesus."

Ephesians 5:1-6 "Be therefore followers of God, as dear children; And walk in love, as Christ also has loved us, and has given himself for us as an offering and a sacrifice to God for a sweet smelling savor. But fornication, and all uncleanness, or covetousness, let it not be named among you, as becometh saints; Neither filthiness, nor foolish talking, nor jesting, which are not convenient; but rather the giving of thanks. For this you know, that no whoremonger, nor unclean person, nor covetous man, who is an idolater, has any inheritance in the kingdom of Christ and of God."

Colossians 3:4-6 "When Christ, who is our life, shall appear, then shall you also appear with him in glory. Mortify therefore your members which are upon the earth; fornication, uncleanness, inordinate affection, evil concupiscence, and covetousness, which is idolatry. For which things' sake the wrath of God comes on the children of disobedience."

Revelation 6:14-17 "And the heavens departed as a scroll when it is rolled together, and every mountain and island were moved out of their places. And the kings of the earth and the great men, and the rich men, and the chief captains, and the mighty men, and every bondman, and every free man, hid themselves in the dens and in the rocks of the mountains. And said to the mountains and rocks, fall on us, and hide us from the face of him that sits on the throne, and from the wrath of the Lamb. For the great day of his wrath is come: and who shall be able to stand.

LIE NUMBER 10 UNITY IN THE BODY OF CHRIST INVOLVES PRAYING WITH OTHER RELIGIONS

No where in the Bible, are the people of God commanded to unite themselves with false god worshippers, pagans, multiple god worshippers, false religions, witches, wizards, and cultists. If we are foolish to engage in prayer meetings with cultists, and other god worshippers, and idol worshippers, we are opening ourselves up to the demons they are contacting when they pray to their false gods. They are praying to the devil and you are trying to pray to the Lord. Because you have the Holy Spirit of God and they have demonic spirits affiliated with their cult and occult practices, you are grieving the Holy Spirit by being there.

You cannot serve the Lord and another god at the same time. You have to choose this day who you will serve. There is a cult that tries to combine Christianity with Islam. Islam serves the God of Forces- Allah and not the God of the Bible. Since they are not the same God, and people are worshipping the real God and a false god, they are not serving either God. Serving God and Satan doesn't get you into heaven. You are breaking the first commandment. Stop it Now, in Jesus Name.

You cannot say you are a Christian when you are serving Satan by buying and reading Harry Potter Books, watching demonic movies, delving into witchcraft, sorcery, tarot cards, horoscopes, Ouija boards, demonic video games, voodoo, spell casting, watching the "Good witch," watching porn, etc… Isn't it time you burn up the occult items, get into a right relationship with the God who Created You, and serve Him Only?

> Deuteronomy 18:9-14 "When you are come into the land which the Lord your God gives you, you shall not learn to do after the abominations of those nations.

There shall not be found among you any one that makes his son or his daughter to pass through the fire, or that uses divination, or an observer of times, or an enchanter, or a witch,

Or a charmer, or a consulter with familiar spirits, or a wizard, or a necromancer.

For all that do these things are an abomination unto the Lord: and because of these abominations the Lord your God does drive them out from before you. You shall be perfect with the Lord your God.

For these nations, which you shall possess, hearkened unto observers of times, and unto diviners; but as for you, the Lord your God has not suffered you to do so."

WE see here that there is "NO SUCH THING AS A GOOD WITCH." A witch is AN ABOMINATION TO GOD. A Wizard- HARRY POTTER IS AN ABOMINATION TO GOD. THERE IS NO SUCH THING AS A GOOD WIZARD. People who sacrifice their children to false gods are an ABOMINATION TO God. In this scripture, the example of burning children in the fire is used as an example of child sacrifice. ABORTION IS THE SACRIFICE OF AN INNOCENT CHILD TO BAAL. IT is the Lord God who is forming the child in the womb of their mother. To murder that child is a sacrifice to another false god.

Abomination, as per Webster's New World Dictionary Fourth Edition means "1. An abominating; great hatred and disgust; loathing2. Anything hateful and disgusting. People who engage in occult practices become an ABOMINATION TO GOD.

IF you have had an abortion, repent, receive Jesus Christ as your Savior and Lord. You can be forgiven. Your sin is no greater than anyone else's sin. Ask God's forgiveness for killing your baby. IF you are truly sorry, He will forgive you through the Blood of Jesus Christ shed for you on the Cross. IF you have occult items in your home, on your property, in your basement, attic, garage, or shed, burn them up as soon as possible. Destroy them fully so no one else takes them into their house.

> Deuteronomy 7:25-26 "The graven images of their gods shall you burn with fire; you shall not desire the silver or gold that is on them, nor take it unto you, lest you be snared therein; for it is an abomination to the Lord your God. Neither shall you bring an abomination into your house, lest you be a cursed thing like it: but you shall utterly detest it, and you shall utterly abhor it; for it is a cursed thing." Anything used in false god worship, occult games, spell casting books, pictures of false gods, crazy Greek Myths, occult jewelry, occult objects, shrines to false gods, dragon statues, wizard dolls, etc…you need to get out of your house. Otherwise, God's Blessings and His Love, and Your Prayers will be withheld from you. You will not have the favor of God on your house, your family, your property, your health, your finances, etc…if you keep abominations instead of getting rid of them.

There should be unity in the Body of Christ means that the people who believe in the Lord and Savior, Jesus Christ, should come together, worship together, serve Him together, love each other, stand together

Church God's Way

in brotherly love and kindness, goodness, etc…The largest Holy Spirit awakenings and revivals have happened when people in the Body of Christ put aside their doctrinal differences, get together and worship the Lord, together, in unity, in the bonds of Christian Love.

When Jesus Christ prayed to the Father for His Church, He prayed for unity. IF we look at John 17:11 "And now I am no more in the world, but these are in the world, and I come to thee. Holy Father, keep through thine own name: those you have given me, that they may be one, as we are." Jesus was praying for those who believed in Him, not for other god worshippers or religions.

> 1 Peter 1:22 "Seeing you have purified your souls in obeying the truth through the Spirit, unto unfeigned love of the brethren, see that you love one another with a pure heart fervently."

> 1 John 4:7 "Beloved, let us love one another: for love is of God: and every one that loves is born of God, and knows God. He that loves not, knows not God; for God is love."
> We are to love our neighbors as ourselves.

If love is of God, then HATRED IS OF THE DEVIL. IF hate is ruling you, whether it is racial hatred, hatred of a parent, a sibling, an ex-spouse, an ex-neighbor, a boss, someone who has stolen from you, hurt you, insulted you, beaten you, abused you, murdered someone you loved, lied against you, etc…that Hatred is not of God. Be willing to give it up and ask the Lord to remove it from your heart and life.

I have been to many churches and have seen racial hatred on the faces of brethren, in some of the black churches, here in America. Many people have taught their children racial hatred instead of love. Martin Luther King was right when he was trying to get people of all races to love each other, work together side by side, respect each other, and live together in peace.

The wicked KKK, is just as evil because they are white people who hate black skinned people. God is not a racist. He made all people and loves every race, kindred, and tongue. The churches in Kenya, Uganda, Tanzania, Rwanda and Burundi had very loving brethren who appreciated the Word of God, even through the mouth of a white woman. They were precious, loving brethren that had no racial hatred, bigotry, and evil intentions toward me, a white woman. I loved them all with the Love of God and preached and taught messages to bless them, encourage them, and grow them in the Christian Faith.

> Revelation 7:9-17 describes the multitudes of people who believed in Jesus from every kindred, nation, and tongue. There were black people, brown people, white people, Hispanic people, Indian people, Asian people, olive skinned people, from every Nation who had put their faith in Jesus Christ and had their robes washed white in the blood of the Lamb, Jesus. They were all serving God, before His Throne in heaven, together, as the children of God.

LIE NUMBER 11 TRUTH IS RELATIVE

This lie goes like this: "Your truth isn't the same as my truth or someone else's truth. Truth is whatever you deem as true at any given time." This is totally contrary to the Son of God, Father God, the Holy Spirit and the Word of God.

REAL TRUTH IS NOT FOUND IN AN IDEALOGY, A CONCEPT, A HEAD KNOWLEDGE OF WHAT YOU WANT TRUTH TO BE at any given time , depending upon your circumstances. REAL TRUTH IS FOUND IN THE PERSON OF JESUS CHRIST; KNOWING HIM IN YOUR HEART AND LIFE, AND HAVING HIM AND HIS DIVINE TRUTH LIVING INSIDE OF YOU. There is no truth outside of God's Truth. God's Truth is Eternal Truth. His Truth Never Changes. His truth is ALWAYS TRUE FOR EVERY PERSON ON PLANET EARTH, no matter what their education, their social status, their circumstances, their ethnic background, their job, etc…God's Eternal Truths Never Change. They Are True Forever.

A man can continually change his mind on what truth he wants to believe, or what truth he chooses to be true; depending on his circumstances, his friends opinions, his own intellect or his own reasoning. If the truth you believe today isn't the same as the truth you believe tomorrow, and it is subject to change depending upon your circumstances, some of the "truth" you are believing is lies. If truth isn't always true, then sometimes, it is a lie.

John 14:6 Jesus said, "I am the way, the truth, and the life; no man comes to the Father but by me." Truth is Not Relative. Truth is found in the person of Jesus Christ. He is the Truth. The Words He spoke and Taught are truth.

Psalm 31:5-6 Into your hand I commit my spirit: you have redeemed me, O Lord God of truth. I have hated them that regard lying vanities but I trust in the Lord."

Psalm 119:142 Your righteousness is an everlasting righteousness, and your law is truth."

Psalm 119:160 "Your word is true from the beginning: and every one of your righteous judgments endures for ever."

John 14:15-17 Jesus said, "IF you love me, keep my commandments. And I will pray the Father, and he shall give you another Comforter that he may abide with you for ever; Even the Spirit of truth; whom the world cannot receive because it sees him not, neither knows him; for he dwells with you, and shall be in you." This scripture is describing God the Holy Ghost/Holy Spirit as the Spirit of Truth. He dwells with and in the people who repent of their sins and receive Jesus Christ as their Lord and Savior. People who reject Jesus Christ do not have the Spirit of Truth living inside of them. Instead, they have the lying spirit of the world. They cannot know real truth until they really belong to Jesus Christ.

John 18:36-37 Jesus said, "My kingdom is not of this world; if my kingdom were of this world, then would my servants fight, that I should not be delivered to the Jews: but now is my kingdom not from hence." Pilate said to Jesus, "Are you a king then?" Jesus answered "You say I am a king. To this end was I born, and for this cause came I into the world that I should bear witness unto the truth. Every one that is of the truth hears my voice."

There are eternal truths that Almighty God has ordained for now and for all eternity. These truths never change, never alter, never wane, never are deleted, null or void, and are NEVER ERASED BY ignorant human beings that refuse to believe the truth and want to change the truth of God's Word into a lie of their own design.

> Isaiah 5:20 "Woe to them that call evil good, and good evil; that put darkness for light, and light for darkness; that put bitter for sweet, and sweet for bitter!" This woe is for those who deny God's Truth by calling God's Truth evil; and embrace Satan's lies and promote the lies as good. They will answer to God for their wickedness.

LIE NUMBER 12 THAT MARY AND JOSEPH NEVER HAD SEX TOGETHER

> Matthew 1:23-25 "Behold, a virgin shall be with child, and shall bring forth a son, and they shall call his name Emmanuel, which being interpreted is, God with us. Then Joseph being raised from sleep did as the angel of the Lord had bidden him, and took unto him his wife; And knew her not till she had brought forth her firstborn son: and called his name Jesus."

Joseph did not have sex with Mary until after Jesus came out of her womb. The Bible term "know", means an intimate, sexual encounter with another person. Joseph waited until after Jesus was born. Then he knew his wife Mary.

> Galatians 1:19 "But other of the apostles saw I none, except James the Lord's brother."

> John 7:2-5 Now the Jews' feast of tabernacles was at hand. His brethren therefore said unto him, Depart hence, and go into Judea, that your disciples also may see the works that you do. For there is no man that does any thing in secret, and he himself seeks to be known openly. IF you do these things, shew yourself to the world. For neither did his brethren believe in him.

Matthew 13:53-58 "And it came to pass, that when Jesus had finished these parables, he departed. And when he was come into his own country, he taught them in the synagogue, insomuch that they were astonished, and said, "Where has this man this wisdom, and these mighty works? IS this not the carpenter's son? IS not his mother called Mary? And his brethren, James, and Joses, and Simon, and Judas? And his sisters, are they not all with us? Whence then has this man all these things? And they were offended in him. But Jesus said, "A prophet is not without honor, save in his own country and in his own house.' WE see here, that Mary gave birth to four boys and more than one girl, after Jesus came out of her womb. Joseph had sex with his wife Mary. He knew her in the Biblical sense.

When Adam and Eve sinned in the garden of Eden, God spoke to the serpent (Satan, the devil). In Genesis 3:14-15 "And the Lord God said unto the serpent, Because you have done this, you are cursed above all cattle, and above every beast of the field; upon your belly shall you go, and dust shall you eat all the days of your life. And I will put enmity between you and the woman, and between your seed and her seed; it shall bruise your head, and you shall bruise his heel." Here we see that the seed of the woman will bruise Satan's head. A woman's body produces eggs, not seeds. Jesus was never Mary's egg. If he was, he would have had original sin. He would have had the sin nature of Adam. Instead, the Holy Ghost came upon Mary and planted Jesus Christ as the seed of the Word of God; into her womb. Luke 1:35 "And the angel answered and said unto her, The Holy Ghost shall come upon you, and the power of the Highest shall overshadow you; therefore also that holy thing which shall be born of you shall be called the Son of God."

Kathleen Hollop

LIE NUMBER 13 THAT CHRISTIANITY IS ONLY A "WHITE PERSON'S RELIGION."

Jesus came from heaven, and was planted, as a seed, in the womb of a young virgin that was of the lineage of King David, a Jew. Jesus had olive skin, as most people from the mid-east have. Mary and Joseph were Jews with olive skin. The original Christ followers were Jews, by nationality. They were not Gentiles. They were neither black nor white. They were not red skinned, yellow skinned, or brown skinned. They had olive skin. They were faithful to God to spread the Gospel of Jesus Christ to lost souls of every nation, kindred, and tongue. If these first followers of our Lord and Savior Jesus Christ were not faithful in spreading the Gospel of Jesus Christ unto salvation, there would be no Christianity today. IF they were not faithful in recording what God spoke to them, the miracles God did, and the signs and wonders onto scrolls, we would not have any Bibles today. WE would not know who Jesus is, what Jesus did for us on the cross, the fact he rose from the dead, the ascension of Jesus or anything else. IF the Old Testament Jews had not recorded the Books of Genesis, Exodus, Leviticus, Numbers, and Deuteronomy all the books of Moses wouldn't be known. IF the prophecies of the major and minor prophets of God were not written down, we would not have known a Savior was coming. WE owe a big debt of gratitude to the Jews. Most of the Jewish Disciples and Apostles, of Jesus were persecuted and killed while preaching the Gospel of Jesus Christ to lost souls.

> Genesis 12:3 The Lord said to Abraham, "And I will bless them that bless you, and curse him that curses you, and in you shall all families of the earth be blessed." This promise of God to the nation of Israel is still in effect today.

> Revelation 7: 9-17 "After this I beheld, and a great multitude, which no man could number of all nations, and kindreds, and people, and tongues, stood before the throne, and before the Lamb, clothed with white robes, and palms in their hands.

And cried with a loud voice, saying, Salvation to our God which sits upon the throne, and unto the Lamb.
And all the angels stood round about the throne, and about the elders and the four beasts, and fell before the throne on their faces, and worshipped God.

Saying, A-men; Blessing and glory, and wisdom, and thanksgiving, and honor, and power, and might, be unto our God for ever and ever. A-men.

And one of the elders answered, saying unto me, What are these which are arrayed in white robes? And where did they come from?

And I said unto him, Sir, you know. And he said to me, These are they which came out of great tribulation, and have washed their robes, and made them white in the blood of the Lamb.

Therefore they are before the throne of God, and serve him day and night in his temple. And he that sits on the throne shall dwell among them.

They shall hunger no more, neither thirst any more; neither shall the sun light on them, nor any heat,

For the Lamb which is in the midst of the throne shall feed them, and shall lead them unto living fountains of waters; and God shall wipe away all tears from their eyes."

As we can see here, there are people from every nation, kindred, and tongue in heaven. There are olive skinned people, brown people, black people, yellow skinned people, red skinned people, and white people in heaven. All of the people there had one thing in common. They all had repented of their sins and believed that Jesus Christ died for them personally on the cross. Their sins were washed clean in the Blood of the Lamb, Jesus Christ.

LIE NUMBER 14 THAT WE CAN GET TO HEAVEN BY BEING A "GOOD PERSON"

If we could have gotten to heaven by just being a " good person", there would have been no need for Jesus Christ to have left heaven, to have taken human form, to have allowed himself to suffer the punishment and pain for our sins that we deserved to get, and to have suffered the horrible death of crucifixion, bearing our shame, our pain, our sins upon Himself so we could be forgiven. We cannot do enough "Good Deeds" in the sight of a Holy God, to even make up for one sin. God is Perfect. We are sinners. If we ever told a fib, we are a liar in the sight of God. If we ever took someone else's pen home, we are a thief in the sight of God. IF we have ever loved anyone more than we have loved God, we have broken the first Commandment. IF we have ever used God's Name in vain we have broken the third commandment.

THE ONLY SINLESS PERSON WHO EVER WALKED ON PLANET EARTH IS JESUS CHRIST. That is why He could be the sacrificial Lamb of God who could pay for the sins of the world with His Own Righteous, Holy Blood. The lamb had to be Perfect, Without Spot or Wrinkle. IF Jesus Christ did even one sin, He could not have paid for the sins of the world and we all would go to hell. When a person repents of their sins and asks Jesus to come into their heart and life; believing He died for them personally and rose again, the Blood of Jesus is applied to their life, their sins are washed clean, and their names are written in the Lamb's Book of Life.

LIE NUMBER 15 THAT WE CAN LIVE ANY WAY WE WANT AND STILL GET INTO HEAVEN-THE ONCE SAVED ALWAYS SAVED LIE

Revelation 3:5 "He that overcomes the same shall be clothed in white raiment; and I will not blot out his name out of the book of life, but I will confess his name before my Father, and before his angels." Here it says that a name can be blotted out of the Book of Life.

When King David was persecuted by his enemies, he prayed in Psalm 69:24-29 "Pour out your indignation upon them, and let your wrathful anger take hold of them. Let their habitation be desolate; and let none dwell in their tents.

For they persecute him whom you have smitten; and they talk to the grief of those whom you have wounded. Add iniquity unto their iniquity: and let them not come into your righteousness.

Let them be blotted out of the book of the living, and not be written with the righteous."

In the Book of Exodus, the people had sinned and worshipped a golden calf. The Lord was very angry at the people. Moses met with God and tried to plead for the people. Exodus 32:30-35

"And it came to pass on the morrow, that Moses said unto the people, You have sinned a great sin: and now I will go up unto the Lord in the hope I shall make an atonement for your sin.

And Moses returned unto the Lord, and said, Oh, this people have sinned a great sin, and have made them gods of gold. Yet now, if you will forgive their sin-; and if not, blot me, I pray you, out of your book which you have written.

And the Lord said unto Moses, Whosoever has sinned against me, him will I blot out of my book. Therefore now go, lead the people unto the place of which I have spoken unto you; behold, my Angel shall go before you; nevertheless in the day when I visit I will visit their sin upon them. And the Lord plagued the people, because they made the calf, which Aaron made."

There are consequences to sin. When King David sinned with Bathsheba, their first child died. The sword never departed from King David's house because he put Uriah the Hittite (Bathsheba's husband), on the front line of the hottest battle and ordered his men to withdraw from him so he would die. A prophet named Nathan confronted David with his sin, David repented, But the sword never departed from David's house. One of David's sons raped his half sister Tamer. Tamer's Brother Absolom (by the same mother), hated Amnon and hated David for not making the man marry Tamer. Absolom tried to dethrone David and steal the kingdom.

Many people are suffering with broken marriages due to adultery, children are suffering while being bounced between mom and dad feeling unloved and unwanted, pregnancies due to fornication are many, young girls suffer with guilt from the abortions they had, many youth are strung out on drugs and alcohol (living for their next fix), many people are sitting in jail cells due to charges of robbery, assault, arson, murder, many people believe they are nothing more than evolved monkeys and see no reason or meaning for their lives, or anyone else's life, etc…What we believe will effect the choices we make and how we live our lives. Some choices we make are unchangeable. Once you abort your child, you can never get your child back on planet earth. Once you tattoo your body, you will have those marks on your skin the rest of your life. Once you have transgender surgery, you cannot get your body parts back; once they are cut off and removed. You cannot undo the damage that the transgender drugs do to your entire body. They are just finding out the physical and mental and spiritual ramifications of transgender surgeries. If a person is depressed and goes through transgender surgeries, it increases their depression. IT is not the answer. Knowing Jesus Christ and seeing yourself through God's eyes is the answer. Becoming the Person that God Created You to Be is the Answer.

> Hebrews 6:4-6 "For it is impossible for those who were once enlightened, and have tasted of the heavenly gift, and were made partakers of the Holy Ghost, And have tasted the good word of God, and the powers of the world to come,

If they shall fall away, to renew them again unto repentance; seeing they crucify to themselves the Son of God afresh, and put him to an open shame."

> Hebrews 3:12-14 "Take heed, brethren, lest there be in any of you an evil heart of unbelief, in departing from the living God.

But exhort one another daily, while it is called To day; lest any of you be hardened through the deceitfulness of sin.
For we are made partakers of Christ, if we hold the beginning of our confidence steadfast unto the end."

> 1 John 2:15-17 "Love not the world; neither the things that are in the world. IF any man love the world, the love of the Father is not in him.

For all that is in the world, the lust of the flesh, the lust of the eyes, and the pride of life, is not of the Father, but is of the world. And the world passes away, and the lust thereof: but he that does the will of God abides for ever."

> Titus 1:15-16 "Unto the pure all things are pure; but unto them that are defiled and unbelieving is nothing pure; but even their mind and conscience is defiled.

They profess that they know God; but in works they deny him, being abominable, and disobedient, and unto every good work reprobate." These people claim to be "Christians" but are not living for Jesus Christ. They are doing all kinds of evil works that defile even their conscience. Because of how they are living, they are disgracing and denying the Name of Jesus Christ, before men. Other people see the wickedness of the people who are not living for Jesus and think to themselves, "If that thief/liar/adulterer/fornicator/is a Christian, I don't want to be one." IF there is no difference between how you are living and how the wicked world around you is living, you are denying Christ by your actions.

> Matthew 10:32-33 Jesus said, "Whosoever therefore shall confess me before men, him will I confess also before my Father which is in heaven. But whosoever shall deny me before men, him will I deny before my Father which is in heaven." People can deny Jesus Christ by living wicked lives and claiming to be a Christian. Their wicked works and sins deny Christ.

Remember Matthew 25, the parable of the foolish virgins. They represent the Body of Christ. Half were wise and half of them were foolish. The foolish ones were living lives of darkness. Their lamps had gone out. They were left behind. Don't be one of them. REPENT AND GET RIGHT AND LIVE RIGHT.

LIE NUMBER 16 WOKISM ISN'T A SIN

Woks is the lie that it is alright to criticize everyone, hate everyone who doesn't agree with you, silence other people's opinions, throw temper tantrums and riots when you don't get your own way, demand everyone else conform to you or shut up, conform to your beliefs, to your feelings, to your emotions etc… Woks refuse the real history of our nation and believe wicked lies, refuse the great nation we live in to embrace the lies of communism and socialism and Karl Marx, refuse Jesus Christ, refuse the Bible, refuse the fact that our forefathers of this nation were Christians, etc…BECAUSE AFTER ALL, LIFE IS ALL ABOUT YOU AND YOU SHOULD BE THE CENTER OF EVERYONE ELSE'S UNIVERSE. IF you complain about a Company Logo, a Ball Team Name, a Pancake Syrup Name, a Song Title, a Business Name, THEY SHOULD CHANGE IT BECAUSE IT MAKES YOU MAD, MAKES YOU UNHAPPY, MAKES YOU UNCOMFORTABLE, MAKES YOU THINK ABOUT SOMETHING YOU DON'T LIKE TO THINK ABOUT, etc…

It is the crazy belief THAT EVERYONE ELSE SHOULD SERVE you, AGREE WITH YOU, MAKE YOU FEEL COMFORTABLE AT ALL TIMES, AVOID ANY AND ALL CONVERSATIONS THAT MAKE YOU FEEL UNEASY, REFUSE TO TALK ABOUT ANYTHING THAT NEEDS TO BE DISCUSSED, REFUSE TO GROW UP AND FACE Problems, Issues, and LIFE. IT is a REFUSAL TO BELIEVE THE TRUTH ABOUT Any ISSUE, a REFUSAL TO LISTEN TO TRUTH, A REFUSAL TO LISTEN TO ANYONE ELSE WHO KNOWS THE TRUTH, and a TOTAL SELFISH, STUBBORN MINDSET. YOU WILL NEVER BE A HAPPY PERSON WHEN YOU CONTINUALLY LOOK TO FIND FAULT WITH EVERYONE AND EVERYTHING AROUND YOU.

My advice to you is, "GROW UP AND ACT LIKE AN ADULT." "FACE LIFE AND IT'S REAL PROBLEMS INSTEAD OF TRYING TO INVENT PROBLEMS WHERE THERE AREN'T ANY; BUT The ONES YOU DECIDE TO MAKE AN ISSUE OF. IF you are not happy unless you find fault with someone else, or something else, or a logo, or a team name, or a song, or the history of our nation, or something else, YOU NEED TO ASK GOD'S FORGIVENESS FOR HAVING A CRITICAL SPIRIT. WHEN ARE YOU GOING TO APPRECIATE THE GOOD IN LIFE, rather than to INVENT The BAD.

> Proverbs 6:16-19 "These six things does the Lord hate; yes, seven are an abomination unto him. A proud look, a lying tongue, and hands that shed innocent blood, A heart that devises wicked imaginations, feet that are swift in running to mischief, A false witness that speaks lies and he that sows discord among brethren." When a person constantly tries to find fault with other people by using raciest lies about team names, company names, songs, etc…they are serving Satan and not God. When people imagine that everything around them is a racial slur, a racist act, a racist logo, a racist emblem, a raciest statue, etc…they are promoting hatred and trying to divide people. That is a plan of the wicked communist party to destroy the unity in a country AND THE HISTORY OF A COUNTRY, so that they can step in and take it over.

When Hitler took over the German people; he destroyed all of their statues of past leaders, their history, their art, their culture, their past ancestors accomplishments, etc… Once they were left with no past, he was able to re-write their future, according to what he wanted it to be. It was easy for him to take over them when they had no idea who they were, what happened in their nation before, who their ancestors were, who began their country, etc…He wiped out their past-the good things as well as the bad. He erased their past history…and left the German people with no past to study and learn from. They forced people to say Hitler's Name and worship him like he was a god. They forced their indoctrination on the children in the schools and taught them to hate the Jews. AS a result of his brainwashing, millions of innocent Jews along with non Jews who helped the Jews, were slaughtered in gas chambers and ovens. The HOLOAUST REALLY HAPPENED. Some ridiculous people want to deny that fact, but Holocaust Victims have the tattoos of numbers on their arms that Hitler branded them with, in the prison camps.

People who viciously attack others with hurtful, lying words, and gang up on anyone who doesn't agree with them, are trying to silence "FREE SPEECH" and make everyone think like them, talk like them, act like them, and agree with them. That is the practice of witchcraft. When people try to manipulate, control, dominate, intimidate, and put fear into others, they are practicing witchcraft. Most of the media today, practice media mob attacks on people who do not agree with them and their opinions of the news. Gone are the days when reporters just reported the News, and not their biased opinions of the news. They taint everything, they report on, to suit themselves. They do not care whether they are speaking the truth about any issue or not. Most have no fear of God. The Bible says, "ALL LIARS HAVE THEIR PLACE IN THE LAKE OF FIRE." Sadly they do not believe in God or HIS TRUTH.

The students in Communist China were tired of Communism. They gathered to have a peaceful protest against their Communist Government. IT happened in Tanimon Square in Beijing China. The wicked Chinese Government shot down all of the students who were peacefully protesting the tyranny of the Communist Party. All the students wanted was freedom. They wanted freedom to choose their jobs, to choose where they wanted to live, to choose how many babies they wanted to have, to worship the real God instead of an emperor, etc…THEY DIED FOR THE FREEDOMS THAT YOU AND I ENJOY AND TAKE FOR GRANTED. IF we are not vigilant, the Communists will take over our nation and subject us to their tyranny.

LIE NUMBER 17 THAT A HUMAN PRIEST, PASTOR OR MINISTER HAS THE POWER TO PULL JESUS CHRIST DOWN FROM HEAVEN AND PUT HIM INTO A WAFER OR A PIECE OF PHYSICAL BREAD

Jesus Christ is God. HE sits on the right hand of God the Father, in heaven, and makes intercession for us. To believe that Jesus Christ is bouncing back and forth between heaven and earth at the whim of a priest or pastor, is not Biblical.

The lie of physically eating Jesus and physically drinking His Blood comes from a distortion of John Chapter 6.

> John Chapter 6: 32-40 "Then Jesus said unto them, Moses gave you not that bread from heaven; but my Father gives you the true bread from heaven.

For the bread of God is he which comes down from heaven, and gives life unto the world. Then said they unto him, Lord, evermore give us this bread.

And Jesus said unto them, I am the bread of life: HE THAT COMES TO ME SHALL NEVER HUNGER; AND HE THAT BELIEVES ON ME SHALL NEVER THIRST.

But I said unto you, That you also have seen me, and believe not. All that the Father gives me shall come to me; and him that come to me I will in no wise cast out.

For I came down from heaven, not to do my own will, but the will of him that sent me. And this is the Father's will which has sent me, that of all which he has given me I should lose nothing, but should raise it up again at the last day.

And this is the will of him that sent me, that every one which sees the Son and believes on him may have everlasting life; and I will raise him up at the last day."

IT is spiritual Faith in Jesus Christ that gives a person eternal life. Jesus satisfies spiritual thirst and hunger. There is an empty place deep in the hearts and spirits of human beings that only faith in Jesus Christ can fill. People try to fill it with money, material things, relationships, drugs, alcohol, lust, fame, fortune, etc…BUT THEIR HEARTS ARE EMPTY UNTIL THEY BELIEVE ON THE LORD JESUS

CHRIST. A person can take Communion Elements every day of their life and still not get to heaven. Physical bread and Physical wine or juice cannot save anyone from hell. IT IS WITH THE HEART THAT MAN BELIEVES.

> Romans 10:9-10 "That if you shall confess with your mouth the Lord Jesus, and shall believe in your heart that God has raised him from the dead, you shall be saved. For with the heart man believes unto righteousness and with the mouth confession is made unto salvation." Notice that it is with the heart that man believes, not with the stomach.

> I John 5:9-13 "If we receive the witness of men, the witness of God is greater: for this is the witness of God, which he has testified of his Son.

He that believes on the Son of God has the witness in himself; he that believes not God has made him a liar; because he believes not the record that God gave of his Son.

And this is the record, that God has given to us eternal life, and this life is in his Son. He that has the Son has life; and he that has not the Son of God has not life.

These things have I written unto you that believe on the name of the Son of God, that you may know that you have eternal life, and that you may believe on the name of the Son of God."

Eternal life does not come by taking physical bread and juice or wine. IT comes from believing Jesus Christ died on the cross for your sins and rose again. Religion doesn't save anyone from hell. IT is faith in your heart that Jesus died for you personally and receiving Him as your Savior (into your heart and life) that saves you from your sins. IT is a RELATIONSHIP WITH JESUS CHRIST-A DAILY WALK WITH JESUS that saves you. Jesus is the only one who can fill the empty space in the depths of people's hearts.

Jesus makes it clear that he is not speaking about physical bread. People who believe on Jesus still have to eat physical bread and drink physical water to live. He is speaking here about people coming to him and believing on him so that their spiritual hunger and spiritual thirst will be satisfied.

Drinking blood and cannibalism are forbidden in the Bible. Jesus isn't telling people to eat him like a cannibal or to actually drink his blood, like the witchcraft groups do. He is telling people to come to him and believe on him to satisfy their spiritual hunger and thirst.

> In John 6:63 Jesus says, "It is the spirit that quickens; the flesh profits nothing: the words that I speak unto you, they are spirit, and they are life." Jesus is the living Word of God who became flesh and dwelt among us. The Living Word is the Bible. The Bible is a Spiritual Book written by holy men of God as they were moved by the Holy Ghost. Jesus was the Bible in human form. WE are to read it and grow up spiritually to know the deeper things of God. IF we don't read it and study it, we remain baby Christians who never accomplish much to advance God's Kingdom here on earth.

LIE NUMBER 18 THAT A CHRISTIAN CAN BELIEVE IN EVOLUTION

> Genesis 1:1-3 "In the beginning God created the heaven and the earth. And the earth was without form, and void, and darkness was upon the face of the deep. And the Spirit of God moved upon the face of the waters. And God said, Let there be light; and there was light. And God saw the light, that it was good; and God divided the light from the darkness. And God called the light Day, and the darkness he called Night, And the evening and the morning were the first day."

The theory of Evolution attacks the entire Bible and the fact that there is a God who created everything seen and unseen. Evolution says that a pile of chemical soup, after millions of years, became alive and changed into/evolved into this and that This chemical soup became monkeys and then evolved into humans. Evolution IS NOT A SCIENCE. A SCIENCE HAS TO BE PROVEN. THE MISSING LINKS ARE STILL MISSING BECAUSE They NEVER EXISTED.

EVOLUTION IS THE RELIGIOUS THEORY OF ATHEISM. IT is an attempt by men to explain how they came to exist without believing in or acknowledging a DIVINE CREATOR, GOD. Evolution is a DEMONIC ATTACK ON THE ENTIRE GOD OF THE BIBLE, HIS PERSON, AND HIS HOLY WORD.

Evolution denies there is a God who molds every person in their mother's womb for a Divine Plan and Purpose. Evolution says that we are all evolved monkeys with no real reason for our existence. WE are no better than animals. There is no real purpose why we exist.

The Bible says in Jeremiah 1:4-5 "Then the word of the Lord came unto me saying, Before I formed you in the belly I knew you, and before you came forth out of the womb I sanctified you; and I ordained you a prophet unto the nations." As God knew Jeremiah before He formed him in the belly, God knows every baby He is forming in the womb. God has a good plan for everyone's life. WE are not an accident, a product of conception, a blob of protoplasm, a fetus, an evolved ape, or a mistake.

> Psalm 139:13-17 "For you have possessed my reins; you have covered me in my mother's womb. I will praise you ; for I am fearfully and wonderfully made: marvelous are your works, and that my soul knows right well. My substance was not hid from you when I was made in secret, and curiously wrought in the lowest parts of the earth. Your eyes did see my substance, yet being unperfect; and in your book all my members were written, which in continuance were fashioned, when as yet there were none of them. How precious are your thoughts unto me, O God! How great is the sum of them."

As God wrote His Plan for David in his book and then fashioned David according to his plan, God has a plan for every baby He is forming in the womb.

> Genesis 2:26-28 "And God said, Let us make man in our own image, after our likeness; and let them have dominion over the fish of the sea, and over the fowls of the air, and over the cattle, and over all the earth, and over every creeping thing that creeps upon the earth. So God created man in his own image , in the image of God created he him; male and

female created he them. And God blessed them, and God said unto them , Be fruitful and multiply , and replenish the earth, and subdue it; and have dominion over the fish of the sea, and over the fowl of the air, and over every living thing that moves upon the earth." (WE have dominion over the monkeys). Monkeys are not made in the image of God. People are. WE are made in God's Own Image. WE have physical bodies, and a soul which includes our emotions, feelings, will, thoughts, plans, creative abilities, problem solving techniques, etc…and a spirit area which is our heart area-the ability to love or hate, forgive or hold unforgiveness. We are a trinity as God is a Trinity. He is Father, Son, and Holy Spirit.

Ask yourself the following questions: Why is it when human beings mate any species, that God did not create, the result is a sterile creature with no ability to reproduce itself? When a horse is mated with a donkey, the result is a sterile mule. When a zebra and a horse are mated, the end result is a creature that cannot reproduce itself. These things prove that God gave each species the ability to reproduce itself. A dog does not give birth to a cat. A pig does not give birth to a horse. A rat does not give birth to a lion. Everything God created can only reproduce it's own species. Yes there are many different species of dogs but they are still dogs. There is natural alterations within a species, But No Mixture of Species. Humans in cold areas may grow more hair, may have layers of fat under their skin to keep warm (like the Masai Tribe in the Narok Mountains of Kenya), or have other adaptations, BUT THEY ARE STILL HUMANS CREATED BY GOD IN HIS OWN IMAGE. Humans do not produce monkeys and monkeys do not give birth to humans. EVOLUTION IS THE RELIGION OF ATHEISM THAT DENIES GOD AND HIS CREATION OF MANKIND IN GOD'S OWN IMAGE. There is No Monkey God in heaven. People were never monkeys. Our ancestors built entire cities. Monkeys have no intelligence to build a car, a house, an airplane, or anything else for that matter. Monkeys have no concept of right or wrong, good or evil. Monkeys have no plans for the future, no creative ability, no reasoning ability, no ability to create anything etc…They have survival instincts to eat and survive as a species, But they do not have a soul. They have no reasoning ability, no real intelligence, no knowledge of God, no real understanding , cannot read books, cannot create cities (only on the crazy Planet of the Apes Movies), etc…Evolution is a Demonic Satanic Lie. Refuse It In Jesus Name. Amen!

LIE NUMBER 19 THAT A CHRISTIAN CANNOT BE OPPRESSED BY A DEMON

2 Timothy 1:7 "For God has not given us a spirit of fear; but of power, and of love, and of a sound mind." A "spirit of fear" does not come from God. God has not given it to us. IT COMES FROM THE DEVIL. Any fear that is not Fear and Reverence For God; is demonic fear. Fear is one of the main tools of the devil to keep Christians silent, control them, torment them, discourage them, harass them, etc…

Romans 8:14-17 "For as many as are led by the Spirit of God, they are the sons of God. For you have not received the spirit of bondage again to fear; but you have received the Spirit of adoption, whereby we cry, Abba, Father. The Spirit Himself bears witness with our spirit; that we are the children of God. And if children, then heirs with Christ; if so be that we suffer with him, that we may also glorified together."

We see here that the Holy Spirit of God is NOT A spirit of bondage to fear. HE IS THE SPIRIT OF ADOPTION by Which WE Can cry ABBA FATHER. Bondage to Fear is NOT OF GOD. Yet, how many Christians are walking in fear, instead of faith?

Fear of Failure will keep you from trying.

Fear of Rejection will keep you from loving or trusting anyone.

Fear of Heights will keep you from being a pilot, a stewardess on a plane, a construction worker…

Fear of Man will keep you compromising with wickedness, to gain popularity with people, and have you living a life of rebellion against God. The Bible says that fear of man brings a snare. WE need to Fear God and depart from evil.

Fear of Man will keep you from sharing your faith in Jesus Christ with anyone else. IT will keep you silent and disobedient to God's Great Commission To The Church.

In Mark16:15-18 Jesus said, "Go you into all the world, and preach the gospel to every creature. He that believes and is baptized shall be saved; but he that believes not shall be damned. And these signs shall follow them that believe; in my name shall they cast out devils; they shall speak with new tongues; They shall take up serpents; and if they drink any deadly thing, it shall not hurt them; they shall lay hands on the sick, and they shall recover."

Fear of Man causes pastors, ministers, and priests to keep silent on abortion murders, sexual sins, and other issues, to avoid "Offending Anyone." Because they are silent, wickedness abounds. Because they agree with the wickedness, instead of standing with what God's Word says about the issues, they are loved by man but will face the judgment of God, some day.

A false preacher will face more judgment than the average person, because God gave them a place of trust and they have violated God's Commandments, to please people. They have refused to warn the wicked to repent of their sins and get right with God. They are populating hell instead of heaven with the souls that are deceived by them. They will be severely punished by God. IT is a fearful thing to fall into the hands of an angry God.

Fear of losing their (501 C3) tax deductions, keep pastors and preachers under the control of the government and the IRS. They are not free to preach about dishonest politicians, abortion issues, gayness, lust, and many other topics because they fear persecution by the IRS, and other government agencies, or the wicked media mob. May the Lord God deliver them from demonic spirits of fear and Fill Them With the Holy Spirit and Boldness To Preach The Whole Word of God. May the pulpits of America be filled with God's Truth, God's Righteousness, Morality, Decency, God's Judgment on the wicked, etc…May the whole truth of the Word of God be Preached not only the love of God; But also God's Judgment on Wickedness. Love is Not Lust. Truth Must Be Preached TO the Generations Again.

Many Christians suffer with spirits of doubt and unbelief. Doubt and Unbelief are spiritual things. They are also weapons that Satan uses against the Churches. IF Satan can get you to doubt your salvation, doubt the Word of God, doubt that God has forgiven you, etc…he can torment you with your past life before you came to Christ. Fear, doubt, and unbelief are the main weapons of Satan against the Body of Christ today.

> Lets look at Matthew 14:22-32 "And straightway Jesus constrained his disciples to get into a ship, and to go before him unto the other side, while he sent the multitudes away. And when Jesus had sent the multitudes away, he went up into a mountain apart to pray; and when evening was come, he was there alone. But the ship was now in the midst of the sea, tossed with waves for the wind was contrary. And in the fourth watch of the night Jesus went unto them walking on the sea.

And when the disciples saw him walking on the sea, they were troubled, saying, IT is a spirit; and they cried out for fear.

But Jesus spoke unto them saying, Be of good cheer; it is I; be not afraid. And Peter answered him and said, Lord, if it is you, bid me to come unto you on the water.

And Jesus said, Come. And when Peter was come down out of the ship, he walked on the water, to go to Jesus. But when he saw the wind boisterous, he was afraid; and beginning to sink, he cried saying, Lord, save me.

And immediately Jesus stretched forth his hand, and caught him, and said unto him, O you of little faith, wherefore did you doubt?"

We see here that it took a lot of faith for Peter to get out of the ship and begin to walk on water. His natural mind told him that liquid water could not hold up a human being, unless it was frozen ice. Yet, Peter decided to leave the ship and walk on the water. While Peter looked at Jesus, he could walk on the water. When he took his eyes off of Jesus, and looked at the wind and the waves (his situation), he began to let fear take over. When fear took over, Peter began to sink, and doubt set in.

We must KEEP OUR EYES ON JESUS, THE AUTHOR AND FINISHER OF OUR FAITH. We must not let fear, doubt, and unbelief get any place in our hearts, in our minds, or in our lives.

Kathleen Hollop

LIE NUMBER 20 THAT A BABY IN THE WOMB IS NOT A HUMAN BEING YET

No where, in the Bible, is a baby called a fetus, a product of conception, a blob of protoplasm, or any term indicating they are less of a person, less of a human being, less of a unique creation of Almighty God. A baby is called a baby whether in the womb or out of the womb. They are a person in the sight of God, who is forming them. As a matter of fact there are many scriptures that make it clear that Almighty God plans each child in his book and then forms each baby according to His Divine Plan for that child's life.

> I Samuel 1:5-6 "But unto Hannah he gave a worthy portion, for he loved Hannah: but the Lord had shut up her womb. And her adversary also provoked her sore, for to make her fret, because the Lord had shut her womb." We see here that it is the Lord who can open a woman's womb to conceive a child or close her womb according to His Divine Plan.

> I Samuel 1:11 Hannah went into the temple and spoke to God. "And she vowed a vow, and said; O Lord of hosts, if you will indeed look on the affliction of your handmaid, and remember me, and not forget your handmaid, but will give unto your handmaid a man child, then I will give him unto the Lord all the days of his life, and there shall no razor come upon his head."

> I Samuel 1:19-20 "And they rose up in the morning early, and worshipped before the Lord and returned, and came to their house to Ramah: and Elkanah knew Hannah his wife; and the Lord remembered her. Wherefore it came to pass, when the time was come about after Hannah had conceived, that she bare a son, and called his name Samuel, saying, Because I have asked him of the Lord."

> I Samuel 1:24-28 "And when Hannah had weaned him, she took him up with her, with three bullocks and one ephah of flour, and a bottle of wine, and brought him unto the house of the Lord in Shiloh: and the child was young

I Samuel 1:27-28 "For this child I prayed; and the Lord has given me my petition which I asked of Him. Therefore also I have lent him to the Lord; as long as he lives he shall be lent to the Lord. And he worshipped the Lord there." IF you study the scriptures, Samuel served the Lord his entire life. Hannah prayed for a son and God opened her womb and gave her a son. It was Not a Blob of Protoplasm, a fetus, a product of conception, in her womb. Samuel was a human baby in her womb. He was her Son being formed by the Lord, for the Lord's Divine Plans and Purposes.

Zechariah 12:1 "The burden of the word of the Lord for Israel, says the Lord, which stretches forth the heavens, and lays the foundation of the earth, and forms the spirit of man within him, behold I will make Jerusalem a cup of trembling" Here we see that it is the Lord who forms the spirit of man while he is in the womb of his/her mother.

Isaiah 43:1 "But now thus says the Lord that created you, O Jacob, and he that formed you, O Israel, Fear not; for I have redeemed you, I have called you by your name; you are mine."

Isaiah 43:4-7 "Since you were precious in my sight, you have been honorable, and I have loved you; therefore I will give men for you, and people for your life. Fear not; for I am with you; I will bring your seed from the east, and gather you from the west; I will say to the north, Give up; and to the south, Keep not back; bring my sons from far, and my daughters from the ends of the earth; Even every one that is called by my name; for I have created him for my glory, I have formed him; yes, I have made him." IT IS VERY CLEAR THAT GOD FORMS PEOPLE IN THE WOMB OF THEIR MOTHERS. TO MURDER PEOPLE IN THE WOMB THAT GOD IS FORMING FOR HIS GLORY; IS A HORRIBLE SIN AGAINST GOD. If you have killed your baby, ask God's forgiveness and turn to Jesus with your whole heart believing He died on the cross for your sins and rose again.

Jeremiah 1:3-4 "Then the word of the Lord came unto me saying, Before I formed you in the belly I knew you; and before you came forth out of the womb I sanctified you, and I ordained you a prophet unto the nations." As the Lord had a Divine Plan for Jeremiah's life, He has a plan for every person He creates in the womb of their mother.

Psalm 139:13-17 KJB King James Bible King David is speaking to the Lord. "For you have possessed my reins; you have covered me in my mother's womb. I will praise you, for I am fearfully and wonderfully made; marvelous are your works; and that my soul knows right well. My substance was not hid from you, when I was made in secret, and curiously wrought in the lowest parts of the earth. Your eyes did see my substance, yet being unperfect; and in your book all my members were written, which in continuance were fashioned, when as yet there was none of them. How precious also are your thoughts of me, O God! How great is the sum of them." We see here, that God first wrote David's members in a book-what David would look like, what color eyes, hair, height, weight, strengths, weaknesses, etc…and then formed David according to His Plan for David's life. God has a plan for every child's life.

Genesis 1:26-28 "And God said, Let us make man in our image, after our likeness; and let them have dominion over the fish of the sea, and over the fowl of the air, and over the cattle, and over all the earth, and over every creeping thing upon the earth. So God created man in his own image, in the image of God created he him, male and female created he them. And God blessed them, and God said unto them, Be fruitful, and multiply, and replenish the earth, and subdue it."

Human beings are the only ones created by God, in God's own image. Beasts, fish, and birds and creeping things are not. God created people to know Him, fellowship with Him, be part of His spiritual Family. To kill a child in the womb is to commit murder in the sight of God. It is the devil who wants to murder human beings. He hates us because God Loves Us.

LIE NUMBER 21 THAT GOD MAKES GENDER MISTAKES.

Romans 9:15-21 "For God said to Moses, I will have mercy on whom I will have mercy, and I will have compassion on whom I will have compassion. So then it is not of him that wills, nor of him that runs, but of God that shows mercy. For the scripture says unto Pharaoh, Even for this same purposes have I raised you up, that I might show my power in you, and that my name might be declared throughout all the earth. Therefore he has mercy on whom he will have mercy, and whom he will he hardens. You will say then unto me, Why does he yet find fault? For who has resisted his will? No but, O man, who are you that replies against God? Shall the thing formed say to him that formed it, Why have you made me thus? Has not the potter power over the clay, of the same lump to make one vessel unto honor, and another unto dishonor?

Who are we to say to God, You made me a man, but I want to be a woman. I will change myself into a woman, because you made a mistake God? If Almighty God made you a boy, you should get to know God. You should read God's Word and become a mighty man of God. You are supposed to grow up, marry a woman , fertilize her eggs, create babies and be a Godly Father figure to your children. IF God made you a girl, you are supposed to grow into a Blessed Woman of God, who will marry a man, have children, and raise up the next generation to know and honor God. GOD DOES NOT MAKE GENDER MISTAKES. PEOPLE LISTEN TO SATAN AND MAKE LIFE CHANGING MISTAKES, AS THEY TRY TO BECOME SOMEONE GOD DID NOT CREATE THEM TO BE. Satan wants to destroy you physically, emotionally and spiritually by lying to you.

I Corinthians 6:13-20 "Now the body is not for fornication, but for the Lord; and the Lord for the body. And God has both raised up the Lord, and will also raise us up by his own power. Don't you know that your bodies are the members of

Christ? Shall I then take the members of Christ, and make them the members of a harlot? God forbid. Flee fornication. Every sin that a man does is without the body; but he that commits fornication sins against his own body. Your body is the temple of the Holy Ghost which is in you, which you have of God, and you are not your own? For you are bought with a price (the blood of Jesus); therefore glorify God in your body, and in your spirit, which are God's."

To take the body that God has given you and try to cut it up, take harmful transgender drugs, mutilate yourself to change yourself into someone God has not created you to be, is a total insult to the God who created you to be either a boy or a girl. Be happy to be the you that God created you to be. Get to know God, His Love For You and His Plan For Your Life as who He Created You To Be.

LIE NUMBER 22 THERE ARE MANY GENDERS.

There are no human beings alive today that are half horse and half human, half ape and half human, half bird and half human, etc… These ridiculous notions are silly, foolish, Greek Myths that the Bible warns us not to pay heed to. Just because you can identify a dog as a dog, it doesn't make you a dog. Since a dog, cat, horse, bird, creeping thing, sea creature, etc… are all inferior life forms to human beings (who are created by God in God's Own Image), WHY WOULD ANY HUMAN BEING WANT TO LOWER THEMSELVES TO TRY TO ACT LIKE A CAT, A DOG, A RAT, A MONKEY, AN OX, ETC… This insanity must come to a speedy end. Anyone who would suggest that there are more than two genders of human beings(male or female), has been deceived by Satan. Humans are supposed to rule over the birds, the fish, the animals, and the creeping things. God gave us dominion Over them. To suggest that people can identify as a beast, act like a beast, howl like a beast, eat like a beast, sue someone in behalf of a beast that is run over on the road by an accident, sue someone in behalf of a river, a brook, a stream, etc… is insane and desperately needs help.

LIE NUMBER 23 THAT GAYNESS IS A MINORITY AND NOT A SEXUAL SIN.

Leviticus 20:13 "If a man also lie with mankind, as he lies with a woman, both of them have committed an abomination; they shall surely be put to death; their blood be upon them."

Leviticus 20:15-16 "And if a man lie with a beast, he shall surely be put to death; and you shall slay the beast. And if a woman approach unto any beast, and lie down thereto, thou shall kill the woman, and the beast: they shall surely be put to death; their blood shall be upon them."

Genesis 19:1-5 "And there came two angels to Sodom at evening; and Lot sat in the gate of Sodom; and Lot seeing them rose up to meet them; and he bowed himself with his face toward the ground; And he said, Behold now, my lords, turn in, I pray you, into your servant's house, and tarry all night, and wash your feet, and you shall rise up early, and go on your ways. And they said, No, but we will abide in the street all night. And he pressed upon them greatly; and they turned in unto him, and entered into his house; and he made them a feast, and did bake unleavened bread, and they did eat. But before they lay down, the men of the city, even the men of Sodom, compassed the house round, both old and young, all the people from every quarter: And they called unto Lot, and said unto him, Where are the men which came in to you this night? Bring them out unto us, that we may know them."

THEY WANTED TO HAVE SEX WITH THE TWO ANGELS WHO WERE STAYING AT LOT'S HOUSE.

Genesis 19:6-11 "And Lot went out at the door unto them, and shut the door after him. And said, I pray you, brethren, do not so wickedly. Behold now, I have two daughters which have not known men, let me, I pray you, bring them out unto you, and do to them as is good in your eyes: only unto these men do nothing; for they came under the shadow of my roof. And they said, Stand back. And they said again, This one fellow came in to sojourn, and he will be a judge: now will we deal worse with you, than with them. And they pressed sore upon the man, even Lot, and came near to break the door. But the men put forth their hand, and pulled Lot into the house to them, and shut the door. And they smote the men that were at the door of the house with blindness, both small and great; so that they wearied themselves to find the door." EVEN WHEN THE ANGELS SMOTE THEM WITH BLINDNESS, THEY WERE STILL TRYING TO FIND THE DOOR, BREAK IT IN, AND RAPE THE TWO ANGELS THAT WERE INSIDE.

Genesis 19: 12-14 "And the men said unto Lot, Do you have here any more people besides? Son in law, and thy sons, and thy daughters, and whatsoever you have in the city, bring them out of this place. For we will destroy this place, because the cry of them is waxen great before the face of the Lord; and the Lord has sent us to destroy it. And Lot went out, and spoke to his sons in law, which married his daughters and said, Up, get you out of this place, for the Lord will destroy this city. But he seemed as one that mocked unto his sons in law."

Genesis 19:23-26 "The sun was risen upon the earth when Lot entered into Zoar. Then the Lord rained upon Sodom and upon Gomorrah brimstone and fire from the Lord out of heaven; And he overthrew those cities, and all the plain, and all the inhabitants of the cities, and that which grew upon the ground."

Jude Verses 5-8 "I will therefore put you in remembrance, though you once knew this, how that the Lord, having saved the people out of the land of Egypt, afterward destroyed them that believed not. And the angels which kept not their first estate, but left their own habitation, he has reserved in everlasting chains under darkness unto the judgment of the great day. Even as Sodom and Gomorrha, and the cities about them in like manner, giving themselves over to fornication, and going after strange flesh, are set forth as an example, suffering the vengeance of eternal fire."

I have heard some mistaken explanations of why God destroyed Sodom and Gomorrha. This scripture in Jude makes it very clear that SEXUAL SINS OF FORNICATION AND GOING AFTER STRANGE FLESH CAUSED THE WRATH OF GOD TO DESTROY SODOM AND GOMORRHA. God did not create them to be gay and go after strange flesh. They chose to do what they did in rebellion to God.

America Needs To Repent of Sexual Sins And Stop It Now Before We Are Destroyed.

> Romans 1:18-28 "For the wrath of God is revealed from heaven against all ungodliness and unrighteousness of men, who hold the truth in unrighteousness; Because that which may be known of God is manifest in them; for God has shewed it unto them. For the invisible things of him from the creation of the world are clearly seen, being understood by the things that are made, even his eternal power and Godhead; so that they are without excuse: Because that, when they knew God, they glorified him not as God, neither were thankful; but became vain in their imaginations, and their foolish heart was darkened. Professing themselves to be wise, they became fools. And changed the glory of the uncorruptible God into an image made like to corruptible man, and to birds, and four footed beasts, and creeping things. Wherefore God also gave them up to uncleanness through the lusts of their own hearts, to dishonor their own bodies between themselves; Who changed the truth of God into a lie, and worshipped and served the creature more than the Creator, who is blessed for ever. A-men'. For this cause God gave them up unto vile affections for even their women did change the natural use into that which is against nature; And likewise also the men, leaving the natural use of the woman, burned in their lust one toward another; men with men working that which is unseemly, and receiving

in themselves that recompence of their error which was meet. And even as they did not like to retain God in their knowledge, God gave them over to a reprobate mind, to do those things which are not convenient; Being filled with all unrighteousness, fornication, wickedness, covetousness, maliciousness; full of envy, murder, debate, deceit, malignity; whisperers, Backbiters, haters of God, despiteful, proud, boasters, inventors of evil things, disobedient to parents, Without understanding, covenant breakers, without natural affection, implacable, unmerciful: Who knowing the judgment of God, that they which commit such things are worthy of death, not only do the same, but have pleasure in them that do them."

If you are doing this sin and you want to be free, REPENT and find a good Christian Deliverance Ministry to set you free from the spirits that have had you bound. Those who the Son of God sets free are free indeed. Anyone practicing this un-Godly life style should never be allowed to be a pastor, an elder, a deacon, an organist, a youth pastor or have any authority position in any Church. WE NEED TO GET THIS WICKEDNESS OUT OF OUR CHURCHES AND OUT OF OUR SCHOOLS, BEFORE THE WRATH OF GOD COMES UPON AMERICA LIKE IT DID ON SODOM AND GOMORRHA.

LIE NUMBER 24 THAT GOD HAS CHANGED HIS WORD TO AGREE WITH SINFUL PEOPLE

Hebrews 13:8 "Jesus Christ the same yesterday, and to day, and for ever." God's Word has not changed. The same God of the Old Testament is the same God of the New Testament. His Word is True Yesterday, today and forever. He has not changed His Mind about sexual sins and other sins. Fornication, sex outside of marriage, is still a sin today. Adultery, sex with someone else's husband or wife is still sin today. Watching pornography and lusting after women is still a sin today.

> Matthew 5:27-28 "You have heard that it was said by them of old time, Thou shalt not commit adultery: But I say unto you, That whosoever looks on a woman to lust after her has committed adultery with her already in his heart."

We have already covered the sins of Sodom and Gomorrha as to going after strange flesh and fornicating. God has never changed his mind. What was sin in the Old Testament is still sin in the New Testament, now and forever. Just because people say that sin is O.K., doesn't make it right in the sight of Almighty God. God does not change His Mind to conform to wicked people, public opinion, Hollywood, and the media. We are accountable to obey God, not man.

LIE NUMBER 25 THAT YOU CAN SERVE GOD AND OTHER GODS AND STILL GO TO HEAVEN.

> Deuteronomy 5:6-7 "I am the Lord thy God, which brought you out of the land of Egypt, from the house of bondage. You shall have none other gods before me."

> Matthew 22:34-38 "But when the Pharisees had heard that he had put the Sadducees to silence, they were gathered together. Then one of them, which was a lawyer, asked him a question, tempting him, and saying, Master, which is the great commandment in the law? Jesus said unto him, Thou shalt love the Lord your God with all your heart, and with all thy soul, and with all thy mind. This is the first, and great commandment. And the second is like unto it. Thou shalt love thy neighbor as thyself."

If you love the Lord your God with all your heart, your soul, and mind, Why would you want to worship another God who cannot save you from hell?

> II Corinthians 6:14-17 "Be you not unequally yoked together with unbelievers: for what fellowship has righteousness with unrighteousness? And what communion has light with darkness? And what concord has Christ with Belial? Or what part has he that believes with an infidel? And what agreement has the temple of God with idols?

I Corinthians 10:19-22 "What do I say then? That the idol is any thing, or that which is offered in sacrifice to idols is any thing? But I say, that the things which the Gentiles sacrifice, they sacrifice to devils, and not to God, and I would not that you should have fellowship with devils. You cannot drink the cup of the Lord, and the cup of devils: you cannot be partakers of the Lord's table, and of the table of devils." Isn't it time that people in the Body of Christ really love Christ and put the false gods, Greek myths, Evolution (Atheism Lies), Harry Potter movies, books, tapes, etc.. wizardry items, witchcraft books, occult items such as Dungeon and Dragon games, demonic video games, quija boards, tarot cards, horoscopes, spell casting books, "The Good Witch" which doesn't exist out of our homes?

John 14:6-11 Jesus said, "I am the way, the truth and the life; no man comes to the Father but by me. If you had known me, you should have known my Father also; and from henceforth you know him, and have seen him. Philip said unto him, Lord, shew us the Father, and it suffices us. Jesus said unto him, Have I been such a long time with you, and yet you have not known me, Philip? He that has seen me has seen the Father: and how do you say then, Shew us the Father? Believe you not that I am in the Father, and the Father in me? The words that I speak unto you I speak not of myself: but the Father that dwells in me, he does the works. Believe me that I am in the Father, and the Father in me; or else believe me for the very works' sake."

THERE IS ONLY ONE WAY TO GET RIGHT WITH GOD THE FATHER. IT IS THROUGH A RELATIONSHIP WITH JESUS CHRIST AS YOUR PERSONAL SAVIOR AND LORD IN YOUR HEART AND LIFE. JESUS CHRIST'S BLOOD IS THE ONLY SACRIFICE FOR SIN THAT FATHER GOD WILL ACCEPT.

CHOOSE YOU THIS DAY WHO YOU WILL SERVE. AS FOR ME AND MY HOUSE, WE WILL SERVE THE LORD.

LIE NUMBER 26 THAT WATCHING PORNOGRAPHY ON T.V. OR IN MOVIES ISN'T SIN.

Pornography isn't freedom of speech. IT IS FILTHY ACTIONS THAT GET IMPLANTED INTO PEOPLE'S MINDS AND HEARTS THAT RESULT IN FORNICATION, ADULTERY, LUST, GAYNESS, PERVERSION, AND ALL TYPES OF SEXUAL DEPRAVITY INCLUDING CHILD RAPE, MOLESTATION, INCEST, THE SEX TRAFFICING OF CHILDREN, ETC…

Proverbs 23:7 "For as he thinks in his heart, so is he"

Proverbs 6:12-15 "A naughty person, a wicked man (or woman), walks with a forward mouth. He winks with his eyes, he speaks with his feet, he teaches with his fingers; Forwardness is in his heart, he devises mischief continually; he sows discord. Therefore his calamity comes suddenly; suddenly he be broken without remedy." This describes a person who tries to sexually seduce, intimidate, or tempt someone else into a lustful relationship or encounter.

Proverbs 6:23-29 "For the commandment is a lamp; and the law is light; and reproofs of instruction are the way of life: To keep you from the evil woman, from the flattery of the tongue of a strange woman. Lust not after her beauty in your heart; neither let her take you with her eyelids. For by means of a whorish woman a man is brought to a piece of bread: and the adulteress will hunt for precious life. Can a man take fire in his bosom, and his clothes not be burned? Can one go upon hot coals, and his feet not be burned? So he that goes in to his neighbor's wife; whosoever touches her shall not be innocent."

Watching steamy soap operas, reading steamy romance novels that describe sexual experiences, watching pornography, going to adult bookstores to read the latest sex magazines and looking at semi-naked pictures of people, is Sin in the sight of God. These things will open you up to lust. They will destroy any sexual inhibitions and morals you have and infiltrate you with un-Godly lusts that will inhabit you and control your life.

Ephesians 5:1-7 "Be therefore followers of God, as dear children; And walk in love, as Christ also has loved us, and has given himself for us an offering and a sacrifice to God for a sweet smelling savor. But fornication, and all uncleanness, or covetousness, let it not be once named among you, as becometh saints; Neither filthiness, nor foolish talking, nor jesting,, which are not convenient: but rather giving of thanks. For this you know, that no whoremonger nor unclean person, nor covetous man, who is an idolator, has any inheritance in the kingdom of Christ and of God."

If you have been involved in any of these things, REPENT AND ASK GOD TO DELIVER YOU FROM ALL UN-GODLY LUSTS. IF NECESSARY GET RID OF YOUR COMPUTER OR CELL PHONE, ANY LUSTFUL BOOKS, MAGAZINES, ETC… AND STOP WATCHING ANYTHING SEXUAL THAT WILL REKINDLE LUST IN YOU. IF YOU NEED DELIVERENCE, FIND A GOOD CHRISTIAN DELIVERENCE MINISTRY AND GET PRAYED FOR. GET RID OF THE DEMON SPIRITS THAT ARE CONTROLLING YOUR LIFE.

LIE NUMBER 27 THAT GOD CANNOT TRAIN, CALL, AND EQUIP A WOMAN TO BE ONE OF THE FIVE FOLDS OF MINISTRY IN THE CHURCH. PAUL'S PERSONAL OPINIONS HAVE HINDERED GOD'S USE OF WOMEN IN THE BODY OF CHRIST.

Luke 2:36-38 "And there was one Anna, a prophetess, the daughter of Phanuel, of the tribe of Aser: she was of great age, and had lived with a husband seven years from her virginity; And she was a widow of about fourscore and four years, which departed not from the temple, but served God with fasting and prayers night and day. And she coming in that instant gave thanks likewise unto the Lord, and spoke of Jesus to all them that looked for redemption in Jerusalem." We see here, that Anna was a prophetess, a prayer warrior, and an evangelist all wrapped into one. She loved the Lord and served Him faithfully.

Romans 16:1-2 "I commend unto you Phebe our sister, which is a servant of the church which is at Cenchrea: That you receive her in the Lord, as becomes saints, and that you assist her in whatsoever business she has need of you: for she has been a succorer of many, and of myself also." Here Paul, the same Paul that said women should keep silent in the church, has come full circle around. PAUL IS INSTRUCTING THE BRETHREN TO RECEIVE PHEOBE AND ASIST HER IN WHATEVER THE LORD HAS FOR HER to do. He commends Phebe as being a faithful woman of God and instructs them to help her in her mission there.

Romans 16:3-5 "Greet Priscilla and Aquila, my helpers in Christ Jesus; Who have for my life laid down their own necks: unto whom not only I give thanks, but also all the churches of the Gentiles. Likewise greet the church that is in their house." Priscilla and Aquila were both Pastoring the Church that was in their house. Here Priscilla is mentioned first before Aquila. In other scriptures Aquila is mentioned first.

Acts 18:24-28 "And a certain Jew named Apollos, born at Alexandria, an eloquent man, and mighty in scriptures, came to Ephesus. This man was instructed in the way of the Lord; and being fervent in the spirit, he spoke and taught diligently the things of the Lord, knowing only the baptism of John. And he began to speak boldly in the synagogue; whom when Aquila and Prisilla had heard, they took him unto them, and expounded unto him the way of God more perfectly. And when he was disposed to pass into Achaia, the brethren wrote, exhorting the disciples to receive him who, when he was come, helped them much which had believed through grace: For he mightily convinced the Jews, and that publicly, shewing by the scriptures that Jesus was Christ." We see here that BOTH AQUILA AND PRISILLA TAUGHT APOLLOS THE WAY OF GOD MORE PERFECTLY.

The Lie That Women Can't Teach Men or Preach is a Man-Made Lie. God Does Use Women To do Whatever He Desires Them To Do. He Does Choose Faithful Women to be in the Five Folds of Ministry. Male Pastors that hinder, hamper, and stop the Lord's female servants from fulfilling His Call on Their Lives will have to answer to God. WOMEN MUST BE FREE TO USE THEIR GIFTS THAT GOD THE HOLY SPIRIT HAS GIVEN THEM, TO THE GLORY OF GOD. THEY MUST OBEY GOD, NOT MAN.

LIE NUMBER 28 THAT CHRISTIANS SHOULD NOT JUDGE ANYONE OR ANYTHING

I Corinthians 5:8-13 "Therefore let us keep the feast, not with old leaven, neither with the leaven of malice and wickedness; but with the unleavened bread of sincerity and truth. I wrote unto you in an epistle not to company with fornicators: Yet not altogether with the fornicators of this world or with the covetous or extortioners or with idolaters; for then must you go out of the world. But now I have written unto you not to keep company, if any man that is called a brother be a fornicator, or covetous, or an idolater, or a railer, or a drunkard, or an extortioner; with such a one do not eat. For what have I to do to judge them also that are without? Do not you judge them that are within? But them that are without God judges. Therefore put away from among yourselves that wicked person." Here we see that when someone is in the Church claiming to be a brother or sister in Christ, and is doing these things, we are to judge them and put them out from among us. They claim to be of God but are not obeying God. The people in the world do not know Christ. God judges them.

I Corinthians 6:1-7 "Dare any of you, having a matter against another, go to law before the unjust, and not before the saints? Do you not know that the saints shall judge the world? And if the world shall be judged by you, are you unworthy to judge the smallest matters? Know you not that we shall judge angels? How much more things that pertain to this life? IF then you have judgments of things pertaining to this life, set them to judge who are least esteemed in the church. I speak to your shame. Is it so, that there is not a wise man among you? No, not one that shall be able to judge between the brethren? But brother goes to law with brother, and that before the unbelievers. Now therefore there is utterly a fault among you, because you go to law one with another. Why do you not rather take wrong? Why do you not rather suffer yourselves to be defrauded? Here Paul was saying that the Church should judge if there is a problem between believers. Believers should not be going to secular courts to settle their differences.

It is the responsibility of the Pastors and elders to judge those within the Church who are into wickedness, and put the wicked people out of their Churches.

Galatians 6:1 "Brethren, if a man be overtaken in a fault, you which are spiritual, restore such a one in the spirit of meekness; considering yourself, lest you also be tempted."

Matthew 18:15-17 "Moreover if thy brother shall trespass against you, go and tell him his fault between you and him alone; if he shall hear you, you have gained your brother. But if he will not hear you, then take with you one or two more, that in the mouth of two or three witnesses every word may be established. And if he shall neglect to hear them, tell it to the church: but if he neglect to hear the church, let him be unto you as a heathen man and a publican."

II John Verses 9-11 "Whosoever transgresses and abides not in the doctrine of Christ, has not God. He that abides in the doctrine of Christ, he has both the Father and the Son. IF any come unto you and bring not this doctrine, receive him not into your house, neither bid him God speed; For he that bids him God speed is partaker of his evil deeds." We are not to let religious cultists into our homes with false beliefs and false doctrines.

> II Thessalonians 3:14-15 "And if any man obey not our word in this epistle, note that man, and have no company with him, that he may be ashamed. Yet count him not as an enemy, but admonish him as a brother."

Christians have the responsibility to register to vote and to vote for people who are promoting what God says is right and what God says is good. We are responsible to elect Godly men and women to lead us into God's Word and Godly lives. IF we don't vote for Godly people, we are letting the wicked rule over us.

> Matthew 7:15-20 "Beware of false prophets, which come to you in sheep's clothing, but inwardly they are ravening wolves. You shall know them by their fruits. Do men gather grapes of thorns, or figs of thistles? Even so every good tree brings forth good fruit; but a corrupt tree brings forth evil fruit. A good tree cannot bring forth evil fruit, neither can a corrupt tree bring forth good fruit. Every tree that brings not forth good fruit is hewn down, and cast into the fire. Wherefore by their fruits you shall know them."

We are to look at the fruit of people's lives to see if they are living right and walking right in the sight of God. We are to weigh what they say and do, to see if they are really following Jesus Christ and the Holy Bible. If they are preaching or teaching things that are contrary to the Word of God, they are wicked and not of God. Weigh The Fruit and you will see who they are. The Pharisees talked the talk, but didn't do what they said. A person who speaks the Word and hears the Word and Does Not Live The Word has deceived themselves. A pastor, priest, bishop, minister, reverend, who tickles people's ears and makes them feel good on their way to hell, is not a preacher of God's Righteousness and Holiness. A preacher who preaches racial hatred, bitterness, and division in the Body of Christ is not of God at all. By their fruits, you will know them.

Jesus warns about false prophets, false teachers, false Christs, false apostles, wolves in sheep's clothing, deceivers, etc…We can know them by their fruits.

LIE NUMBER 29 THE LIE THAT GOD WON'T JUDGE THE WICKED BECAUSE HE IS A GOD OF LOVE. HE IS ALSO A GOD OF HOLINESS AND JUDGMENT.

> Matthew 13:37-43 Jesus answered and said, "He that sows the good seed is the Son of man; The field is the world; the good seed are the children of the kingdom; but the tares are the children of the wicked one; The enemy that sowed them is the devil; the harvest is the end of the world; and the reapers are the angels. As therefore the tares are gathered and burned in the fire; so shall it be in the end of this world. The Son of man shall send forth his angels, and they shall gather out of his kingdom all things that offend, and them which do iniquity; And shall cast them into a furnace of fire: there shall be wailing and gnashing of teeth. Then shall the righteous shine forth as the sun in the kingdom of their Father. Who has ears to hear, let him hear."

Here we see that the wicked people, that do iniquity, will be cast into a furnace of fire to burn for all eternity. The righteous will shine with the light and glory of Father God.

> Jude verses 3-8 "Beloved, when I gave all diligence to write you of the common salvation, it was needful for me to write unto you, and exhort you that you should earnestly contend for the faith which was once delivered unto the saints. For there are certain men crept in unawares, who were before of old ordained to this condemnation, ungodly men, turning the grace of our God into lasciviousness, and denying the only Lord God, and our Lord Jesus Christ. I will therefore put you in remembrance, though you once knew this, how the Lord, having saved the people out of the land of Egypt, afterward destroyed them that believed not. And the angels which kept not their first estate, but left their own habitation, he has reserved in everlasting chains under darkness unto the judgment of the great day. Even as Sodom and Gomorrha, and the cities about them in like manner, giving themselves over to fornication, and going after strange flesh, are set forth for an example; suffering the vengeance of eternal fire."

Kathleen Hollop

LIE NUMBER 30 THAT CHRISTIANS SHOULD NOT BE INVOLVED IN OUR GOVERNMENT

Isaiah 9:6-7 "For unto us a child is born, unto us a son is given: and the government shall be upon his shoulder: and his name shall be called Wonderful, Counselor, The mighty God, The everlasting Father, The Prince of Peace. Of the increase of his government and peace there shall be no end, upon the throne of David, and upon his kingdom, to order it, and to establish it with judgment and with justice from henceforth even for ever. The zeal of the Lord of hosts will perform this."

Genesis :27-28 "So God created man in his own image, in the image of God created he him; male and female created he them. And God blessed them, and God said unto them, Be fruitful, and multiply, and replenish the earth, and subdue it: and have dominion over the fish of the sea, and over the fowl of the air, and over every living thing that moves upon the earth. " God gave man the ability to govern the earth. It is up to us to take the seats of power and authority and govern this earth according to God's Word, God's wisdom, and God's understanding.

Psalm 50: 14-20 "Offer unto God thanksgiving: and pay your vows unto the most High. And call upon me in the day of trouble, I will deliver you, and you shall glorify me.

But unto the wicked God says, What have you to do to declare my statutes, or that you should take my covenant in your mouth? Seeing you hate instruction, and casts my words behind you. When you saw a thief, then you consented with him, and have been partaker with adulterers. You give your mouth to evil, and your tongue frames deceit. You sit and speak against your brother; you slander your own mother's son."

Jeremiah 2:11 "Has a nation changed their gods, which are yet no gods? But my people have changed their glory for that which does not profit."

Why should we allow wicked people to rule over us with un-Godly decrees, wicked laws that justify evil, wicked devices, evil minds and hearts. CHRISTIANS NEED TO TAKE OVER OUR GOVERNMENT POSITIONS AND TURN THIS NATION BACK TO GOD, IN JESUS NAME. CHILDREN NEED TO BE TAUGHT THE WORD OF GOD IN OUR SCHOOLS AGAIN; AND PRAYER TO THE REAL GOD OF HEAVEN NEEDS TO BE ENCOURAGED. THE FALSE GREEK GODS AND MYTHS, VAIN PHILOSOPHIES, AND THE ATHEIST LIE OF EVOLUTION NEEDS TO BE THROWN OUT OF OUR SCHOOLS ALONG WITH FALSE MID-EASTERN RELIGIONS. JESUS CHRIST NEEDS TO BE EXAULTED IN OUR SCHOOLS, OUR COLLEGES, OUR BUISINESSES, OUR ENTERTAINMENT, OUR GOVERNMENT, OUR MILITARY, OUR MEDIA, OUR CHURCHES AND OUR FAMILIES. WITHOUT JESUS THERE IS NO SAVIOR. WITHOUT GOD'S WISDOM, WE HAVE NO WISDOM AT ALL; JUST CONFUSION AND CRAZINESS.

LIE NUMBER 31 THAT YOUNGER GENERATIONS SHOULD NOT RESPECT THEIR PARENTS OR TRY TO BE LIKE THEM.

Deuteronomy 6: 1-2 "Now these are the commandments, the statutes, and the judgments which the Lord your God commands to teach you, that you might do them in the land whither you go to possess it: That you might fear the Lord your God, to keep all his statutes and his commandments, which I command you, you, and your son, and your son's son , all the days of your life, and that your days may be prolonged."

Deuteronomy 11:16-21 "Take heed to yourselves, that your heart be not deceived, and you turn aside, and serve other gods, and worship them; And then the Lord's wrath be kindled against you, and he shut up the heaven, that there be no rain, and that the land yield not her fruit; and lest you perish quickly from off the good land which the Lord gives you. Therefore shall you lay up these my words in your heart and in your soul, and bind them for a sign upon your hand, that they may be as frontlets between your eyes. And you shall teach them to your children, speaking of them when you sit in your house, and when you walk by the way, when you lay down, and when you rise up. And you shall write them upon the door posts of your house, and upon your gates; That your days may be multiplied, and the days of your children, in the land which the Lord swore unto your fathers to give them, as the days of heaven upon the earth."

We have a responsibility to teach our children the Bible, God's Truths, God's Commandments, God's statutes, God's Principles, etc…Otherwise, our children will be deceived by he devil, the world, and Hollywood.

Ephesians 6: 1-4 "Children, obey your parents in the Lord: for this is right. Honor your father and mother; which is the first commandment with promise; That it may be well with you, and you may live long on the earth. And, you fathers, provoke not your children to wrath; but bring them up in the nurture and admonition of the Lord."

Colossians 3:20 "Children, obey your parents in all things; for this is well pleasing unto the Lord."

There is a WICKED INSURANCE COMPANY that has advertisements on television, that tell the younger generations not to be like their parents. It projects the idea that parents are old fashioned, out of date, too old to give good advice, senile, of no value, stupid, and ignorant. THESE ADS ARE DEMONIC ATTACKS ON THE WISDOM, BIBLICAL TRUTHS, GOD, VALUES, MORALS, DECENCY, INSTRUCTION, CHRISTIAN FAITH, LOVE OF GOD, LOVE OF COUNTRY, LOVE OF NEIGHBORS, ETC.. THAT SHOULD BE PASSED FROM ONE GENERATION TO ANOTHER. These ads teach the younger generations to refuse the wisdom, knowledge, and values, and morals of their parents and do their own thing. These ads ae demonic as hell and teach rebellion against real wisdom-God's Wisdom.

LIE NUMBER 32 THAT WE HATE PEOPLE WHEN WE TRY TO WARN THEM TO REPENT OF SIN

> Jonah 1: 1-3 "Now the word of the Lord came unto Jonah the son of Amittal, saying, Arise, go to Nineveh, that great city, and cry against it; for their wickedness is come up before me. But Jonah rose up to flee unto Tarshish from the presence of the Lord, and went down to Joppa; and he found a ship going to Tarshish; so he paid the fare thereof, and went down into it, to go from the presence of the Lord."

Jonah Hated The People of Nineveh and did not want to warn them of God's anger and wrath that would come upon them, if they did not repent of their wickedness. JONAH WANTED NINEVAH TO BE DESTROYED BY GOD. Instead of obeying God and going to Nineveh, Jonah went in the opposite direction. He ran from God's Presence.

The Lord sent a mighty wind to toss the ship Jonah was on, and the people feared that the ship would be broken. They cast lots to see why the evil had come upon them and the lot fell on Jonah. In verse 15, the men took up Jonah and cast him into the sea. Jonah was swallowed up by a whale and was in the whale's belly for three days and three nights.

Some people say, it is impossible for a person to be swallowed up by a whale. LAST YEAR OR A FEW YEARS AGO, A MAN SAID HE WAS SWALLOWED UP BY A WHALE. ALSO TWO WOMEN WHO WERE KYAKING WERE SWALLOWED UP BY A WHALE. They escaped when the whale opened his mouth. Google it and see for yourself.

Jonah prayed to the Lord, in his distress. He had to smell the dead fish in the whale's belly. Sea weeds were wrapped around his head. It took him three days and nights to call out to God for help. When he did, the Lord spoke to the fish, and it vomited out Jonah upon the dry land.

> Jonah 3:1-10 "And the word of the Lord came unto Jonah the second time, saying, Arise, go unto Nineveh, that great city, and preach unto it the preaching that I bid you. So

> Jonah arose, and went into Nineveh, according to the word of the Lord. Now Nineveh was an exceeding great city of three days' journey. And Jonah began to enter into the city a day's journey, and he cried, and said, Yet forty days, and Nineveh shall be overthrown. So the people of Nineveh believed God, and proclaimed a fast, and put on sackcloth, from the greatest of them even to the least of them. For the word came unto the king of Nineveh and he arose from his throne, and he laid his robe from him, and covered him with sackcloth, and sat in ashes. And he caused it to be proclaimed and published through Nineveh by the decree of the king and his nobles, saying, Let neither man nor beast, herd nor flock, taste any thing: let them not feed, nor drink water; But let man and beast be covered with sackcloth, and cry mightily unto God; yes, let them turn every one from his evil way, and from the violence that is in their hands. Who can tell if God will turn and repent, and turn away from his fierce anger, that we perish not?"

We see here that the people of Nineveh repented of their wickedness and turned from it. As a result, God had mercy on them and did not destroy Nineveh at that time.

> Jonah 4:1-4 "But it displeased Jonah exceedingly, and he was very angry. And he prayed unto the Lord, and said, I pray you, O Lord, was not this my saying when I was yet in my country? Therefore I fled before unto Tarshish: for I knew that you are a gracious God, and merciful, slow to anger, and of great kindness, and would repent of the evil. Therefore now, O Lord, take, I beseech you, my life from me; for it is better for me to die than to live."

> Jonah 4:10-11 "Then said the Lord, You have had pity on a gourd, for the which you have not labored, neither made it to grow; which came up in a night, and perished in a night; And should not I spare Nineveh, that great city, wherein are more than six score thousand persons that cannot discern between their right hand and their left hand; and also much cattle."

JONAH DID NOT WANT TO WARN NINEVEH TO REPENT. HE KNEW IF NINEVEH REPENTED THAT GOD WOULD HAVE MERCY ON THE PEOPLE OF NINEVEH. JONAH WANTED THEM DESTROYED BY GOD.

> Ezekiel 3:17-19 "Son of man, I have made you a watchman unto the house of Israel: therefore hear the word at my mouth, and give them warning from me. When I say unto the wicked, You shall surely die; and you give him not warning, nor speak to warn the wicked from his wicked way, to save his life; the same wicked man will die in his iniquity; but his blood will I require at your hand. Yet if you warn the wicked, and he turn not from his wickedness, nor from his wicked way, he shall die in his iniquity; but you have delivered your soul."

> Ezekiel 3:20-21 "Again, When a righteous man does turn from his righteousness, and commit iniquity, and I lay a stumbling block before him, he shall die: because you have not given him warning, he shall die in his sin, and his righteousness which he has done shall not be remembered; but his blood will I require at your hand. Nevertheless if you warn the righteous man, that the righteous sin not, and he does not sin, he shall surely live, because he is warned; also you have delivered your soul."

We HAVE A God GIVEN RESPONSIBILITY TO WARN THE WICKED TO REPENT AND GET RIGHT WITH GOD. WE ARE NOT LOVING THEM BY LETTING THEM CONTINUE IN WICKEDNESS AND LETTING THEM END UP IN HELL FOR ALL ETERNITY. IF WE REALLY LOVE THEM, WE WILL TELL THEM WHAT GOD'S WORD SAYS IN THE HOPE THEY WILL REPENT. WE WANT THEM TO GO TO HEAVEN AND NOT HELL IF WE REALLY LOVE THEM. If we condone their wickedness and approve of it, we are condemning them to hell for all eternity. The people who won't tell them the truth, really hate them like Jonah hated Nineveh.

LIE NUMBER 33 THE LIE THAT JESUS CHRIST IS NOT GOD.

John I: 1-5 "In the beginning was the Word, and the Word was with God, and the Word was God. The same was in the beginning with God. All things were made by him; and without him was not any thing made that was made. In him was life; and the life was the light of men. And the light shined in the darkness; and the darkness comprehended it not." We see here that the Word always was in the beginning and that the Word was God. He, the Word, created all things.

John I: 6-9 "There was a man sent from God, whose name was John. The same came for a witness, to bear witness of the Light, that all men through him might believe. He was not that Light, but was sent to bear witness of that Light. That was the true Light, which lights every man that comes into the world." This speaks of John the Baptist who testified of Jesus Christ. The True Light is Jesus Christ.

John I: 10-13 "He was in the world, and the world was made by him, and the world new him not. He came unto his own, and his own received him not. But as many as received him, to them gave he power to become the sons of God, even to them that believe on his name; Which were born, not of blood, nor of the will of the flesh, nor of the will of man, but of God." Jesus was in the world and the world was made by Him. He came unto the Jews, but many did not receive him. Then salvation was given to the Gentiles. Whether a Jew or a Gentile believer in Jesus Christ, we have been given the power to be sons of God.

John I:14 "And the Word was made flesh, and dwelt among us, (and we beheld his glory, the glory as of the only begotten of the Father,) full of grace and truth."

These scriptures show the deity of Jesus Christ, that He is God. He is the Word of God who became flesh and dwelt among us. He is the creator, the light of the world, and the life.

I Timothy 3:16 "And without controversy great is the mystery of godliness: God was manifest in the flesh, justified in the Spirit, seen of angels, preached unto the Gentiles, believed on in the world, received up into glory."

John 8: 52-59 "Then said the Jews unto Jesus, Now we know that you have a devil. Abraham is dead, and the prophets; and you say, If a man keep my saying, he shall never taste of death. Are you greater than our father Abraham, which is dead? And the prophets are dead; who do you make yourself?

Jesus answered, If I honor myself, my honor is nothing: it is my Father that honors me; of whom you say that he is your God; Yet you have not known him; but I know him: and if I should say, I know him not I shall be a liar like unto you; but I know him, and keep his saying. Your father Abraham rejoiced to see my day: and he saw it, and was glad. Then said the Jews unto him, You are not yet fifty years old, and have you seen Abraham? Jesus said unto them, Verily, verily I say unto you, Before Abraham was I am.

Then they took up stones to cast at him: but Jesus hid himself, and went out of the temple, going through the midst of them, and so passed by." Jesus was telling them that he was God, that he always was, and that Abraham was alive, not really dead.

There are many other scriptures that prove the deity of Jesus Christ. Daniel 3:19-30 tells how the three men (Shadrach, Meshach, and Abednego) were cast into the Firey furnace. The king saw four men in the flames walking and he said, "I see four men loose, walking in the midst of the fire, and they have no hurt; and the form of the fourth is like the Son of God." The flames didn't touch them, neither was there any smell of fire on them when they came out. Jesus Christ protected them because they trusted in him and refused to bow to false gods. JESUS CHRIST IS GOD. HE ALWAYS EXISTED AND ALWAYS WILL EXIST.

LIE NUMBER 34 THAT GOING TO CHURCH AND HAVING RELIGION WILL SAVE YOU

Having just head knowledge about God and of God is not enough. That is all vain religion will give a person. The lie that you don't have to repent of your sins and believe on the Lord Jesus Christ in your heart and life has infiltrated many churches. People sit in the pews every week, but they do not have a heart to heart relationship with JESUS CHRIST HIMSELF.

> Romans 10:9-13 "That if you shall confess with your mouth the Lord Jesus, and shall believe in your heart that God has raised him from the dead, you shall be saved. For with the heart man believes unto righteousness; and with the mouth confession is made unto salvation. For the scripture says, Whosoever believes on him shall not be ashamed. For there is no difference between the Jew and the Greek: for the same Lord over all is rich unto all that call upon him. For whosoever shall call upon the name of the Lord shall be saved."

There are about 17 inches between the head and the heart. Everyone needs Jesus Christ in their heart and life to belong to him and be a child of God.

> Revelation Chapter 21 speaks of the beautiful new Jerusalem There will be no more crying, death, pain in the new Jerusalem. But Revelation 21:27 "And there shall in no wise enter into it any thing that defiles, neither whatsoever works abomination, or makes a lie; but they which are written in the Lamb's book of life." We see here that the Book of Life belongs to Jesus Christ.

> John 1:29 "The next day John saw Jesus coming unto him, and said, Behold the Lamb of God, which takes away the sin of the world." The book of life belongs to Jesus Christ. Have you believed on Jesus Christ? Have you ever repented of your sins and asked Jesus Christ to come into your heart and life and save you? Are you sure your name is written in His Book of Life?

John 3:16 "For God so loved the world, that he gave his only begotten Son, that whosoever believes in him should not perish, but have everlasting life." Jesus Christ is God the Father's gift to us. A gift must be accepted in order to belong to you. IF you have never accepted Jesus Christ as your Personal Savior and Lord, he is not yours, yet. If you physically die without Jesus Christ in your heart and life, you die in your sins and have to pay for them yourself in hell.

John 5:39 Jesus said, "Search the scriptures; for in them you think you have eternal life; and they are they which testify of me. And you will not come to me, that you might have life." It is not enough to be religious and read the scriptures. **YOU MUST COME TO JESUS CHRIST HIMSELF IN ORDER TO HAVE ETERNAL LIFE.** If you realize that you haven't repented of your sins and asked Jesus Christ to come into your heart and life, you can pray this prayer. Don't wait. None of us know if we have tomorrow. Just pray this prayer and mean it, and Jesus will receive you.

"Father God, I am sorry for my sins. I believe that Jesus Christ died on the cross to save me. I believe His Sinless Blood was shed for me, in payment for my sins. Lord Jesus, Come into my heart. Come into my life. Be my Savior and be my Lord. I receive you now. Cleanse me from all my sins and all my unrighteousness. Help me to live a life that will honor you, in your Holy Name. Amen."

Now Jesus will reveal Himself to you in deeper ways as you study the Bible, hear His Voice, and be led by His Holy Spirit.

LIE NUMBER 35 THE LIE OF SEPERATION OF CHURCH AND STATE BEGAN IN 1948

Our first text book was the Holy Bible. School children were taught to read from the pages of God's Word. They were taught Salvation by the Blood of Jesus Christ. They were taught about Adam and Eve and how sin entered planet earth. They were taught what was right from what was wrong from God's Holy Bible. They were not open to Satan's lies because they were taught God's Truths.

Yale, Harvard and Princeton were once Bible Colleges used to train missionaries to spread the Gospel of Jesus Christ to other nations. Their students were made to read the Holy Bible and were trained up to follow God, obey God, and live Godly lives. Prayer to the God of The Bible used to be prayed by our students. They would ask God's Blessings upon their families, their teachers, their school s, their school work, and on America. NOW STUDENTS ARE TAUGHT THE WICKED IDEOLOGIES OF COMMUNISM/SOCIALISM MARXIST THEOLOGIES, AND ALL KINDS OF WICKEDNESS AND PERVERSIONS. TEACHERS, DEANS, AND PROFESSORS NEED TO REPENT AND STOP TEACHING SATAN'S LIES TO THE FUTURE GENERATIONS. THEY MUST REPENT AND TURN BACK TO GOD OR ELSE GOD'S JUDGMENT WILL COME UPON THEM. Sadly, many of our politicians, lawyers, and judges have gone to these wicked colleges and have been brainwashed into the devil's deceptions. As a result, Our Nation is ruled by wicked, un-Godly men and women that have corrupt minds and hearts. They are ignorant of God, God's Word, God's Commandments, and God's Judgments and Wrath on the un-Godly.

WICKED JUDGES BEGAN THE LIE OF SEPERATION OF CHURCH AND STATE IN 1948. THEY DELIBERATELY WANTED TO SEPARATE OUR GOVERNMENT AND OUR PEOPLE FROM THE CHRISTIAN FAITH AND THE GOD OF THE BIBLE. THE ONLY NAME THAT CANNOT BE MENTIONED IN OUR SCHOOLS, OUR GOVERNMENT, OUR SOCIETY, ETC…IS THE NAME OF JESUS CHRIST. ANY OTHER RELIGION OR NAME IS PERMITTED, BUT THE NAME OF JESUS.

THE ATHEIST RELIGION OF EVOLUTION THAT SAYS THERE IS NO GOD; WE ARE ALL EVOLVED MONKEYS, AND THERE IS NO DIVINE PLAN OR FUTURE FOR OUR LIVES, BRINGS PEOPLE WHO ARE MADE IN THE IMAGE OF GOD; DOWN TO THE LEVEL OF BEASTS. It gives no hope to those who believe it's lies. THE WICKED OCCULT PRACTICES OF WITCHES, WIZARDS, ZOMBIES, VOODOO, SPELL CASTING, AND NECROMANCY, FORTUNE TELLING, TARROT CARD READING, ARE ALLOWED IN OUR

SCHOOLS. Some schools even have Satan clubs. Harry Potter wizard books were sold in the hallways of our schools and were required reading for many classes. NOW ALL KINDS OF SEXUAL PERVERSIONS ARE ALLOWED IN OUR SCHOOLS; BUT NOT JESUS CHRIST, THE HOLY BIBLE, AND BIBLE TEACHING, PRAYER TO THE GOD OF THE BIBLE, AND WORSHIP TO HIM; MORALITY, DECENCY, HONESTY, BROTHERLY LOVE, KINDNESS, GOODNESS…

Our Pilgrims, Separatists, Huguenots, Ana-Baptists, and others came to America for RELIGIOUS FREEDOM TO WORSHIP THE GOD OF THE BIBLE WITHOUT PERSECUTION. Now, because of un-Godly, Wicked Politicians , Judges, Lawyers, DA's, State Attorney generals, mayors, governors, etc…Christians can be hauled into court and sued for their faith in the Holy Bible and their stand for God and His Righteousness. This is a violation of our Constitution and Amendment 1. There is No Real Separation of Church and State. It Is a Man-Made Demonic concept and lie.

Prior to 1948, our laws were based on God's Laws. When a pornographer tried to go onto a college campus, the courts threw him out and decreed that he could not corrupt the morals of our youth. When the Mormons wanted to have multiple wives, they were told no, due to what the Bible says in I Timothy 3:2-5 "A bishop then must be blameless, the husband of one wife, vigilant, sober, of good behavior, given to hospitality, apt to teach, Not given to wine no striker, not greedy of filthy lucre; but patient, not a brawler, not covetous: One that rules well his own house, having his children in subjection with all gravity; (For if a man does not know how to rule his own house, how shall he take care of the church of God)."

> I Timothy 3:12-13 "Let the deacons be the husbands of one wife, ruling their children and their own houses well. For they that have used the office of a deacon well purchase to themselves a good degree, and great boldness in the faith which is in Christ Jesus."

A person must stand for his or her convictions and live them out every day. Christianity is a life style, not a religion. If you are a real Christian, you must be a Christ Follower every day. The things that

Almighty God says are wrong, in His Holy Bible, you must agree with God and believe they are wrong. The things Almighty God says are right and true, you must agree with Almighty God and believe they are right and true. The Bible Must Be The Standard Of How You Live Your Life. You must believe that God's Word is True and it should be the basis of your thought patterns, your decisions, and how you live your daily life. A relationship with God, His Word, and His Holy Spirit will keep you from the lies, deceptions, and pit falls of your enemy, Satan. He wants to destroy you. The Bible and what God says should be read, studied, and obeyed as the Ultimate Guidance and Direction For Your Life. The Holy Ghost/Holy Spirit wrote the Bible. It Is Direction and Guidance From Almighty God Himself. God's Wisdom is real wisdom. Anything outside of God's Wisdom is Satan's Lies.

LIE NUMBER 36 THE LIE THAT ONCE YOU ASK JESUS INTO YOUR HEART, YOU DON'T HAVE TO REPENT ANY MORE OF YOUR SINS. IT IS ALL UNDER THE BLOOD (THE SLOPPY GRACE LIE).

> I Corinthians 15:34 "Awake to righteousness, and sin not; for some have not the knowledge of God: I speak this to your shame."

> 11 Corinthians7:1 "Having therefore these promises, dearly beloved, let us cleanse ourselves from all filthiness of the flesh and spirit, perfecting holiness in the fear of God."

> Ephesians 5: 1-12 "Be Therefore followers of God, as dear children; And walk in love, as Christ also has loved us, and has given himself for us an offering and a sacrifice to God for a sweet smelling savor. But fornication, and all uncleanness, or covetousness, let it not be named among you as becometh saints; Neither filthiness, nor foolish talking, nor jesting, which are not convenient; but rather giving of thanks. For this you know, that no whoremonger, nor unclean person, nor covetous man, who is an idolater, has any inheritance in the kingdom of Christ and of God. Let no man deceive you with vain words; for because of these things comes the wrath

of God upon the children of disobedience. Be not partakers with them. For you were sometimes darkness, but now you are light in the Lord: walk as children of light. (For the fruit of the Holy Spirit is in all goodness and righteousness and truth. Proving what is acceptable unto the Lord. And have no fellowship with the unfruitful works of darkness, but rather reprove them. For it is a shame even to speak of those things which are done of them in secret."

James 1:20-22 "For the wrath of man works not the righteousness of God. Wherefore lay apart all filthiness and superfluity of naughtiness, and receive with meekness the engrafted word which is able to save your souls. But be doers of the word, and not hearers only, deceiving your own selves."

1 John 1:5-10 "This then is the message which we have heard of him, and declare unto you, that God is light, and in him is no darkness at all. If we say that we have fellowship with him, and walk in darkness, we lie, and do not have the truth; But if we walk in the light as he is in the light, we have fellowship one with another, and the blood of Jesus Christ his Son cleanses us from all sin. If we say that we have no sin, we deceive ourselves, and the truth is not in us. If we confess our sins, he is faithful and just to forgive us our sins, and to cleanse us from all unrighteousness. If we say that we have not sinned, we make him a liar, and his word is not in us." SOME T.V. PREACHERS HAVE TOLD PEOPLE THAT 1 John 1:5-10 is not for believers in Jesus Christ. It is just for the unsaved. They have taught that every sin is under the Blood of Christ Already and We Don't Have To Repent Of Our Sins Any More. That is a lie from hell.

IF BELIEVERS IN CHRIST DON'T HAVE TO REPENT ANY MORE, THEN WHY DID THE HOLY SPIRIT OF GOD TELL FIVE OF THE SEVEN CHURCHES IN REVELATION 2 AND 3 TO REPENT AND GET RIGHT WITH GOD? The majority of the people in these churches were not walking right or living right. They were warned to repent of their wickedness, and stop it.

IF a believer sins, and the Holy Spirit convicts them to repent and put that sin out of their life; they need to obey the Holy Spirit. If they continually ignore the prompting of God the Holy Spirit, eventually they will grieve him away, their heart will harden like Pharaoh's heart, and their conscience will be seared like the people mentioned in Titus 1:15-16. "Unto the pure all things are pure; but unto them that are defiled and unbelieving is nothing pure; but even their mind and conscience is defiled. They profess that they know God; but in works they deny him, being abominable, and disobedient, and unto every good work reprobate."

REPENT OF YOUR SINS RIGHT AWAY. DON'T LET SINS MULTIPLY AND DESTROY YOUR CLOSENESS WITH GOD, YOUR WALK WITH GOD, AND YOUR FUTURE WITH GOD. PUT SIN OUT OF YOUR LIFE AND OBEY GOD.

LIE NUMBER 37 THAT IF YOU SPANK YOUR CHILDREN, THEY WILL HATE YOU.

Hebrews 12: 5-11 "And you have forgotten the exhortation which speaks as unto you as children, My son despise not the chastening of the Lord, nor faint when you are rebuked of him; For whom the Lord loves he chastens, and scourges every son whom he receives. IF you endure chastening God deals with you as with sons; for what son is he whom the father chastens not? But if you be without chastisement, whereof all are partakers, then are you bastards, and not sons. Furthermore we have had fathers of our flesh which corrected us, and we gave them reverence; shall we not much rather be in subjection unto the Father of spirits, and live? For they verily for a few days chastened us after their own pleasure, but he for our profit, that we might be partakers of his holiness. Now no chastening for the present seems to be joyous, but grievous: nevertheless afterward it yields the peaceable fruit of righteousness unto them which are exercised thereby."

Proverbs 3: 11-12 "My son, despise not the chastening of the Lord; neither be weary of his correction: For whom the Lord loves he corrects; even as a father the son in whom he delights."

II Timothy 3: 12-17 "Yes, and all that will live godly in Christ Jesus shall suffer persecution. But evil men and seducers shall wax worse and worse, deceiving, and being deceived. But continue in the things which you have learned and have been assured of, knowing of whom you have learned them; And that from a child you have known the holy scriptures, which are able to make you wise unto salvation through faith which is in Christ Jesus. All scripture is given by inspiration of God, and is profitable for doctrine, for reproof, for correction, for instruction in righteousness: That the man of God may be perfect, thoroughly furnished unto all good works."

We notice here that God's Word, God's holy scriptures make people wise to faith in Jesus Christ and to salvation. Without God's Words-God's holy scriptures, there is no moral compass of right and wrong. People are deceived into thinking that evil things are good and good things are evil. The world is full of deceptions, half-truths, and lies. TEACH YOUR CHILDREN THE WORD OF GOD SO THEY WILL HAVE GOD'S WISDOM AND GOD'S UNDERSTANDING INTO THE ISSUES OF OUR DAY. CORRECT YOUR SONS AND YOUR DAUGHTERS. STOP TRYING TO BE THEIR PAL AND BE THEIR GODLY PARENT.

Proverbs 22: 15 "Foolishness is bound in the heart of a child; but the rod of correction shall drive it far from him."

Proverbs 23: 13-14 "Withhold not correction from the child; for if you beat him with the rod, he shall not die. You shall beat him with the rod, and shall deliver his soul from hell."

Proverbs 29:15-17 "The rod and reproof give wisdom; but a child left to himself brings his mother to shame. When the wicked are multiplied, transgression increases: but the righteous shall see their fall. Correct your son, and he shall give you rest; yea, he shall give delight unto your soul."

There is a right way to correct children and a wrong way. Here are some helpful rules:

1. Never Hit A Child In Anger. Calm down completely first.
2. Ask the child why they deserve a spanking. Most times they already know why.
3. Tell them you love them and you have to correct them so they won't go to hell.
4. Take a paddle to their behind. IF they rise up in rebellion while you are spanking them, spank them some more. IF they weep and lay there over your lap in submission, stop the spanking.
5. After the spanking, give them a tissue to wipe their eyes, hug them and pray with them that God will forgive them for whatever it was they did. Tell them you love them enough to correct them. Never spank or hit a child anywhere but on the rear end.

We had our nephew living with us for three years. He had some anger in him. He began beating up other children on the school bus. I showed him a ping pong paddle and told him that if he beat up anyone else, he would get that paddle on his bare behind. He didn't believe me. While I was at work he hit my son with a plastic bat making welts on my son's arm. I went into his room, woke him up, and proceeded to throw him over my lap and spank him with the ping pong paddle. I said, "I promised you a spanking if you beat up anyone else. You made welts on Brian's arm. Now you are having the spanking I promised you."

After I spanked him, I gave him a tissue, hugged him, and we prayed and asked God to forgive him for hitting his cousin with the bat. After that, he never beat up anyone else again. Years later, when he was fully grown, he came up to me and said, "Thank you Aunt Kathy for correcting me when I was little. You made me a better person."

If we look at the scriptures in I Samuel 3: 11-14, we see an example of what not to do. "And the Lord said to Samuel, Behold I will do a thing in Israel, at which both the ears of every one that hears it shall tingle. In that day I will perform against Eli all things which I have spoken concerning his house; when I begin I will also make an end. For I have told him that I will judge his house for ever for the iniquity which he knows; because his sons made themselves vile, and he restrained them not. And therefore I have sworn unto the house of Eli, that the iniquity of Eli's house shall not be purged with sacrifice nor offering for ever."

What did Eli and his sons do to anger God to the point that God would destroy Eli and his sons and their descendants? I Samuel 2:12 " Now the sons of Eli were sons of Belial; they knew not the Lord." They worshipped and served another God.

> I Samuel 2: 13-16 Eli's sons were stealing the offerings that belonged to the Lord. Verse 17 "Wherefore the sin of the young men was very great before the Lord: for they abhorred the offering of the Lord."

> I Samuel 2: 22-25 "Now Eli was very old, and heard all that his sons did unto Israel; and how they lay with the women that assembled at the door of the tabernacle of the congregation. And he said unto them, Why do you do such things? For I hear of your evil dealings by all this people. No, my sons; for it is no good report that I hear; you make the Lord's people to transgress. If one man sin against another, the judge shall judge him: but if a man sin against the Lord, who shall intreat for him? Notwithstanding they hearkened not unto the voice of their father, because the Lord would slay them."

They were fornicating and committing adultery at the door of the tabernacle of the Lord. They had no fear of God, no love for God, no respect for their father, no relationship with the real God, and they served false gods. They pretended to be of God, but served Belial. How many pretenders do we have in the churches today?

> I Samuel 4: 10-11 "And the Philistines fought, and Israel was smitten, and they fled every man into his tent: and there was a very great slaughter; for there fell of Israel thirty thousand footmen. And the ark of God was taken; and the two sons of Eli, Hophni and Phinehas, were slain."

> I Samuel 4:15-18 " Now Eli was ninety and eight years old; and his eyes were dim, that he could not see. And the man said unto Eli, I am he that came out of the army, and I fled to day out of the army. And he said, What is there done,

my son? And the messenger answered and said, Israel is fled before the Philistines, and there has been also a great slaughter among the people, and your two sons also, Hophni and Phinehas, are dead, and the ark of God is taken. And it came to pass, when he made mention of the ark of God, that he fell from off the seat backward by the side of the gate, and his neck broke, and he died; for he was an old man, and heavy. And he had judged Israel forty years." Eli died.

I Samuel 4: 19-22 "And his daughter in law, Phinehas wife, was with child, near to be delivered: and when she heard the tidings that the ark of God was taken, and that her father in law and her husband were dead, she bowed herself and travailed; for her pains came upon her. And about the time of her death, the women that stood by her said unto her, Fear not; for you have born a son. But she answered not, either did she regard it. And she named the child I-cha-bod, saying, The glory is departed from Israel; because the ark of God was taken, and because of her father in law and her husband. And she said, The glory is departed from Israel; for the ark of God is taken."

Because Eli failed to impart to his sons faith in God, they became false god worshippers. Because Eli failed to teach them that stealing was wrong, they stole God's offerings. Because Eli failed to teach them that fornication (sex outside of marriage) and adultery was wrong, they were having sex with women at the door of God's Tabernacle. Instead of teaching people the things of God, Eli's sons were teaching people to rebel against God, to disregard the God of Heaven, to worship other gods, to lust after women, to steal from the temple, etc…THEY CAUSED THE JUDGMENT OF GOD TO COME UPON THEIR OWN FAMILY AND ON ISRAEL.

We must teach our children and grandchildren to love God, honor God, obey God, serve God, and live Godly lives. IF we don't, we will have wicked sons and daughters like Eli had. Eventually God will judge them and destroy them. If we don't teach them right, God will hold us accountable. You may have taught your children right and they have walked away from God. If they are adults, they are responsible to God for the way they have chosen to live. You did your best.

It is not up to a teacher, a pastor, a minister, a reverend, a priest, a pope, another adult, etc…to teach your children to love God, to fear God, to read God's Word the Bible, to impart God's truths, to apply God's truths to their lives, etc… It must be taught and lived in the home. A child will imitate a parent. If their mom or dad curse, they will curse. If their mom and dad take drugs, the child will copy them. IF the mom and dad drink a lot of alcohol, the child will drink a lot of alcohol. Children learn by what they see and hear in the home. If they hear a lot of arguments and fighting, they will grow up angry, pick fights with other people, and expect to fight with their spouse. If they see a lot of love and affection between their parents and experience a lot of love from their parents, they will grow up a loving person. If they are taught hatred, violence, anger, etc…they will grow up with these things in their hearts.

People spend a lot of time trying to get their children into the right professions, the right schools, have a good job, have money and a good future here on earth; But they fail to prepare them to know God, God's Commandments, God's Word, God's wisdom, God's Truths, and have a daily relationship with God Himself.

> Mark 8: 34-38 "And when Jesus had called the people unto him with his disciples also, he said unto them, Whosoever will come after me, let him deny himself, and take up his cross, and follow me. For whosoever will save his life shall lose it; but whosoever shall lose his life for my sake and the gospel's, the same shall save it. For what shall it profit a man, if he shall gain the whole world, and lose his soul? Or what shall a man give in exchange for his soul? Whosoever therefore shall be ashamed of me and of my words in this adulterous and sinful generation; of him also shall the Son of man be ashamed, when he comes in the glory of his Father with the holy angels."

It will not prosper your children if they go after wealth, fame, fortune, and all of the things of this world and lose their souls, in hell. They need a real relationship with Jesus Christ in their hearts and lives, every day. Only you can teach and impart saving faith into your children and future generations. If we fail to teach them God's Truths, they will serve other gods and be destroyed for all eternity. We must impart to them strong Biblical Faith in Father God, Jesus Christ, and Holy Spirit/Holy Ghost.

Kathleen Hollop

LIE NUMBER 38 THE GIFTS OF THE HOLY SPIRIT ARE NOT FOR TODAY

I Corinthians 13: 9-12 "For we know in part, and we prophecy in part. But when that which is perfect is come, then that which is in part shall be done away. When I was a child, I understood as a child, I thought as a child: but when I became a man, I put away childish things. For now we see through a glass darkly; but then face to face; now I know in part; but then shall I know even as also I am known."

One time someone quoted the above scripture and said, "The Bible is here. The Bible is perfect. No Need For The Gifts. The gifts Are Not For Today." I said, "If someone comes to your church and needs to be healed, is there no hope of their being healed?" She said, "Believe me, the gifts are not for today."

The above scripture is not talking about when the Bible is written. It is saying that when we are face to face with Jesus, in heaven, there will be no need for the gifts. There are no sick people or demonized people in heaven. There will be no need for preaching, evangelism, teaching, etc...because God Himself will be there and we will see Him face to face. Everyone in heaven knows the Lord personally.

In the meantime, the Holy Spirit Gifts Are For Today. WE Need The Full Baptism in the Holy Ghost/Holy Spirit in order for the healing and deliverance gifts to operate in us and through us. There are many people, here on planet earth, who need to be healed physically, emotionally, and spiritually. There are many people who need deliverance from addictions to drugs, alcohol, lust, etc...

The devil has mis-used God's Scriptures and taken them out of context to convince people that only the original disciples had the gifts. The gifts are for all believers in Christ and can manifest in and through us, once we are baptized by Jesus , in the Holy Ghost.

I personally have seen the Holy Spirit work through me to cast a legion of demons out of a woman in Nairobi, raise a dead boy back to life in Butere Kenya, see a broken finger healed in seconds, watch burns disappear from skin, watch babies who were almost dead of malaria healed, etc...

Get Baptized in the Holy Spirit and let His Divine Giftings flow in and through you. Become a vessel God can use to do mighty things, on planet earth today.

LIE NUMBER 39 THAT A PERSON CANNOT APPROACH FATHER GOD THEMSELVES.

> Matthew 27:50-53 "Jesus, when he had cried again with a loud voice, yielded up the ghost. And behold, the veil of the temple was rent in half from the top to the bottom: and the earth did quake, and the rocks rent; And the graves were opened; and many bodies of the saints which slept arose. And came out of the graves after his resurrection and went into the holy city , and appeared unto many."

Prior to Jesus Christ's death on the cross, no one could go through the temple veil into the Holy of Holies, but the high priest. If anyone else tried to enter, where the Ark of the Covenant was kept, they would die. Only the high priest could approach Father God with a sacrifice for his own sins and the sins of the people. The average person could not enter or approach Father God themselves. Once Jesus Christ's Blood had been shed and Jesus said, "It is Finished" and died, the temple veil that divided people from being able to approach Father God was torn in half. Now everyone has access to approach Father God through Jesus Christ.

> Hebrews 10: 17-23 "And their sin and iniquities will I remember no more. Now where remission of these is, there is no more offering for sin. Having therefore, brethren boldness to enter into the holiest by the blood of Jesus, By a new and living way, which he has consecrated for us, through the veil, that is to say, his flesh; And having a high priest over the house of God; Let us draw near with a true heart in full assurance of faith, having our hearts sprinkled from an evil conscience, and our bodies washed with pure water. Let us hold fast the profession of our faith without wavering; (for he is faithful that promised).

I John 1:7-10 "But if we walk in the light, as he is in the light, we have fellowship one with another, and the blood of Jesus Christ his Son cleanses us from all sin. If we say that we have no sin, we deceive ourselves, and the truth is not in us. If we confess our sins, he is faithful and just to forgive us our sins, and to cleanse us from all unrighteousness. IF we say that we have not sinned, we make him a liar, and his word is not in us." We can go right to Father God ourselves.

LIE NUMBER 40 THAT THERE ARE OTHER MEDIATORS, BESIDES JESUS, BETWEEN GOD AND MAN

I Timothy 2:5 "For there is one God, and one mediator between God and men, the man Christ Jesus; Who gave himself a ransom for all, to be testified in due time."

Hebrews 9:11-15 "But Christ being come a high priest of good things to come, by a greater and more perfect tabernacle, not made with hands, that is to say, not of this building; Neither by the blood of goats and calves, but by his own blood he entered in once into the holy place; having obtained eternal redemption for us. For if the blood of bulls and of goats, and the ashes of a heifer sprinkling the unclean, sanctified to the purifying of the flesh; How much more shall the blood of Christ, who through the eternal Spirit, offered himself without spot to God, purge your conscience from dead works to serve the living God? And for this cause he is the mediator of the new testament, that by means of death, for the redemption of the transgressions that were under the first testament, they which are called might receive the promise of eternal life."

There is only one mediator between God and men. Only Jesus Christ can redeem us, save us, deliver us, and make us acceptable to Father God. When Jesus taught the disciples to pray, he had them pray to the Father. He never had them pray to anyone else. He also told them to ask in His Name.

John 14:13-14 "And whatsoever you shall ask in my name, that will I do, that the Father may be glorified in the Son. If you shall ask any thing in my name, I will do it."

John 16:23 "And in that day you shall ask me nothing, Verily, Verily, I say unto you, Whatsoever you shall ask the Father in my name, he will give it you. Hitherto have you asked nothing in my name; ask, and you shall receive, that your joy may be full."

LIE NUMBER 41 WE DON'T HAVE TO PREACH JESUS CHRIST TO THE JEWS

In the time of Jesus Christ's Ministry on earth, there were some Jews who believed on Him and other Jews who rejected Him. He told the scribes and Pharisees , "If you don't believe I am he, you will die in your sins." There is a lie of the devil saying that all Jews are saved and going to heaven so it is unnecessary to share the Gospel of Jesus Christ with them. The Jews who don't receive faith in Jesus Christ as their personal Savior and Lord; are going to hell, along with the Gentiles who reject Jesus. Satan Hates the Nation of Israel and the Jewish People. We must reach them for Yeshua, Jesus, the Jewish Messiah.

Romans 11: 27-31 "For this is my covenant unto them, when I shall take away their sins. As concerning the gospel, whey are enemies for your sakes, but as touching the election, they are beloved for the fathers' sakes. For the gifts and calling of God are without repentance. For as you in times past have not believed God, yet have obtained mercy through their unbelief: Even so have these also now not believed, that through your mercy they also may obtain mercy." We are to share the Gospel of Jesus Christ with the Jews so they will be saved and receive God's mercy through our witness to them.

John 5: 39-40 Jesus was speaking to the Jews. "Search the scriptures; for in them you think you have eternal life: and they are they which testify of me. And you will not come to me, that you might have life." He was telling them that just studying the scriptures would not give them eternal life. They had to come to faith in Jesus Christ Himself. We must reach the Jews for Jesus.

LIE NUMBER 42 THAT THE ROCK IS PETER AND NOT JESUS CHRIST HIMSELF

Deuteronomy 32: 3-4 "Because I will publish the name of the Lord: ascribe ye greatness unto our God. He is the Rock, his work is perfect: for all his ways are judgment; a God of truth and without iniquity, just and right is he."

Samuel 22:32 and Psalm 18:31 "For who is God, save the Lord? And who is a rock, save our God?

Matthew 16: 13-18 "When Jesus came into the coasts of Caesarea Philippi, he asked his disciples, saying, Whom do men say that I the Son of man am? And they said, Some say that you are John the Baptist; some, Elias; and others, Jeremias, or one of the prophets. He said unto them, But whom do you say I am? And Simon Peter answered and said, Thou art the Christ, the Son of the living God. And Jesus answered and said unto him, Blessed art thou, Simon Barjona: for flesh and blood has not revealed it unto you, but my Father which is in heaven."

Peter got a revelation, from God the Father, that JESUS IS THE CHRIST, THE SON OF THE LIVING GOD. Upon Jesus Christ being the Son of the Living God, God builds His Church and the gates of hell will not prevail against it.

Jesus continued on to say, "Thou art Peter, and upon this rock (the revelation that Jesus is the Christ, the Son of The Living God) I will build my church and the gates of hell shall not prevail against it.

Matthew 16: 19-20 Jesus said to Peter "And I will give unto you the keys of the kingdom of heaven; and whatsoever you shall bind on earth shall be bound in heaven and whatsoever you shall loose on earth shall be loosed in heaven." GOD GAVE THESE KEYS TO THE BODY OF CHRIST, HIS PEOPLE, HIS CHURCH. We have the Power to bind demonic spirits, in the Name of Jesus. We have the power to loose God's angels into the atmosphere and into our situations. WE DO NOT HAVE THE POWER TO CHANGE OR ALTER GOD'S WORD, THE HOLY BIBLE. "Then Jesus charged his disciples that they should tell no man that he was Jesus the Christ.

Matthew 16: 21-23 "From that time forth began Jesus to shew unto his disciples, how that he must go unto Jerusalem, and suffer many things of the elders and chief priests and scribes, and be killed, and be raised again the third day. Then Peter took him, and began to rebuke him, saying, Be it far from thee, Lord: this shall not be unto you. But Jesus turned, and said unto Peter, Get thee behind me, Satan: you are an offense unto me; for you savor not the things that be of God, but those that be of men." The discouraging words coming out of Peter's mouth were of Satan. Jesus rebuked Peter. PETER WAS NEVER INFALLIBLE.

I Corinthians 10: 1-4 "Moreover, brethren, I would not that you should be ignorant, how that all our fathers were under the cloud, and all passed through the sea; And were all baptized unto Moses in the cloud and in the sea; And did all eat the same spiritual meat; And did all drink the same spiritual drink: for they drank of that spiritual Rock that followed them and that Rock was Christ."

JESUS CHRIST IS GOD. HE IS THE ROCK. THE REVELATION THAT JESUS WAS THE CHRIST, THE SON OF THE LIVING GOD; IS THE ROCK ON WHICH GOD HAS BUILT HIS CHURCH. THE CHURCH IS PURCHASED BY THE BLOOD OF JESUS, IS SAVED BY JESUS, IS DELIVERED BY JESUS, AND BUILT BY JESUS CHRIST HIMSELF. THERE IS NO OTHER ROCK BUT OUR GOD.

Kathleen Hollop

CHAPTER 11
DON'T ACCEPT A WRONG COVERING

Isaiah 30:1-3 "Woe to the rebellious children, says the Lord, that take counsel, but not of me; and that cover with a covering, but not of my Spirit, that they may add sin to sin: That walk to go down into Egypt, and have not asked at my mouth; to strengthen themselves in the strength of Pharaoh, and to trust in the shadow of Egypt! Therefore shall the strength of Pharaoh be your shame, and the trust in the shadow of Egypt your confusion."

As we look at this scripture, we see that God's children were not seeking Him for guidance and direction for their lives. They were taking advice from human beings, Pastors, Priests, Bishops, Elders, Deacons, fortune tellers, tarot card readers, psychics, mediums, witches, wizards, and the worldly media, Hollywood, and other people; rather then praying to God and asking His Counsel.

They were not seeking God the Holy Spirit to be their covering, but they were seeking human beings to cover them. Back in the 1980's there was a lie that rose up in the Body of Christ. It goes like this, "Everyone Should Be Under A Pastor." "Everyone Should BE Covered By A Pastor". IT is un-Biblical to put a pastor over the other four folds of ministry, Evangelist, Apostle, Prophet, and Teacher so he can deny them access to impart their folds to the sheep. All five folds of ministry are supposed to be operating in the Church and growing the sheep into unity of the faith. When a pastor, priest, bishop, elder etc…deprives the sheep of the other four folds of ministry, the sheep are weak, under nourished, under fed, and starving spiritually.

Mature believers, in Christ, who can discern the voice of God, are baptized in the Holy Ghost, and skilled in the Word of God; are supposed to be covered by God's Holy Spirit, led by God's Holy Spirit, and Filled by God's Holy Spirit. They are supposed to be free to hear and obey God the Holy Ghost, and fulfill Father God's Plan and Purpose for their lives. When a pastor, priest, board of elders, deacon, pope, bishop, etc…refuses to allow a mature believer to hear from God the Holy Spirit and be led by Him, they are hindering the work of God in a believer's heart and life. When a believer can discern the voice of God, they need to obey God rather than man.

> I Corinthians 7:22-24 "For he that is called in the Lord, being a servant, is the Lord's freeman; likewise also he that is called , being free, is Christ's servant. You are bought with a price; be you not the servants of men. Brethren, let every man, wherein he is called, therein abide with God."

> Romans 8:14-18 "For as many as are led by the Spirit of God; they are the sons of God. For you have not received the spirit of bondage again to fear; but you have received the Spirit of adoption, whereby we cry, Abba, Father. The Spirit Himself bears witness with our spirit, that we are the children of God. And if children, then heirs; heirs of God, and joint-heirs with Christ; if so be that we suffer with him, that we may be also glorified together." Are those not led by the Spirit of God really sons of God? We must be led by the Spirit of God to be a son of God.

> Romans 8:8-9 "So then they that are in the flesh cannot please God. But you are not in the flesh, but in the Spirit, if so be that the Spirit of God dwell in you. Now if any man have not the Spirit of Christ, he is none of his." Here we see that the Spirit of Father God and the Spirit of Jesus Christ is the same Spirit. He is the Holy Spirit.

> John 16:13-15 "When he, the Spirit of truth is come, he will guide you into all truth: for he shall not speak of himself; but whatsoever he shall hear, that shall he speak: and he will shew you things to come. He shall glorify me; for he shall receive of mine, and shall shew it unto you."

The Holy Spirit guides the believer into all truth, speaks of Jesus, tells the believer what he hears Father God and Jesus saying in heaven, guides the believer into Father's Will, glorifies Jesus and shows the believer the future. Without being led by the Holy Spirit of God, the believer doesn't know the will of Father God for his life. Only the Holy Spirit can reveal Father God's Will to the believer.

> Luke 11:9-13 "And I say unto you, Ask, and it shall be given you; seek, and you shall find, knock and it shall be opened unto you. For every one that asks receives; and he that seeks finds; and to him that knocks it shall be opened. If a son shall ask bread of any of you that is a father, will he give him a stone? Or if he ask a fish, will he for a fish give him a serpent? Or if he shall ask an egg, will he offer him a scorpion? IF you then, being evil, know how to give good gifts unto your children; how much more shall your heavenly Father give the Holy Spirit to them that ask him? We Can Ask For More OF The Holy Spirit and Know that Our Father in heaven will give us More OF the Holy Spirit. We won't get a demon or a wrong spirit.
>
> Ephesians 4:30 "And grieve not the Holy Spirit of God, whereby you are sealed unto the day of redemption." We are to hear and obey the Holy Spirit of God, rather than man.

A MATURE, MALE OR FEMALE BELIEVER, IN CHRIST, SHOULD BE COVERED BY THE HOLY SPIRIT AND OBEY HIM. THE HOLY SPIRIT WILL LEAD HIM OR HER INTO FATHER'S WILL AND PURPOSE FOR THEIR LIFE. A MARRIED, FEMALE BELIEVER, IN CHRIST, SHOULD BE COVERED BY THE HOLY SPIRIT AND HER HUSBAND. If the Lord has called her into ministry, the Lord will also confirm this to her husband and he will agree to release her into ministry. She is not to rebel against her husband and the Holy Spirit, by listening to any other human being. No other human being has the right to interfere in her walk with God the Holy Spirit.

Acts 2:1-4 "And when the days of Pentecost were fully come, they were all with one accord in one place. And suddenly there came a sound from heaven as of a rushing mighty wind, and it filled all the house where they were sitting. And there appeared unto them cloven tongues like as of fire, and it sat upon each of them. And they were all filled with the Holy Ghost, and began to speak with other tongues, as the Spirit gave them utterance."

Acts 2:16-21 "But this is that which was spoken by the prophet Joel: And it shall come to pass in the last days, saith God, I will pour out my Spirit upon all flesh; and your sons and daughters shall prophesy, and your young men shall see visions, and your old men shall dream dreams: And on my servants and on my handmaidens I will pour out in those days of my Spirit; and they shall prophesy: And I will shew wonders in heaven above, and signs in the earth beneath; blood, and fire, and vapor of smoke; The sun shall be turned into darkness, and the moon into blood, before that great and notable day of the Lord come: And it shall come to pass, that whosoever shall call on the name of the Lord shall be saved."

Acts 4:29-33 When the disciples were threatened by a counsel to stop preaching or teaching the Gospel of Jesus Christ, they prayed. "And now, Lord, behold their threatening's: and grant unto your servants that with all boldness they may speak thy word. By stretching forth your hand to heal: and that signs and wonders may be done by the name of your holy child Jesus. And when they had prayed, the place was shaken where they were assembled together; and they were all filled with the Holy Ghost, and they spoke the word of God with boldness. And the multitude of them that believed were of one heart and of one soul: neither said any of them that anything was his own; but they had all things common. And with great power gave the apostles witness of the resurrection of the Lord Jesus, and great grace was upon them all."

Why were they able to have great power to witness and do mighty things. They had all been filled with the Holy Ghost more than once. We can ask Father God to give us more of the Holy Spirit, in Jesus' Name. Amen. Without the Holy Spirit, we cannot do the work of Christ on planet earth. The flesh profits nothing. The Spirit is life.

> Luke 11: 9-13 Jesus said, "And I say unto you, Ask, and it shall be given you; seek, and you shall find; knock and it shall be opened unto you. For every one that asks receives; and he that seeks finds; and to him that knocks it shall be opened.

If a son shall ask for bread of any of you that is a father, will he give him a stone? Or if he asks for a fish, will he for a fish give him a serpent? Or if he shall ask for an egg will he offer him a scorpion? If you then, being evil, know how to give good gifts unto your children: how much more shall your heavenly Father give the Holy Spirit to them that ask him?"

WHEN WE ASK GOD FOR MORE OF THE HOLY SPIRIT, WE WILL RECEIVE MORE OF THE HOLY SPIRIT. WE CAN ASK FOR MORE THAN A DOUBLE PORTION OF THE HOLY SPIRIT. Personally, I ask very frequently for more, more, more, of the Holy Spirit. Without Him, my flesh profits nothing. I need God the Holy Spirit's Power, and Anointing, and guidance, and direction; in order to fulfill Father God's Will and purpose for my life.

> The Disciple Paul said in I Corinthians 2:1-5 "And I brethren, when I came to you, I came not with excellency of speech or of wisdom, declaring unto you the testimony of God. For I determined not to know any thing among you, save Jesus Christ, and him crucified. And I was with you in weakness, and in fear, and in much trembling. And my speech and my preaching was not with enticing words of man's wisdom, but in demonstration of the Spirit and of power: That your faith should not stand in the wisdom of men, but in the power of God." Our faith should not be in man, but in the power of God."

The brethren in the early church were directed, guided, instructed, and empowered by the Holy Spirit/Holy Ghost. He Is The Power of the Godhead. Without Him, the Body of Christ is powerless to stand with boldness, in the faith. Without Him, there are no signs, wonders, and miracles happening in our Churches. WE NEED THE HOLY SPIRIT'S COVERING, DIRECTION, AND INSTRUCTION TO FULFILL THE CALL OF GOD ON EACH OF OUR LIVES. WE ARE ALL CALLED TO ADVANCE GOD'S KINGDOM ON PLANET EARTH. WE CANNOT ADVANCE GOD'S KINGDOM WITHOUT THE HELP OF HOLY SPIRIT. WE NEED THE HOLY SPIRIT BACK IN OUR CHURCHES. WE NEED THE HOLY GHOST BAPTISM MENTIONED IN ALL FOUR GOSPELS (MATTHEW 3:11, MARK 1:6-11, LUKE 3: 15-22, JOHN 1: 26-34). IT IS JESUS CHRIST WHO BAPTISES US WITH THE HOLY GHOST, IF WE ASK HIM TO. WE NEED TO BE COVERED BY THE HOLY SPIRIT, RATHER THAN ANY HUMAN BEING. NO ONE ELSE IS ALMIGHTY, ALL KNOWING AND ALL POWERFUL, BUT GOD HIMSELF. THE HOLY SPIRIT IS GOD THE HOLY SPIRIT. WE MUST LISTEN TO HIM, BE LED BY HIM, AND OBEY HIM, rather than any human being.

CHAPTER 12
OUR WORDS HAVE SPIRITUAL POWER

Proverbs 18:21 "Death and life are in the power of the tongue; and they that love it shall eat the fruit thereof." Our words have the power to either build up, encourage, strengthen, and impart truth to other people, or they have the power to discourage, tear down, wound, lie, and destroy other people.

There is an old saying, "Sticks and stones may break my bones, but names will never hurt me." That saying is not true. Words spoken in anger can cut worse than a knife, into the heart and soul of another person. They can bear destructive fruit, in their life, for years to come; Maybe even forever. Proverbs 18:21 says that our words bear fruit in people's lives. Words are released into the atmosphere and do effect those who hear them.

> Psalm 34:12-14 "What man is he that desires life, and loves many days, that he may see good? Keep your tongue from evil, and your lips from speaking guile. Depart from evil, and do good, seek peace, and pursue it." We have to be careful with the words we speak.
>
> Psalm 39:1 "I said, I will take heed to my ways that I sin not with my tongue; I will keep my mouth with a bridle, while the wicked is before me. "
>
> Proverbs 12:13-14 "The wicked is snared by the transgression of his lips; but the just shall come out of trouble. A man shall be satisfied with good by the fruit of his mouth; and the recompence of a man's hands shall be rendered unto him."
>
> Proverbs 12:17-19 "He that speaks truth shews forth

righteousness; but a false witness deceit. There is he that speaks like the piercings of a sword; but the tongue of the wise is health. The lip of truth shall be established for ever; but a lying tongue is but for a moment."

Proverbs 15:4 "A wholesome tongue is a tree of life; but perverseness therein is a breach in the spirit."

Proverbs 21:23 "Whoso keeps his mouth and his tongue keeps his soul from troubles."

As we can see here, there are many scriptures that mention the tongue, our words, and whether our words are true and righteous or lies and cutting.

Years ago, a teenager, about seventeen, was brought to my house. Before he came, I had been phoned and told that the boy was thinking of killing himself. I prayed and asked the Holy Spirit to come and help me to minister to the boy. When he entered my house, the Holy Spirit said, "Ask him if anyone ever told him he was useless, worthless and would never amount to anything." I said to the boy, "Did any one ever tell you that you are useless, worthless, and would never amount to anything?" Immediately he began to cry and said, "My dad used to tell me that all the time from the time I was four years old." I TOLD HIM THAT GOD NEVER CREATES ANYONE TO BE USELESS, WORTHLESS, AND OF NO VALUE. Almighty God Loved Him and Wanted him. God Wanted Him to Have a Relationship with Jesus, Father God in Heaven, and Holy Spirit.

I showed him Psalm 139:13-18 from the King James Bible. King David said to the Lord, "For you have possessed my reins; you have covered me in my mother's womb. I will praise you; for I am fearfully and wonderfully made: marvelous are your works; and that my soul knows right well. My substance was not hid from you, when I was made in secret, and curiously wrought in the lowest parts of the earth. Your eyes did see my substance, yet being unperfect; and in your book all my members were written, which in continuance were fashioned, when as yet there were none of them. How precious also are your thoughts unto me, O God! How great is the sum of them! IF I should count them, they are more in number than the sand: when I awake, I am still with you."

We see from this scripture that God makes a plan for each person in His book and then forms the person in their mother's womb according to His Plan and His Purpose for their life. No one is an accident. No one is a nobody or useless or worthless. Jesus Bled and Died on the Cross For Us All. The Blood of Almighty God was paid for our sins so He could forgive us, save us, and redeem us back to Himself. He made the way for us to know him personally, and to become His sons and daughters.

Satan used this teenager's earthly dad to lie to him and wound him. Because he believed the lie, he almost took his own life. He had dropped out of school, was homeless, was living in doorways, and ready to kill himself; all over a lie that he believed about himself. The words of his dad wounded him and almost destroyed him. It was thirteen years later, but those hurtful, painful words that were spoken to him were still destroying his life.

I was able to share the truth with him and he received Jesus Christ into his heart as his Savior and Lord. He got a job with a cab company and has a family now.

This is just one example of how words can hurt worse than a knife. Lying words, false accusations, and half-truths; can ruin a person's life and future; if the person believes them.

This is why a person should get to know the Lord and realize that Jesus Christ (God) was willing to leave heaven , come to earth in human form, die on a cross to save you personally. Jesus Loves You. Jesus wants A Relationship With You , and You Are Valuable To God Himself. You are no accident. God Wanted you. If God Almighty Created You, Loves You Enough to Die For Your Sins So You Can Live In Heaven with Him Some Day, then you need to realize that you are special and important, no matter what any other human being says about you, or to you.

> Proverbs 14:1 "Every wise woman builds her house; but the foolish pluck it down with her hands." The Bible says with her hands. I also believe a foolish woman plucks her house down with her lips, her anger, her complaints, her nagging, her railing at her husband and children, her bad attitude, etc…

When we consider Solomon, the King, who had 300 wives and 700 concubines, we can learn many things. There were many fights, squabbles, arguments, contention, among all the women. Imagine competing with 999 other women for a chance to see your husband or sleep with him? It was horrible for those women. Some of them only slept with Solomon once in their entire life and were condemned to remain in his harem forever. Frankly, I would have refused his proposal and probably would have chosen death rather than to be 'one of his harem girls.' Solomon wrote the Book of Proverbs. Lets look at some of them written by Solomon.

> Proverb 21:9 "It is better to dwell in a corner of the housetop, than with a brawling woman in a wide house."

> Proverbs 21:19 "It is better to dwell in the wilderness, than with a contentious and an angry woman."

> Proverbs 25:24 It is better to dwell in the corner of the housetop, than with a brawling woman and in a wide house."

As we can see from these proverbs, Solomon did not have a peaceful existence with all his many wives and concubines. He wanted to live in the wilderness or hide on the roof to get away from angry, brawling, contentious women.

If you find yourself to be an angry, brawling, contentious woman, REPENT AND ASK THE LORD TO DELIVER YOU FROM THESE THINGS. YOU ARE CAUSING YOUR HUSBAND TO RUN AWAY FROM YOU. IF YOU HAVE CHILDREN, YOU ARE CAUSING THEM TO TRY TO GET AWAY FROM ALL OF THE FIGHTING, RAGE, ANGER, ARGUMENTS, AND STRIFE IN YOUR HOME. You are tearing down your husband, your children, and your marriage, and your family. Remember a wise woman builds her house, but a foolish woman plucks it down.

> Proverbs 15:1 "A soft answer turns away wrath but grievous words stir up anger." In my over 50 years of marriage, the Lord has given me wisdom in how a Christian woman should handle situations if your spouse and you disagree. Here are a few examples of how to wisely handle issues, God's Way.

Ephesians 5:22-24 "Wives, submit yourselves unto your own husband, as unto the Lord. For the husband is the head of the wife, even as Christ is the head of the church: and he is the savior of the body. Therefore as the church is subject unto Christ, so let the wives be to their own husbands in every thing."

My husband was sent to Florida for a few weeks on a business trip. We live in New York. When he returned from Florida he said, "I want to move to Florida. I like the boss in Florida better." At the time, I was a firm believer in Christ, but my husband was not saved, yet. He only had religion, but not a saving relationship with Jesus Himself.

I did not believe that it was the will of God for us to sell our house and move to Florida. But, I said, "You are my husband. I go where you go." I didn't say, "I refuse to go to Florida", or I'm Not Going To Florida And That's Final." Instead, I went into another room and said, "Lord, I don't believe that you want us to move to Florida. What am I to do about this?" I heard the Lord say, "Make a list of the things you need to consider, if you want to move to Florida, and show him the list." I sat down and composed a list of about 24 things that we needed to consider, and showed him the list. Houses were not selling here and if we didn't sell our home ; we would have no money to purchase a home down there. Our children were in Christian school. Where would they go to school there? Our widowed mothers were both here in the Northeast. How could we help them if we moved so far away? All our friends were here. WE knew no one in Florida. After Paul looked at the long list, he said, "I've changed my mind. I don't want to move to Florida." That was the peaceful end of that.

One day I was in our daughter's room praying with her. My Husband Paul did not know Jesus, in his heart, at that time. He came into the room and said, "The Kids Are Not Going To Church With You And That IS Final." I did not argue with him or answer him. Later, I prayed and took it before the Lord. I said, "Lord, my children are going to know you. IF I have to leave my husband in order for them to be saved and go to heaven, I will. Please change his mind and heart in this matter." The very next day, I drove to his job to pick up his paycheck to do errands. He came outside with me and said, "The kids can go to church with you." God changed his heart and his mind overnight, 180 degrees. IF I had screamed "These kids are going to church with me and you can't stop me," his heart would have been hardened and the Lord would have had to deal with me. Because I did things God's Way and held my tongue and took it before the Lord, the Lord worked on Paul and changed his heart and mind. Paul got saved in 1990.

A lot of times we pray, "God Change My Spouse", and it is our own attitudes that need to change first. If our attitudes and hearts are right, then God will work on our spouses.

> Ephesians 5:25-31 "Husbands, love your wives, even as Christ also loved the church, and gave himself for it: That he might sanctify and cleanse it with the washing of water by the word, That he might present it to himself a glorious church, not having spot, or wrinkle, or any such thing; but that it should be holy and with out blemish. So ought men to love their wives as their own bodies. He that loves his wife loves himself. For no man ever yet hated his own flesh; but nourishes and cherishes it, even as the Lord the church: For we are members of his body, of his flesh, and of his bones. For this cause shall a man leave his father and mother, and shall be joined unto his wife, and they two shall be one flesh."

> Proverbs 13:2-3 "A man shall eat good by the fruit of his mouth; but the soul of the transgressors shall eat violence. He that keeps his mouth keeps his life; but he that opens wide his lips shall have destruction."

We see that husbands are to love their wives, encourage their wives, cherish their wives, and appreciate their wives. Men need to show their wives that they appreciate them, and not take them for granted. Women do much work around the house, help raise the children, clean the house, do laundry, errands, etc…and some of them have jobs outside the home. For a husband to never say, "thank you for all you do. I appreciate you. I love you," to his wife; he is failing to encourage and build her up.

Sadly, many marriages fail because once a husband courts his wife and she becomes his wife, he forgets to romance her. He forgets to show her that he loves her with kind words of appreciation, hugs, kisses, holding hands, buying her a flower, taking her out to eat, and spending time with her alone. IF he refuses to speak good, loving, kind words to his wife, he makes her vulnerable to another male who will speak kind words, good words, encouraging words to lure his wife's affections and heart. Wake Up Men! Appreciate Your Wives And Tell Them You Love Them, More Often.

Many husbands and wives live for the children and forget to spend time alone with each other. Those children will go off to college, get married, and move away. Eventually the nest will be empty and all you will have left is the husband and wife. Many older couples end up divorced, once the children leave, because they have lost the love for each other that they once had. They have lost communication, lost what they had in common, lost each other in the business of raising the kids. Husbands and wives should set aside a date night where they go out together and enjoy each other. It is very important to stay close to your spouse. No matter how busy life gets, make sure you don't neglect your relationship with your spouse. Your spouse should come first. Then the children. It takes both of you and your love for each other to cause the children to feel loved, secure and valued in the home. Your children are learning how to relate to their future spouses by what they see their mom and dad do. Set a good example for your children to follow. They are watching you and learning from you.

STOP SPEAKING YOUR PROBLEM AND SPEAK GOD'S WORD INSTEAD

There have been many times that I have heard Christians speak in doubt and unbelief. There was a woman who said, "My husband ALWAYS gets a job and loses it." That poor man had fourteen different jobs and lost them all. He worked for a short time and was laid off, or the company went out of business, or closed it's local branch, or cut it's staff down and he was laid off. He couldn't seem to keep a job, because his wife had said that he ALWAYS would get a job and lose it. The devil was happy to bring her words to pass.

The same woman said, "Every winter, I Always Get The Flu." Every winter she got sick with the flu. Satan was happy to oblige her words and bring them to pass.

I would pray for another woman's business and finances. Right after I got done praying, she would say, "I'm ALWAYS struggling to make ends meet. I ALWAYS have a lack of funds." She should have said, "Thank You Jesus You Are Healing My Finances. You Are My Provider and I Thank You that You are Now Increasing My Business And I will have an abundance of funds to pay my bills and tithe." Her doubt and unbelief that God could increase her finances negated the prayers I had prayed for her.

> James 1:5-8 "If any of you lack wisdom, let him ask of God, that gives to all men liberally, and upbraids not; and it shall be given him, But let him ask in faith, nothing wavering. For he that wavers is like a wave of the sea driven with the wind and tossed. For let not that man think that he shall receive any thing of the Lord. A double minded man is unstable in all his ways."

Whatever we need, we must ask in faith believing we will have what we are asking for. If we are praying that we will be healed, we must believe we have received our healing and thank the Lord for it. IF we have doubt in our minds and hearts, we won't receive any thing. It is faith that moves God. Without faith it is impossible to please God. IF we are double minded, we will not receive any thing from God. Don't negate your prayers by speaking words of doubt and unbelief.

There was an 80 year old woman in Kenya who had fallen and broken her hip. I went to pray for her. First the Lord told me she had unforgiveness in her heart. She had to forgive her husband for leaving her and the children. Then she asked Jesus Christ to forgive her sins and come into her heart and life. Then, I prayed for the bones in her hip to be healed, in Jesus Name. I told her to say, "Thank You Jesus For Healing My Hip. No matter if you feel pain or not, command the pain to leave in Jesus Name and Confess Only Healing over your hip, in Jesus Name. Don't speak anything else." I left to preach in other towns. A few months later I went back to Kenya and asked about the woman. I was told that she was totally healed by the Lord and was outside planting her crops to feed her grandchildren. If she had said any words of doubt or unbelief, the devil would have robbed her of her healing. We must speak faith words.

Kathleen Hollop
THE POWER OF DECREES

Genesis 1:3 "And God said, Let there be light; and there was light."

Genesis 1:9 And God said, Let the waters under the heaven be gathered together unto one place, and let the dry land appear; and it was so."

Genesis 14 "And God said, Let there be lights in the firmament of heaven to divide the day from the night; and let them be for signs, and for seasons, and for days, and years; And let them be for lights in the firmament of the heavens to give light upon the earth: and it was so. And God made two great lights; the greater light to rule the day, and the lesser light to rule the night; he made the stars also. And God set them in the firmament of the heaven to give light upon the earth."

If we look at God speaking "Let There Be" and everything came into existence because God spoke it into existence. All God needed to do was speak His Words, and all creation heard and obeyed His Voice. He spoke things into existence when they didn't exist before. The believers, in Jesus Christ, also have His Authority and His Power to speak things into existence.

Job 22: 21-30 "Acquaint now yourself with him, and be at peace; thereby good shall come unto you. Receive, I pray you, the law from his mouth, and lay up his words in your heart. If you return to the Almighty, you shall be built up, you shall put away iniquity far from your tabernacle. Then shall you lay up gold as dust, and the gold of Ophir as the stones of the brooks. Yes, the Almighty shall be your defense, and you shall have plenty of silver. For then shall you have your delight in the Almighty, and shall lift up your face unto God. You shall make your prayer unto him, and he shall hear you, and you shall pay your vows. You shall also decree a thing, and it shall be established unto you; and the light shall shine upon your ways. When men are cast down then you shall say, There is a lifting up, and he shall save the humble person. He shall deliver the island of the innocent; and it is delivered by the pureness of your hands."

It was immediately after I preached Job 22:21-31, in a church in Butere, Kenya, that a woman was outside screaming, "My boy is dead. My Boy is dead." The Holy Spirit took over me and I went outside. I spoke over the boy, "You spirit of death leave this boy now, in Jesus Name. In Jesus Name, you will live and not die. You will fulfill all your days and they will not be shortened, in Jesus Name." With that, the dead boy's spirit came back into his body and he sat up alive and well. Because I walk close to the Lord and understand the Authority I have in Jesus Name and the Power I have in the Holy Spirit, I was able to speak life back into that dead boy and see him restored to health. If I had not been obeying the Lord, I could not have decreed life back into that boy. Because I try to live right with God, I seek Him every day, and He is my delight, He hears me. I have the power to decree a thing and it is established. There are benefits to living right and walking right with the Lord.

In my walk with my Jesus, I have decreed and commanded rain clouds to leave the area, and they obeyed me. I have commanded high winds to get out of my town and they left. I have spoken God's Word and have seen Him be true to his word to perform it.

> Psalm 119:160 "Thy word is true from the beginning; and every one of thy righteous judgments endures for ever."

> Jeremiah 29:10-11 "For thus says the Lord, That after seventy years be accomplished at Babylon I will visit you, and perform my good word toward you, in causing you to return to this place." If we read the Books of Daniel, Ezra, and Nehemiah we see that God kept His Word to Israel and caused them to return to Jerusalem to rebuild the city and the temple wall.

There are over 8,800 promises in the Bible, for believers in Jesus Christ. The promises are written in God's Word and God cannot lie. He is true to His Word to perform it. Even all of the promises in the Old Testament to God's people apply to us today.

If we speak God's Word and agree with the promises that He has given to us, He will perform them. The Old Testament Promises and the New Testament Promises are ours, if we speak them, believing that we have them. I BELIEVE I HAVE EVERYTHING GOD SAYS I HAVE. I SPEAK HIS PROMISES OVER MY LIFE, MY HEALTH, MY FINANCES, ETC…HE CANNOT LIE. WHAT HE HAS PROMISED , HE WILL DO.

When Jesus Christ was tempted of the devil in the wilderness, He answered Satan with the Word of God. Jesus said, "It is Written" and Quoted the Bible every time Satan tempted him. We must stand on the scriptures when we are tempted, face persecution for our faith, suffer illnesses, have problems, need a job, need help in times of trouble, etc… We Must Speak The Promises of God into our situations. Here are some examples of how to stand on the Word:

One day, a shirt got stuck in the back of my clothes drier. I reached into the hot drier and tried to free the shirt and severely burnt three of my fingers. The pain was intense. My skin turned red, blisters filled with fluid began rising up; I went to the sink and began running cold water over my fingers. The Holy Spirit reminded me of a scripture I had read in Isaiah. I didn't remember the exact chapter or verse, but I knew what the scripture said. I said, "It is written I will not be drowned and I shall not be burned; neither shall the flame kindle upon me. You burns leave my skin now, in Jesus Name. I stand on the Word of God that I WILL NOT BE BURNED. YOU BURNS HAVE TO GET OFF OF MY SKIN, THIS REDNESS AND BLISTERS MUST GO, THIS FLUID RISING UP MUST GO, I CANNOT BE BURNED, IN JESUS NAME. I COMMAND THESE FINGERS TO RETURN TO NORMAL IN JESUS NAME. AMEN." Immediately the fluid left and my fingers returned flat, the blisters and redness left, the pain left, and it was as if my fingers were never burned.

If I didn't know God's Promise, I would have spent my day at the emergency room being treated for severe burns on three fingers. Because I knew God's Promises and could stand on them and speak them over my body, I was completely healed and restored, instantly.

If I am under any attack by anyone or anything, I speak God's Promise of Isaiah 54:17 It is Written, "No weapon that is formed against me shall prosper; and every tongue that shall rise against me in judgment

I shall condemn. This is my heritage as a servant of the Lord, and my righteousness is of the Lord."

One night, while preaching in Kenya, I awoke in my hotel room; with someone growling and stomping around my bed. Holy Spirit told me it was Satan. I said, "Satan get out of this hotel room, in Jesus Name, and never come back." I got out of bed, turned on the light, saw that Satan was gone, and shut the light and went back to sleep.

> Luke 10: 19 Jesus said, "Behold, I give unto you power to tread on serpents and scorpions, and over all the power of the enemy, and nothing shall by any means hurt you." The Holy Ghost Power, I have, is greater than Satan, my enemy. He couldn't hurt me and I knew it. He has to bow before My Jesus. Every knee shall bow to My Jesus. I have power over all the power of the enemy. It is Written. So It Is.

READ GOD'S WORD. KNOW HIS PROMISES ARE FOR YOU, SPEAK HIS WORD AND HIS PROMISES OVER YOUR LIFE AND WALK IN VICTORY AND NOT DEFEAT, IN JESUS' NAME. AMEN. WATCH CAREFULLY WHAT YOU SPEAK INTO BEING. You are either releasing God's angels to help you by standing on God's Word and Promises; or you are releasing Satan's fallen angels to bring about the negative words that are coming out of your own mouth.

> Psalm 103: 30 "Bless the Lord, ye his angels, that excel in strength that do his commandments, hearkening unto the voice of his word." God's angels go into action when we speak God's Word. When we speak words of doubt, unbelief and negativity, we release the fallen angels and Satan to attack us, with our permission.

> Matthew 12:36-37 "But I say unto you, That every idle word that men shall speak, they shall give account thereof in the day of judgment. For by your words you shall be justified, and by your words you shall be condemned."

People who swear all the time will have a lot to answer for, in the day of judgment. There are seven things God hates in the Book of Proverbs

6:16-19. Three of these things are sins done with our mouths. "These six things does the Lord hate; yes, seven are an abomination unto him. A proud look, a lying tongue, and hands that shed innocent blood, A heart that devises wicked imaginations, feet that are swift in running to mischief, A false witness that speaks lies, and he that sows discord among brethren." A lying tongue, a false witness that speaks lies, and he that sows discord among brethren. Discord means strife, anger, causes trouble, sets people against each other, etc....

It is important to put yourself and your family members into the scriptures and believe they are for you, if you are a believer in Jesus Christ. I pray, "It is written no weapon formed against my husband, my Son Brian or myself shall prosper. No weapon formed against our health, our finances, our peace, our bodies, our souls, our spirits, our emotions, our feelings, our wills, our pets, our home, our vehicles or anything else pertaining to us will prosper, in Jesus Name. Father sent angels of protection around us continually and be with us today and every day, in Jesus Name. Amen." It is Vital that we speak the promises of God, out loud, into our situations.

> II Corinthians I: 18-20 "But as God is true, our word toward you was not yes and no. For the Son of God, Jesus Christ, who was preached among you by us, even by me and Silvanus and Timotheus, was not yes and no, but in Christ was yes. For all the promises of God in Christ are yes, and in him, Amen, unto the glory of God by us." The promises are for the believers today.

> 2 Peter 1: 1-4 "Simon Peter, a servant and an apostle of Jesus Christ, to them that have obtained like precious faith with us through the righteousness of God and our Savior Jesus Christ; Grace and peace be multiplied unto you through the knowledge of God, and of Jesus our Lord. According as his divine power has given unto us all things that pertain unto life and godliness, through the knowledge of him that has called us to glory and virtue: Whereby are given unto us exceeding great and precious promises that by these you might be partakers of the divine nature, having escaped the corruption that is in the world through lust." These promises are for us today. They are eternally ours through Jesus Christ.

WHEN YOU MAKE A PROMISE TO GOD/ A VOW/ PAY IT

> ECCLESIASTES 5: 4-6 "When you vow a vow unto God, defer not to pay it; for he has no pleasure in fools; pay that which you have vowed. Better it is that you should not vow, than that you should vow and not pay. Suffer not your mouth to cause your flesh to sin; neither say before the angel that it was an error; wherefore should God be angry at your voice, and destroy the work of your hands?"

Many Christians have made vows to God and have not kept them. They sing, "I Surrender All. I Surrender All. All to Thee My Blessed Savior, I Surrender All. Yet, they refuse to trust God with their finances, their children, their future, their emotions, their feelings, their own will, their own selfish wants and desires, and their own lives. They say, " I surrender all", but they refuse to do so; and have lied to God.

Many sing, "Here I Am, send me." If the Lord tried to send them to witness and share their faith with their neighbor; they wouldn't go. They have lied to God.

THREE OF THE SEVEN ABOMINATIONS ARE WITH THE TONGUE

There are seven things the Lord hates. Three of them involve using your words to sin and commit abominations.

> Proverbs 6:16-19 "These six things does the Lord hate; yes, seven are an abomination unto him. A proud look, a lying tongue, and hands that shed innocent blood, A heart that devises wicked imaginations, feet that be swift in running to mischief, A false witness that speaks lies, and he that sows discord among brethren."

Gossip is a Sin. IF someone tells you something about someone else, You should ask them if they have prayed for that person and that situation. You should refuse to tell anyone else the rumor, and make it a point to pray. IF you spread the rumor, you may be slandering that other person and causing them, their marriage, and their family to be destroyed. Even if what you heard is true, you are accountable to God to do the right thing. If they are in the church, you should tell the pastor and allow him or her to handle the situation. You should not spread the thing.

Years ago, a teenage girl lied about a man and accused him falsely of raping her. He lost his job, lost his marriage, lost his family, and it turned out the girl had lied. Nothing was done to the liar who ruined his life. Newspapers printed the lies against this man. People gossiped and spread the lies to his wife and children. Other people believed the lying teenager and sent her large sums of money, feeling sorry for her. She should have been jailed for what her lies cost this innocent man. She lied, was a false witness, and destroyed an innocent man. Don't let the devil use your mouth.

A person that deliberately tries to pit people against each other by in sighting strife, disagreements, and divisions is also doing an abomination, to the Lord.

> Proverbs 18: 6-8 "A fool's lips enter into contention, and his mouth calls for stokes. A fool's mouth is his destruction, and his lips are the snare of his soul. The words of a talebearer are as wounds, and they go down into the innermost parts of the belly."

THERE IS AN OLD SAYING THAT IS RELEVANT FOR US TO REMEMBER: IF YOU CAN'T SAY ANYTHING GOOD, ENCOURAGING, UPLIFTING, ETC… DON'T SAY ANYTHING AT ALL.

DON'T SIN WITH YOUR MOUTH BY MURMURING AND COMPLAINING

> Exodus 16: 6-8 "And Moses and Aaron said unto all the children of Israel, At evening, then you shall know that the Lord has brought you out from the land of Egypt; And in the morning then you shall see the glory of the Lord; for that he hears your murmurings against the Lord and what are we, that you murmur against us? And Moses said, This shall be, when the Lord shall give you in the evening flesh to eat, and in the morning bread to the full; for that the Lord hears your murmurings which you murmur against him: and what are we? Your murmurings are not against us, but against the Lord."

Because the children of Israel kept murmuring and complaining, they spent 40 years in the wilderness. IF they had controlled their tongues, and not murmured, they could have been in the promised land in a few short months. Because of their murmuring, they kept going around the mountain for 40 years. If we murmur and complain, we will continue to go through the same problems and troubles that we are complaining about. Stop complaining and murmuring and pray and ask the Lord to help you to learn what He is trying to show you; in the difficulty and in the problem. Once you understand, He will remove it. Praise Him even when it is difficult to Praise Him.

> Psalm 106: 21-27 "They forgot God their savior, which had done great things in Egypt; Wonderous works in the land of Ham, and terrible things by the Red Sea. Therefore he said that he would destroy them, had not Moses his chosen stood before him in the breach, to turn away his wrath, lest he should destroy them. Yes, they despised the pleasant land, they believed not his word: But murmured in their tents, and hearkened not unto the voice of the Lord." As a result, they wandered in the wilderness 40 years until the generation that murmured had died. They never saw the Promised Land. Only Joshua and Caleb were left of that generation. They led the younger generations into the Promised Land. Even Moses Himself saw it in the distance, from a mountaintop, but he did not enter into it.

> Philippians 2:14-15 "Do all things without murmurings and disputing; That you may be blameless and harmless, the sons of God, without rebuke, in the midst of a crooked and perverse nation, among whom you shine as lights in the world."

CHAPTER 13

DON'T BE A FOOLISH VIRGIN, BE SANCTIFIED AND READY

Matthew 25:1-8 "Then shall the kingdom of heaven be likened unto ten virgins, which took their lamps, and went forth to meet the bridegroom. And five of them were wise, and five were foolish. They that were foolish took their lamps, and took no oil with them: But the wise took oil in their vessels with their lamps. While the bride groom tarried; they all slumbered and slept. And at midnight there was a cry made,, Behold, the bridegroom comes; go out to meet him. And all those virgins arose, and trimmed their lamps. And the foolish said unto the wise, Give us of your oil; for our lamps are gone out."

These were not people in the world. These virgins were people in the churches are waiting. Only people in the churches are waiting for Jesus to return. Half of the Body of Christ was wise and half were foolish. The foolish ones were not shining as lights, in this world. Their lamps had gone out. They were no longer filled with the Holy Spirit's oil. They had no oil.

I Samuel 16: 13 "Then Samuel took the horn of oil, and anointed David in the midst of his brethren: and the Spirit of the Lord came upon David from that day forward." Oil is symbolic of God the Holy Spirit. If the foolish virgins had no oil, they did not have the Holy Spirit's Anointing. They were the fleshly, intellectual Christians.

Matthew 5:14-16 Jesus said, "You are the light of the world. A city that is set on a hill cannot be hid. Neither do men light a candle, and put it under a bushel, but on a candlestick; and it gives light unto all that are in the house. Let your light so shine before men, that they may see your good works, and glorify your Father which is in heaven."

The foolish virgins were in darkness, doing works of darkness, because they had no oil and their lamps had gone out. They were not shining as lights; in this dark world. They had compromised, had agreed with the evils of this world, and were not living lives that would glorify God. They refused to fear God and depart from evil.

Proverbs 24:20 "For there shall be no reward to the evil man; the candle of the wicked shall be put out."

I asked the Lord, "WHAT MADE THE WISE, WISE, AND WHAT MADE THE FOOLISH, FOOLISH?" Immediately he led me to Proverbs 1: 20-23 "Wisdom cries without; she utters her voice in the streets; She cries in the chief place of concourse, in the openings of the gates; in the city she utters her words saying, How long, you simple ones, will you love simplicity? And the scorners delight in their scorning, and fools hate knowledge? Turn you at my reproof, behold, I will pour out my Spirit unto you, I will make known my words unto you." God is pleading with these people. He had given them His Words and His Spirit, but they refused to read the Word, obey Him , and be filled with the Holy Spirit.

Proverbs 1:24-33 " Because I have called, and you have refused; I have stretched out my hand, and no man regards; But you have set at nought all my counsel, and would none of my reproof: I also will laugh at your calamity; I will mock when your fear comes; When your fear comes as desolation, and your destruction comes as a whirlwind; when distress and anguish comes upon you. Then shall they call upon me, but I will not answer; they shall seek me early, but they shall not find me: For that they hated knowledge, and did not choose the fear of the Lord. They would none of my counsel: they despised all my reproof, Therefore shall they eat of the fruit of their own way; and be filled with their own devices. For the turning away of the simple shall slay them, and the prosperity of fools shall destroy them. But whoso hearkens unto me shall dwell safely, and shall be quiet from fear of evil."

The Wise Virgins read the Word of God and allowed the Word of God to instruct, correct, and change them to be more like Jesus. The wise virgins had been filled with the Holy Spirit and obeyed Him; allowing Holy Spirit to convict them if they sinned and bring them speedily to repentance. The foolish virgins refused the Word of God and the Holy Spirit's Correction. They were not ready when Jesus Returned.

> Proverbs 15:31-32 "The ear that hears the reproof of life abides among the wise. He that refuses instruction despises his own soul; but he that hears reproof gets understanding. The fear of the Lord is the instruction of wisdom; and before honor is humility."
>
> II Timothy 3:16-17 "All scripture is given by inspiration of God, and is profitable for doctrine, for reproof, for correction, for instruction in righteousness: That the man of God may be perfect, thoroughly furnished unto all good works."

The foolish virgins didn't read the Bible. The foolish virgins continued to accept to believe in, and condone the lies of Hollywood, the media, and the world. They walked in darkness, did works of darkness, and had no light at all.

> Matthew 25:8-13 "And the foolish said unto the wise, Give us of your oil; for our lamps are gone out. But the wise answered, saying, No; lest there be not enough for us and you: but go rather to them that sell, and buy for yourselves. And while they went to buy, the bridegroom came; and they that were ready went in with him to the marriage: and the door was shut. Afterward came also the other virgins, saying Lord, Lord, open to us. But he answered and said, Verily I say unto you, I know you not. Watch therefore, for you know neither the day nor the hour wherein the Son of man comes." Don't Be A Foolish Virgin.

BE SANCTIFIED AND READY

> Ephesians 24:23-27 "Therefore as the church is subject unto Christ, so let the wives be to their own husbands in every thing. Husbands, love your wives, even as Christ also loved the church, and gave himself for it. That he might sanctify and cleanse it with the washing of water by the word. That he might present it to himself a glorious church, not having spot or wrinkle, or any such thing; but that it should be holy and without blemish."

Notice that the church is sanctified and cleansed by the Word of God so that it will be holy and without blemish. How many pastors, priests, and ministers have left the Word of God; and are preaching their vacations, current events, and worldly things? IS it no wonder that the sheep in the pews won't be ready when Christ returns?

> John 17:15-19 Jesus Prayed For Us: "I pray not that you should take them out of the world, but that you should keep them from the evil. They are not of the world, even as I am not of the world. Sanctify them through thy truth; thy word is truth. As you have sent me into the world, even so have I also sent them into the world. And for their sakes I sanctify myself that they also might be sanctified through the truth."

God's Word is Truth. IF we do not read the word of God, we will not be sanctified into the truth of God. We must read the Bible in order to be sanctified and cleansed and ready.

> Hebrews 10: 10-17 "We are sanctified through the offering of the body of Jesus Christ once for all. And every priest stands daily ministering and offering oftentimes the same sacrifices, which can never take away sins; But this man, after he had offered one sacrifice for sins for ever, sat down on the right hand of God; From henceforth expecting till his enemies be made his footstool. For by one offering he has perfected for ever them that are sanctified." Faith in the shed blood of Jesus Christ sanctifies us.

> *I Peter 1: 1-2 "Peter, an apostle of Jesus Christ, to the strangers scattered throughout Pontus, Galatia, Cappadocia, Asia, and*

Bithynia, Elect according to the fore-knowledge of God the Father, through sanctification of the Spirit, unto obedience and sprinkling of the blood of Jesus Christ: Grace unto you, and peace be multiplied."

Notice that they were sanctified by the Holy Spirit unto obedience to the word of God. They were also sanctified by the Blood of Jesus.

> John 16: 7-11 "Nevertheless I tell you the truth; It is expedient for you that I go away: for if I go not away, the Comforter will not come unto you; but if I depart; I will send him unto you. And when he is come, he will reprove the world of sin, and of righteousness, and of judgment."

It is God the Holy Ghost/Holy Spirit that corrects us by showing us when we need to repent of our sins. He brings us into obedience to the word of God.

> II Thessalonians 2:13-14 "But we are bound to give thanks always to God for you, brethren beloved of the Lord, because God has from the beginning chosen you to salvation through sanctification of the Spirit and belief of the truth. Whereunto he called you by our gospel, to the obtaining of the glory of our Lord Jesus Christ."

> I Corinthians 1:29-31 "That no flesh should glory in his presence. But of him are you in Christ Jesus, who of God is made unto us wisdom, and righteousness, and sanctification, and redemption: That, according as it is written, He that glories, let him glory in the Lord."

> I Corinthians 6: 9-20 "Know you not that the unrighteous shall not inherit the kingdom of God? Be not deceived: neither fornicators, nor idolaters, nor adulterers, nor effeminate, nor abusers of themselves with mankind, nor thieves, nor covetous, nor drunkards, nor revilers, nor extortioners, shall inherit the kingdom of God. And such were some of you: but you are washed, but you are sanctified, but you are justified in the name of the Lord Jesus, and by the Spirit of our God. All things are lawful unto me, but all things are not expedient: all things are lawful for me, but I will not be brought under the power of any. Meats for the belly, and the belly for meats; but God shall

destroy both it and them. NOW THE BODY IS NOT FOR FORNICATION, BUT FOR THE LORD; AND THE LORD FOR THE BODY. And God has both raised up the Lord, and will also raise us up by his own power. KNOW YOU NOT THAT YOUR BODIES ARE THE MEMBERS OF CHRIST? SHALL I THEN TAKE THE MEMBERS OF CHRIST, AND MAKE THEM THE MEMBERS OF A HARLOT? GOR FORBID. WHAT? KNOW YOU NOT THAT HE WHICH IS JOINED TO A HARLOT IS ONE BODY? FOR TWO, SAYS HE, SHALL BE ONE FLESH. BUT HE THAT IS JOINED UNTO THE LORD IS ONE SPIRIT. FLEE FORNICATION. EVERY SIN THAT A MAN DOES IS WITHOUT THE BODY; BUT HE THAT COMMITS FORNICATION SINS AGAINST HIS OWN BODY. WHAT? KNOW YOU NOT THAT YOUR BODY IS THE TEMPLE OF THE HOLY GHOST, WHICH IS IN YOU, WHICH YOU HAVE OF GOD, AND YOU ARE NOT YOUR OWN? For you are bought with a price; (the blood of Jesus) THEREFORE GLORIFY GOD IN YOUR BODY AND IN YOUR SPIRIT, WHICH ARE GOD'S."

The foolish virgins were not ready when Jesus Christ came. They refused to read their Bibles. They refused the correction, instruction, and wisdom of the Word of God. They refused to repent and put their sins out of their lives. They refused to fear God (Reverence Him As God), and obey Him. They refused to repent when God the Holy Spirit was showing them their sin. They grieved and wounded the Holy Spirit until He departed from them and they had no oil. They were involved with the world's darkness, lusts, corruption, and wickedness. They were not sanctified by God's Word and God's Spirit. Proverbs Chapter One calls them foolish. They were locked out of heaven. They were left behind.

Don't Be A Foolish Virgin. Let God's Word and His Spirit fully sanctify you to be ready when Jesus returns to take up those who are His. Put sexual sin out of your life. Stop IT Now; Before You Are Left Behind. Be Ready For The Bridegroom. He Will Come Quickly!

Kathleen Hollop

CHAPTER 14
BE A FAITHFUL PRIEST TO GOD

The Bible describes the work of Jesus Christ on planet earth. The same work Jesus did, is our work to carry out, here on earth. We are to be His people, His hands and His feet to do the works of Father God on earth. We are His Current Day Disciples.

> Isaiah 61:1-6 "The Spirit of the Lord God is upon me; because the Lord has anointed me to preach good tidings unto the meek; he has sent me to bind up the broken hearted, to proclaim liberty to the captives, and the opening of the prison to them that are bound; To proclaim the acceptable year of the Lord, and the day of vengeance of our God: to comfort all that mourn; To appoint unto them that mourn in Zion, to give unto them beauty for ashes, the oil of joy for mourning, the garment of praise for the spirit of heaviness; that they might be called trees of righteousness, the planting of the Lord, that he might be glorified. And they shall build the old wastes, they shall raise up the former desolations, and they shall repair the waste cities, the desolations of many generations. And strangers shall stand and feed your flocks, and the sons of the alien shall be your plowmen and your vinedressers. But you shall be named the Priests of the Lord; men shall call you the Ministers of our God: you shall eat the riches of the Gentiles, and in their glory shall you boast yourselves."

In Luke 4:18-21, Jesus quoted this Isaiah 61:1-6 scripture and told them "This day this scripture is fulfilled in your ears." This scripture is about Jesus. This scripture is about the believers in Jesus Christ today; who have the Word of God and the Spirit of God living inside them. We are to carry on the work of Jesus. We are to be Priests of the Lord and Ministers of God. We are to do these same works that Jesus did. We are to be current day disciples.

Matthew 22: 34-40 "But when the Pharisees had heard that he had put the Sadducees to silence, they were gathered together. Then one of them, which was a lawyer, asked him a question, tempting him, and saying, Master, which is the great commandment in the law? Jesus said unto him, Thou shall love the Lord your God with all your heart, and with all your soul, and with all your mind. This is the first and great commandment. And the second is like unto it, Thou shall love thy neighbor as thyself. On these two commandments hang all the law and the prophets."

HOW MANY CHRISTIANS REALLY LOVE THE LORD THEIR GOD WITH ALL THEIR HEART, AND WITH ALL THEIR SOUL AND WITH ALL THEIR MIND? Very few really love Him and put Him first. One day I prayed, "Father God, I don't know how to love you with my whole being. Put that kind of love into me that I would love you the way you deserve to be loved, in Jesus Name. Amen!

Father God, help me to love my neighbor as myself. I don't know how to do that, but I want to obey you. Put that kind of love in me for my neighbor, in Jesus Name. Amen! IF you love your neighbor, you don't lie against them, slander them, steal from them, covet what they have, lust after their husband or wife, etc… You want to bless, encourage, and help your neighbor.

Matthew 10: 37-39 Jesus said, "He that loves father or mother more than me is not worthy of me; and he that loves son or daughter more than me is not worthy of me. And he that takes not his cross, and follows after me, is not worthy of me. He that finds his life shall lose it: and he that loses his life for my sake shall find it. He that receives you receives me, and he that receives me receives him that sent me." JESUS MUST BE NUMBER ONE IN OUR HEARTS AND LIVES. WE MUST LET JESUS LEAD US, BY HIS HOLY SPIRIT, INTO FATHER GOD'S WILL AND PURPOSE FOR OUR LIVES.

Mark 8: 34-38 Jesus said, "Whosoever will come after me, let him deny himself and take up his cross, and follow me. For whosoever will save his life shall lose it; but whosoever shall lose his life for my sake and the gospel's, the same shall save it. For what shall it profit a man, if he shall gain the whole world, and lose his own soul? OR what shall a man give in exchange for his soul? Whosoever therefore shall be ashamed of me and of my words in this adulterous and sinful generation; of him also shall the Son of man be ashamed, when he comes in the glory of his Father with the holy angels."

Galatians 2:20-21 The disciple Paul said, "I am crucified with Christ, nevertheless I live; yet not I, but Christ lives in me. And the life which I now live in the flesh I live by the faith of the Son of God, who loved me, and gave himself for me. I do not frustrate the grace of God: for if righteousness come by the law, then Christ is dead in vain."

PAUL WAS SAYING THAT HE WAS DEAD TO HIMSELF, HIS OWN PLANS, HIS OWN AGENDAS, HIS OWN WILL, HIS OWN PURPOSES AND THAT JESUS CHRIST WAS ALIVE IN HIM DOING THE FATHER'S WILL PLAN AND PURPOSE. HE WAS SAYING THAT HIS LIFE AND EVERY AREA OF HIS LIFE BELONGED TO JESUS CHRIST, NOT HIMSELF. HE HAD SURRENDERED HIS ENTIRE LIFE AND FUTURE TO JESUS CHRIST AND THE WILL OF FATHER GOD.

Revelation 12: 7-11 "And there was war in heaven: Michael and his angels fought against the dragon, and the dragon fought and his angels, And prevailed not, neither was their place found any more in heaven. And the great dragon was cast out, that old serpent, called the devil, and Satan, which deceives the whole world: he was cast out into the earth, and his angels were cast out with him. And I heard a loud voice saying in heaven, Now is come salvation, and strength, and the kingdom of our God, and the power of his Christ; for the accuser of our brethren is cast down, which accused them before our God day and night. AND THEY OVERCAME HIM BY THE BLOOD OF THE LAMB, AND BY THE WORD OF THEIR TESTIMONY; AND THEY LOVED NOT THEIR LIVES UNTO THE DEATH."

I hear many Christian say, "We overcame the devil by the blood of the Lamb and the word of our testimony, BUT THEY FORGET THE THIRD THING-THEY LOVED NOT THEIR LIVES UNTO THE DEATH. They had surrendered their entire lives to the Lordship of Jesus Christ. They were dead to themselves, their own agendas, their own plans, etc…and had given their entire life and will over to Jesus and Father's Will. God created us to do His Will, not our own will.

Jesus Surrendered His Own Will To Do The Father's Will. Matthew 26:39 Jesus said, "O my Father, if it be possible, let this cup pass from me; nevertheless not as I will, but as you will."

Mark 14:36 Jesus said, "Abba, Father, all things are possible unto you; take away this cup from me: nevertheless not what I will, but what you will."

Luke 22: 42-45 Jesus said, "Father, if you be willing, remove this cup from me: nevertheless not my will, but thine, be done. And there appeared an angel unto him from heaven, strengthening him. And being in an agony he prayed more earnestly: and his sweat was as it were great drops of blood falling down to the ground. And when he rose up from prayer, and was come to his disciples, he found them sleeping for sorrow."

I received Jesus Christ as my personal Savior and Lord in 1984. In 1996, while on a CBN TOUR of Israel, I had an encounter with God. I was in the Church of The Nations with the CBN Tour Group. My Son Brian was also on the tour. Inside the Church of The Nations, there was a large, flat, rock that was roped off by ropes; on the floor of the Church. The Holy Spirit led me to go under the ropes and touch that rock. Immediately, I was convicted that I did not know Father God's Will for my life. I was convicted that I had not surrendered my entire life to

Jesus Christ as the Lord of my life. Yes, Jesus was my Savior for twelve years, but He was not the one leading my life; I was. I began weeping in the Lord's Presence and Repenting of living for myself, and not for Him. I surrendered me. I surrendered my body, my soul, my mind, my spirit, my family, my finances, my will and my life, fully to Jesus Christ. I said to my Father in Heaven, "Father I give you everything. Not My Will, Your Will BE Done. This Life is Yours. Use IT To Your Glory."

After I surrendered my own plans and my entire life, I began having dreams. I saw myself standing on platforms preaching Jesus to millions of people. The dreams were so real that I knew the Lord's Will was for me to Preach and Teach His Word.

I got a phone call from TBN. They wanted me to answer prayer calls and pray with people. I said, "I must pray about this and see if this is what the Lord has for me. I also got a phone call from the Crisis Pregnancy Center offering to train me to be a counselor. I said, "Let me pray about this and see if this is what the Lord has for me." When I prayed, the Lord said, "No," to both things. While these things were Godly things, they were not His Will for me. There were other people He had chosen to do those things. His plan for my life was different.

The next day, I saw Marilyn Hickey on television looking for people to go with her ministry to China, Hong Kong, and the Philippines, as part of her prayer team. When I prayed and asked the Lord if He wanted me to go, HE said, "Yes." That was in 1996. In 1997, the Lord sent me again with Marilyn's Ministry to Mombasa, Kenya, Comoros, Zanzibar and Madagascar. While in Kenya, doing a street outreach, the Lord had me give my contact information to a member of Jesus Celebration Center Church and take their contact information. Before I got on the plane to come home from Kenya, the Lord said, "I am sending you back here." After many confirmations from the Lord through prophets, through His Word, and by His Spirit, I wired funds to my contact to set up crusades in Kenya, got on a plane and preached at crusades, etc…when I had never preached before in my life. The Lord opened doors for me to do crusades, revival meetings, preach in many churches, camp meetings, do Pastors Seminars for Kenya City Mission Churches, officiate at Pastor's Ordination Ceremonies, Preach on Jesus is Lord Radio, Nakuru, Kenya, Preach on Sayre, Voice of Mercy Radio and Television out of Eldoret, Kenya, Preach on local Cablevision here in N.Y. etc…Through radio and T.V. I could have reached many millions of people. Through radio the possibility was 11 million people. Through T.V., the possibility was 3.3 million people. ALL THESE THINGS HAPPENED AFTER I SURRENDERED MY WILL AND MY LIFE FULLY TO JESUS CHRIST AS LORD OF MY LIFE.

Any areas, of your life, that you refuse to trust Jesus with; are under the control of self and Satan. You will never have Victory in these areas until Jesus Christ is Lord over them. If you surrender your will and entire life to Jesus, there will be no place for self and Satan to be on the throne of your heart or life. You will have the VICTORY IN JESUS THAT YOU ARE SUPPOSED TO WALK IN.

> John 8:12 Jesus said, "I am the light of the world: he that follows me shall not walk in darkness, but shall have the light of life."

> Matthew 5:14-16 Jesus said to the disciples, "You are the light of the world. A city that is set on a hill cannot be hid. Neither do men light a candle, and put it under a bushel but on a candlestick; and it gives light unto all that are in the house. Let your light so shine before men, that they may see your good works, and glorify your Father which is in heaven."

As Jesus was the Light of the world, we are called to be lights. We are called to reach others, for Jesus, so that they will have the light of life and not stumble in darkness and be destroyed by Satan.

> Mark 16:15-20 (King James Bible) Jesus gave the Body of Christ a Great Commission. He said, "Go ye into all the world, and preach the gospel to every creature. He that believes and is baptized shall be saved; but he that believes not shall be damned. And these signs shall follow them that believe: In my name they shall cast out devils; they shall speak with new tongues; They shall take up serpents; and if they drink any deadly thing, it shall not hurt them, they shall lay hands on the sick, and they shall recover." WE, AS THE BODY OF CHRIST, SHOULD BE DOING THESE THINGS. IF WE ARE NOT, WE ARE REFUSING TO OBEY JESUS CHRIST AND HIS COMMISSION TO US AS BELIEVERS IN HIM.

We are not to play with poisonous snakes or drink poison to put the Lord to the test. There have been believers, on mission fields, who were bitten by snakes and suffered no harm. There have been others who were given poisonous food to eat and suffered no harm. Still others accidentally took wrong medication and pled this scripture over the situation and suffered no harm.

> Matthew 28: 18-20 Jesus Gave Us Another Great Commission. Jesus said, "All power is given unto me in heaven and in earth. Go ye, therefore, and teach all nations, baptizing them in the name of the Father, and of the Son, and of the Holy Ghost: Teaching them to observe all things whatsoever I have commanded you: and, Lo, I am with you always, even unto the end of the world. Amen."

Back in the 1970's and 1980's there was a Holy Ghost move of God. Many youth received Jesus Christ as their Savior and Lord. Our youth came to Jesus Christ and received Him into their hearts and lives, BUT THEIR MINDS WERE NOT RENEWED BY THE WORD OF GOD. WE FAILED TO TEACH THEM ALL THINGS JESUS CHRIST COMMANDED US. AS A RESULT, WE HAD SAVED YOUTH, BUT NOT DISCIPLED YOUTH. THEIR MINDS WERE NOT RENEWED BY THE WORD OF GOD AND THE TEACHINGS OF JESUS CHRIST. AS A RESULT, OUR SOCIETY WAS TAKEN OVER BY SECULAR HUMANISM, COMMUNISM, SOCIALISM, MARXISM, FALSE GOD WORSHIP, EVIL IDEALOGIES, AND DEMONIC FALSE GODS...THESE THINGS GOT INTO OUR GOVERNMENT, OUR SCHOOLS, OUR COLLEGES, AND CONTINUED TO FUNCTION IN THE SAVED YOUTH'S MINDS. THIS IS WHY PEOPLE CLAIMING TO BE CHRISTIAN CAN CONDONE ABORTION, GAYNESS, FORNICATION, PORNOGRAPHY, LUSTS, PERVERSIONS, ETC...WE CANNOT AFFORD TO MAKE THE SAME MISTAKE AGAIN. AS THE LORD SENDS US A GREAT AWAKENING, WE MUST DISCIPLE THE BELIEVERS IN THE TEACHINGS OF JESUS CHRIST SO WE WON'T LOSE ANOTHER GENERATION TO WORLDLY LUSTS, VAIN PHILOSOPHIES, HOLLYWOOD, AND CRAZINESS. WE MUST TEACH THE YOUTH OF AMERICA

THE WORD OF GOD AND NOT ALLOW WICKED PEOPLE TO INDOCTRINATE THEM INTO THE FILTH, GREED, AND LUST OF THIS WICKED WORLD. THEIR MINDS NEED TO BE RENEWED.

> Revelation 1: 4-6 "John to the seven churches which are in Asia; Grace be unto you, and peace, from him which is, and which was, and which is to come; and from the seven Spirits which are before his throne; And from Jesus Christ, who is the faithful witness, and the first begotten of the dead, and the prince of the kings of the earth. Unto him that loved us, and washed us from our sins in his own blood. And has made us kings and priests unto God and his Father; to him be glory and dominion for ever and ever. Amen."

We see here that Jesus has washed our sins in His Own Blood and has made us to be kings and priests to Father God. We must be faithful in the calling. Being a king and priest to God, is a holy calling.

> Hosea 4: 6-12 "My people are destroyed for lack of knowledge. I will also reject thee, that you shall be no priest to me; seeing you has forgotten the law of your God, I will also forget your children.. As they were increased, so they sinned against me; there -fore, will I change their glory into shame. They eat up the sin of my people, and they set their heart on their iniquity. And there shall be, like people, like priest and I will punish them for their ways, and reward them their doings. For they shall eat, and not have enough: they shall commit whoredom, and shall not increase: because they have left off to take heed to the Lord. Whoredom and wine and new wine take away the heart. My people ask counsel at their stocks, and their staff declares unto them: for the spirit of whoredoms has caused them to err, and they have gone a whoring from under their God."

God's people are being destroyed because they are worshipping other gods. They have left God, God's Commandments, and God's Presence to walk in sins, iniquities, and wickedness. How many Christians read horoscopes, tarot cards, have Harry Potter movies, books, witchcraft objects, seances, and are living lives contrary to God and His Word? This scripture is not talking about Satan's people. It is talking about God's people that have forsaken Him and are following other gods; committing whoredom in His sight. God tells them that they will be no priest to God. Since they have rejected Him and followed other gods, He will not let them be a priest of His, in heaven. These are the foolish virgins living lives of darkness-not shining with Christ's light.

> II Corinthians 5: 8-11 "We are confident, I say, and willing rather to be absent from the body, and to be present with the Lord. Wherefore we labor, that, whether present or absent, we may be accepted of him. For we must all appear before the judgment seat of Christ; that every one may receive the things done in his body, according to that he has done, whether it be good or bad. Knowing therefore the terror of the Lord, we persuade men; but we are made manifest unto God; and I trust also are made manifest in your consciences."

Believers in Christ; will all appear before the judgment seat of Christ and our works will be looked at.

> I Corinthians 3: 9-17 "For we are laborers together with God; you are God's husbandry, you are God's building. According to the grace of God which is given unto me, as a wise master builder, I have laid the foundation, and another builds thereon. But let every man take heed how he builds thereupon. For other foundation can no man lay than that is laid, which is Jesus Christ. Now if any man build upon this foundation gold, silver, precious stones, wood, hay, stubble; Every man's work shall be made manifest; for the day shall declare it, because it shall be revealed by fire; and the fire shall try every man's work of what sort it is. If any man's work abide which he has built thereupon, he shall receive a reward. IF any man's work shall be burned, he shall suffer loss: but he himself shall be saved, yet so as by fire. Know ye not that you are the temple of God, and that the Spirit of God dwells in you? Let no man defile the temple of God, him shall God destroy; for the temple of God is holy, which temple you are."

Church God's Way

As believers in Christ, our works (since we received Jesus Christ as our Savior and Lord), will be tried in the fire. If we waste our time doing all kinds of things that God has not called us to do, we will have wood, hay and stubble that will burn up. IF we press into God, get filled with the Holy Spirit, be led by the Holy Spirit into Father God's Will, we will have the works that will be of gold, silver, and precious stones that will stand the test of fire. I want my life to advance the Kingdom of God on planet earth. I want to hear Jesus say, "Well done my good and faithful servant." The believers will receive rewards for their works; that do stand the test of fire. Some people's works will all burn up. They will be saved; but have nothing to show for their lives. They will have no crown to cast at Jesus's feet.

Other believers will escape hell and the lake of fire, but they will be locked outside of heaven's gate for all eternity. Is there scripture to confirm this? Yes, there is.

> Revelation 20: 10-15 "And the devil that deceived them was cast into the lake of fire and brimstone, where the beast and the false prophet are, and shall be tormented day and night for ever and ever. And I saw a great white throne, and him that sat on it, from whose face the earth and the heaven fled away; and there was found no place for them. And I saw the dead, small and great stand before God; and the books were opened: and another book was opened, which is the book of life: and the dead were judged out of those things which were written in the books, according to their works. And the sea gave up the dead which were in it; and death and hell delivered up the dead which were in them: and they were judged every man according to their works. And death and hell were cast into the lake of fire. This is the second death. AND WHOSOEVER WAS NOT FOUND WRITTEN IN THE BOOK OF LIFE WAS CAST INTO THE LAKE OF FIRE." This is the fate of all the unbelievers. Every one who rejected Jesus Christ is judged and cast into the lake of fire.

> Revelation Chapter 21 and Chapter 22 describe the new heaven and new earth. The holy city, new Jerusalem, comes

down from God out of heaven. And God shall wipe away all tears from their eyes; and there shall be no more death, neither sorrow, nor crying, neither shall there be any more pain; for the former things are passed away.

Revelation 21:7-8 "He that overcomes shall inherit all things; and I will be his God, and he shall be my son. But the fearful, and unbelieving, and the abominable, and murders, and whoremongers, and sorcerers, and idolaters, and all liars, shall have their part in the lake which burns with fire and brimstone: which is the second death." These were the ones who died in their sins; the unsaved.

Revelation 22:14-15 "Blessed are they that do his commandments, that they may have the right to the tree of life; and may enter in through the gates into the city. For without (outside) are dogs, and sorcerers, and whoremongers, and murderers, and idolaters, and whosoever loves and makes a lie."

WAIT A MINUTE! THE UNSAVED PEOPLE WERE CAST INTO THE LAKE OF FIRE IN REVELATION 20: 14-15. WHO ARE THESE WICKED PEOPLE WHO ARE LOCKED OUTSIDE THE GATES OF HEAVEN FOR ALL ETERNITY AND CANNOT ENTER IN? THESE ARE THE DISOBEDIENT, REBELLIOUS CHRISTIANS, THE FOOLISH VIRGINS, WHO DID NOT PUT THE SINS OUT OF THEIR LIVES AND OBEY GOD'S COMMANDMENTS AND HOLY SPIRIT. THEY REFUSED GOD'S WORD, GOD'S INSTRUCION, GOD'S CORRECTION, GOD'S REPROOF, GOD'S HOLINESS, GOD'S HOLY SPIRIT, GOD'S COMMANDMENTS, AND GOD HIMSELF. As a result they spent eternity locked outside of the New Jerusalem, unable to ever enter in.

John 14: 21 Jesus said, "He that has my commandments, and keeps them, he it is that loves me: and he the loves me shall be loved of my Father, and I will love him, and will manifest myself to him."

John 14:23-24 Jesus said, "If a man love me, he will keep my words; and my Father will love him, and we will come unto him, and make our abode with him. He that loves me not keeps not my sayings: and the word which you hear is not mine, but the Father's which sent me."

How Much Do You Love Jesus? Do you love Him enough to repent and put the sin out of your life? Do you love Him enough to read the Bible and live it? Do you love Him enough to obey His Commandments? Do you love Him enough to surrender your entire life to Him and live a life that will honor Him? Do you love Him enough to be led by the Holy Ghost/Holy Spirit; into Father's Will for your life? Are You a REAL CHRISTIAN, or a FAKE CHRISTIAN? Whether you will enter into the New Jerusalem or spend eternity locked outside of the gate is up to you.

DON'T BE AN UNFAITHFUL PRIEST OR A FOOLISH VIRGIN. HEAR THE LORD SAY "WELL DONE, MY GOOD AND FAITHFUL SERVANT."

CHAPTER 15

YOU ARE IN THE ARMY OF THE LORD. STAND AND FIGHT.

> II Corinthians 10: 3-5 "For though we walk in the flesh, we do not war after the flesh: (For the weapons of our warfare are not carnal, but mighty through God to the pulling down of strongholds;) casting down imaginations, and every thought that exalts itself against the knowledge of God, and bringing into captivity every thought to the obedience of Christ;"

Every sin that tempts us, begins in our minds, as a thought. If we entertain wicked thoughts and vain imaginations; we will eventually do what we are thinking about. The devil will bring about the chance to do it. We must refuse any thought that is not lined up with the word of God, rebuke it, and command it to leave, in Jesus Name. If it comes back, rebuke it again, and again. Eventually, when Satan sees that you are not entertaining it or giving it any place, the thought will go away.

> James 4: 7-8 "Submit yourselves therefore to God. Resist the devil, and he will flee from you. Draw nigh to God, and he will draw nigh to you. Cleanse your hands, you sinners; and purify your hearts, you double minded. Be afflicted, and mourn, and weep; let your laughter be turned to mourning, and your joy to heaviness. Humble yourselves in the sight of the Lord, and he shall lift you up."

Notice, we are NOT TOLD to place ourselves in a sinful situation to resist the sin. We are told to resist the devil and he will flee from us. A recovering alcoholic should not be hanging around bars. A person who was delivered from sexual addictions should not be watching pornography, hanging out in adult bookstores, or subscribing to lustful T.V. stations. We are to resist the devil himself and not put ourselves in compromising situations.

We are to draw near to God by reading the Bible, praying, seeking more of God's Holy Spirit, God's direction for our lives, and repenting when we realize we have sinned. IF we confess our sins to God, He is faithful and just to forgive us our sins, and to cleanse us from all unrighteousness.(1 John 1:9).

> I Peter 5: 9-10 "Be sober, be vigilant; because your adversary the devil, as a roaring lion, walks about, seeking whom he may devour; Whom resist steadfast in the faith, knowing that the same afflictions are accomplished in your brethren that are in the world. But the God of all grace, who has called us unto his eternal glory by Christ Jesus, after that you have suffered a while, make you perfect, stablish, strengthen, settle you."

The devil walks around looking for who he may devour. If you are a believer in Christ, the devil wants to destroy you, your marriage, your family, your friends, your witness for Christ, Your Christian walk, your reputation, your credibility, etc…Resist Him. Don't Open Any Doors To Him.

The devil wants you to be addicted to alcohol, drugs, sex, lust, perversions, lies, deceptions, false ideologies, violence, hatred, and all types of sin, iniquity and wickedness. He will put other people, in your path, to try to tempt you to sin in whatever area you are weak.

My cousin had been addicted to alcohol and drugs. He turned to Jesus, was attending a Salvation Army Church, and walking with the Lord. Then, Satan brought an old friend, who was addicted, over to talk to my cousin. My cousin went with him. He gave my cousin drugs, my cousin took them, and was found dead behind a bush after three days. The mistake my cousin made was going with an old friend. He was tempted more than he could endure and ended up destroying his life, on earth.

People make the mistake of thinking they can go back into the area that God has delivered them from; and reach others there, for the Lord.

Unless the Lord Speaks to them and directs them to try to reach their old friends, they need to avoid them. They can pray the Lord sends someone else to them, but they need to avoid the temptation, their old friends, and their old life style. They are to be that new creature in Christ by putting away the old person they used to be. Find new friends that love the Lord, read the Word, Pray, and will help you to grow in your faith, in Christ Jesus. If there is a Real, Christian Church that preaches a relationship with Jesus Christ, the Baptism of the Holy Spirit, and allows the gifts of God the Holy Ghost to flow, begin attending Church. If there is none in your area, find a real Pastor on T.V. who preaches the Word of God, in truth, and listen to him. Refuse anyone who doesn't line up with the Word of God. Read the Bible yourself and allow the Holy Spirit to teach you the Word. Compare what any priest, preacher, minister, reverend, pope, or elder or deacon says with the Word of God. If they preach contrary to the Word of God, they are a false preacher. Don't listen to them. Find someone else.

> Hebrews 10:21-23 "And having a high priest over the house of God (Jesus); Let us draw near with a true heart in full assurance of faith, having our hearts sprinkled from an evil conscience, and our bodies washed with pure water. Let us hold fast the profession of our faith with out wavering; for he is faithful that promised."

> I Timothy 1: 18-20 "This charge I commit unto you, son Timothy, according to the prophecies which went on you before, that you by them might war a good warfare; Holding faith, and a good conscience, which some having put away concerning faith have made shipwreck. Of whom is Hymenaeus and Alexander; whom I have delivered unto Satan, that they may learn not to blaspheme."

> Timothy was told to stand on the prophecies that were spoken over his life. He needed to proclaim them, believe for them, and pray for them to come to pass. He was told to continue to have faith and a good conscience toward God.

> Habakkuk 2: 1-3 "I will stand upon my watch, and set me upon the tower, and will watch to see what he will say unto

> me, and what I shall answer when I am reproved. And the Lord answered me, and said, Write the vision, and make it plain upon tables, that he may run that reads it. For the vision is yet for an appointed time, but t the end it shall speak, and not lie: though it tarry, wait for it; because it will surely come, it will not tarry."

IT is very important that when the Lord speaks something to you, you write it down and put the date that he said it to you. Keep a log book of any scriptures the Lord personally speaks to you, everything the Lord says to you, and any dreams or visions that you know are from the Lord. Put the date on it so you will know when the Lord said it to you. Through the years, I have written many log book pages of scriptures and things the Lord has spoken to me as well as the prophecies that I know came from genuine prophets of God concerning me and my life. In times of discouragement, persecution, betrayal, or disappointment, I re-read these prophecies, these Words from the Lord to me, and the scriptures that I know are Mine to claim. They encourage me greatly and give me strength to go on. I pray into what the Lord has spoken to me and ask Him to bring it to pass, in Jesus' Name.

> II Timothy 2: 1-5 "You therefore, my son, be strong in the grace that is in Christ Jesus. And the things that you have heard of me among many witnesses, the same commit to faithful men, who shall be able to teach others also. You therefore endure hardness, as a good soldier of Jesus Christ. No man that wars entangles himself with the affairs of this life; that he may please him who has chosen him to be a soldier. And if a man also strive for masteries, yet is he not crowned, except he strive lawfully."

Timothy was told to impart to faithful people the things he was taught; so they could in turn teach others. He was also told to endure whatever persecution or trouble that came his way as a good soldier of Jesus Christ.

> II Corinthians 11:21-28 The Disciple Paul said, "I speak as concerning reproach, as though we had been weak. Howbeit wherein so ever any is bold, I am bold also. Are they Hebrews? So am I. Are they Israelites? So am I. Are they the

seed of Abraham? So am I. Are they ministers of Christ? I am more; in labors more abundant, in stripes above measure, in prisons more frequent, in deaths often, Of the Jews five times I received forty stripes save one. Thrice was I beaten with rods, once was I stoned, thrice I suffered shipwreck, a night and a day I have been in the deep; In journeyings often, in perils of waters, in in perils of robbers, in perils by my own countrymen, in perils by the heathen, in perils in the city, in perils in the wilderness, in perils in the sea, in perils among false brethren. In weariness and painfulness, in watching often, in hunger and thirst, in fasting often, in cold and nakedness. Beside those things that are without, that which comes upon me daily, the care of the churches."

As we can see here, the disciples and Apostles of Jesus Christ suffered much persecution, for His Name Sake. How Much Are You Willing To Suffer For The Cause of Christ? Are you willing to go on mission trips to places with no electricity, no running water, no indoor plumbing, no creature comforts, severe heat of the deserts, the cold of the mountain tops, the change of culture, weather, food, and everything you are familiar with to follow Jesus? Are you willing to trust the Lord and walk with Him to places you have never been? Are you willing to trust Him with everything that happens in your life? Only you know the answer to these questions.

Not everyone is called to go on mission trips. Some are called to fight for truth in our Congress and Senate. Others are called to fight for Jesus in our school systems, in our businesses, in the public arena, at a job, or in a store. Others are called to be salt and light in the sports teams and stadiums, or in the health care industry, or on the social media platforms. Wherever the Lord has placed you, you need to be faithful to Jesus Christ above all.

II Timothy 1:7 "For God has not given us the spirit of fear, but of power, love and of a sound mind." Fear is a demonic spirit. It doesn't come from God. It is one of the tools the enemy uses to stop us from obeying God. Here is an example from my own life: One day the Lord spoke to me and told me to take a Bible to the post office and give it to whom he would show me. I took a Bible and drove to the post office. I went in and heard nothing more. I came outside and got into my car. I asked, "Lord, who am I supposed to give this Bible to?" Immediately a car pulled up alongside my car. A woman got out and went into the post office. A man was sitting at the drivers seat. The Lord said, "Give the Bible to that man." Immediately the devil began saying, "What if the man won't take the Bible? What if he gets angry at you when you knock on his window? What if he screams at you? I had a choice of obeying God, or listening to the "What IF'S of Satan. I went outside and knocked at his car window. He rolled down the window. I said, "Good morning sir. The Lord told me to give you this." He said, "Oh, a Bible. I'll Read It. I said, "Have a Great Day," and drove off.

When The Lord Jesus called me to go to Kenya, with Him, to do crusades; the devil said, "What if the people are not at the airport when you get off the plane in Kenya? What if you get on the crusade platform and get tongue tied and can't speak? What if this and what if that. I Said, "Shut up Satan. I can do all things through Jesus Christ who strengthens me." I had to completely trust the Lord with everything. He moved mightily and didn't let me down. He directed me through twenty three trips to Africa, six weeks at a time. He gave me the messages to preach and teach His People. He gave me the Salvation Messages for the lost souls. He saved, delivered and healed people in the Churches and in the marketplaces.

If I had let fear of man, fear of airplane travel, fear of diseases, fear of witch doctors, fear of robbers, fear of tribal hatreds, fear of failure, fear of death, or any other fear get any hold on me, I would not have been able to go and obey God. Fear is Our Enemy.

> Matthew 10:28 Jesus said, "And fear not them which kill the body, but are not able to kill the soul; but rather fear him which is able to destroy both soul and body in hell." People would say to me aren't you afraid to go to Africa? Aren't you afraid to travel all those hours by plane? Aren't you afraid of the diseases, the robbers, the poisonous snakes, the crocodiles, the devil worshippers, the witches, the road accidents? I said, "No! Death has no meaning for me. I

know I have eternal life through Jesus Christ. The most that anyone can do to me is kill me, and I will be with My Jesus Forever. We are not to fear people. We are to fear God; Reverence Him as God, and depart from evil.

Ephesians 6: 12 "For we wrestle not against flesh and blood, but against principalities, against powers, against the rulers of the darkness of this world, against spiritual wickedness in high places." THIS IS THE KEY TO SPIRITUAL WARFARE AND THE SAFETY OF THE SAINTS. OUR BATTLE IS NOT AGAINST THE HUMAN BEINGS. OUR BATTLE IS AGAINST SPIRITUAL WICKEDNESS. IT IS THE DEMONS IN THE PEOPLE THAT WANT TO ATTACK US. ONCE WE BIND THE DEMONS, IN THE PEOPLE, IN JESUS NAME, WE RENDER THEM POWERLESS TO DO ANYTHING AGAINST US. IT IS LIKE WE HAVE TIED UP THE DEMONS SO THEY CANNOT MANIFEST IN AND THROUGH THE HUMAN BEINGS WHO ARE HOUSING THEM. Here are two examples in my own life so that you will remember them and apply them to your life, if you ever feel threatened by anyone.

I was in a horrible hotel in Tanzania. IT was the only hotel in the town of Tarumi, Tanzania where people could stay. It was a few doors down from the church. Fornication, prostitution, drugs, alcoholism, etc…were going on in this hotel. I was sharing a room with a woman, named Jane, who made the audio tapes of the meetings, for the brethren. The little latch hook lock on the door would not have kept any intruders out. I realized we were not safe there. I barricaded the beds, the luggage, a table and everything I could find from the door to the wall across the room; to keep people from being able to push the door open and get to us. I said, "Lord, I have done all I can to keep us safe. Now I am standing in faith." In the wee hours of the morning, I heard three drunk men outside the window talking the word mazoongu meaning white person. I was the only white person there. I said, "In the Name of Jesus, I bind the demons in these men outside of my window, that they cannot manifest against us, in Jesus Name. Amen! Right after I bound the demons, the men went away. The demons were tied up and couldn't use those men to attack us.

I was in a village in Uganda, staying at a pastor's house. He had huge fences around his property with barbed wire on top. The fences had huge gates with heavy chains and huge padlocks that were locked for our protection. There were thieves (in that area of Uganda), who would put chemicals in the air conditioners of people's homes to cause the people not to breathe and have to run out of their homes. Then the thieves would go inside and rob the homes. In the middle of the night, I heard someone trying to cut the chains on the gates to get into the compound. I said, " I bind the demons in the people who are at the gate, trying to break into this compound that they cannot do it, in Jesus Name. Amen! Right after I bound the demons in the people. The people left.

I heard of a horrible situation that could have ended differently. If the Christian woman had known that she could bind the demons, in the man who kidnapped her and her daughter, they would not have been raped and her daughter would not have been murdered. WE WAR NOT AGAINST FLESH AND BLOOD BUT AGAINST PRINCIPALITIES, POWERS, RULERS OF DARKNESS AND SPIRITS OF WICKEDNESS IN HIGH PLACES. ONCE THESE DEMONS ARE BOUND, IN THE NAME OF JESUS, AND COMMANDED NOT TO MANIFEST AGAINST US, IN JESUS NAME, THERE IS NOTHING THEY CAN DO AGAINST US. THEY ARE RENDERED POWERLESS, IN JESUS NAME.

Just speaking the Name Jesus, if you feel threatened in any way, will put the demons to flight. The demons have to submit to the Name of Jesus.

> Philippians 2:5-11 "Let this mind be in you, which was also in Christ Jesus; Who being in the form of God, thought it not robbery to be equal with God: But made himself of no reputation, and took upon him the form of a servant, and was made in the likeness of men: And being found in fashion as a man, he humbled himself, and became obedient unto death, even the death of the cross. Wherefore God also has highly exalted him, and given him a name which is above every name: That at the name of Jesus every knee should bow, of things in heaven and things in earth, and things under the earth; And that every tongue should confess that Jesus Christ Is Lord, to the glory of God the Father."

As we can see here, every knee with bow to Jesus and every tongue will confess that Jesus Christ is Lord. Hitler will bow to Jesus and confess that Jesus Christ is Lord. The anti-Christ will bow to Jesus and confess that Jesus Christ is Lord. The principalities will bow to Jesus and declare that Jesus Christ is Lord.. The fallen angels will bow to Jesus and confess that Jesus Christ is Lord. Satan himself will bow to Jesus and confess that Jesus Christ is Lord, to the glory of God the Father. THERE IS NO NAME MORE POWERFUL THAN THE NAME OF JESUS.

> Luke 10:19 (KJB) Jesus said to the believers, "Behold, I give unto you POWER to tread on serpents, and scorpions, and over all the power of the enemy: and nothing shall by any means hurt you." Some Bibles have changed the word "power" to the word" authority". Authority with no power is useless. This is why I recommend the King James Bible over the other versions of the Bible. I stood on this scripture many times, while in Africa. I Have no fear of witch doctors, demonized people, illnesses, etc…because I believe I have power over all the power of Satan and he could not harm me.

Once, while in a hotel room in Kisumu, Kenya, Satan was stomping around the bed in the middle of the night huffing and puffing. The Holy Spirit said, "It is Satan." I said, "Satan get out of this hotel room now and don't you ever return, in Jesus Name." I got up, turned on the light, saw that he left, shut the light off and went back to sleep. I had no fear of the devil because I know he cannot harm me. I believe Jesus has given me power over all the power of the devil and nothing can harm me. Jesus Christ is God. God cannot lie. His Word is true for ever.

> Ephesians 6:13-16 "Wherefore take unto you the whole armor of God, that you may be able to withstand in the evil day, and having done all, to stand. Stand therefore, having your loins girt about with truth, and having on the breastplate of righteousness; And your feet shod with the preparation of the gospel of peace; Above all, taking the shield of faith, wherewith you shall be able to quench all the fiery darts of the wicked. And take the helmet of

salvation, and the sword of the Spirit, which is the word of God: Praying always with all prayer and supplication in the Spirit, and watching thereunto with all perseverance and supplication for all saints." People cannot pray in the Spirit unless they receive the Holy Ghost/Holy Spirit Baptism and receive a prayer language.

We must stand on the truth of God's Word. WE must realize that we have Christ's Righteousness that has been applied to our lives. Man's righteousness is filthy rags. None of us could reach heaven without Jesus Christ's Blood and His Righteousness applied to our lives. Feet shod with the Gospel of Peace is the Gospel of Jesus Christ unto salvation. We are to spread the gospel message. Our shield of faith must be in Christ alone. His Word is true and he is faithful; who promised us eternal life. The helmet of salvation is our minds. WE must renew our minds and thoughts to agree with God and His Word. Our Sword is the Word of God. We must memorize the scriptures that pertain to our situations and speak God's Word. When Jesus was tempted in the wilderness, he said, "IT is written". He answered the tempter with the Word of God. WE must read the Word of God to have a sharp sword of the Spirit, to wield against the devil and his agents.

> Hebrews 4:12 "For the Word of God is quick, and powerful, and sharper than any two edged sword, piercing even to the dividing asunder of soul and spirit, and of the joints and marrow, and is a discerner of the thoughts and intents of the heart." IT is the Word of God spoken into situations that touch people's souls and spirits and bring about change. Pastors who do not preach the Bible, are not helping anyone to change. They need to get out of the pulpits of America and stop pretending to be of God. They are serving the enemy of our souls, when they preach nonsense from the pulpit. God will hold them accountable, more than the average lay person.

> Hebrews 5:12-14 "For when for the time you ought to be teachers, you have need that one teach you again the oracles of God; and are become such as have need of milk and not

of strong meat. For every one that uses milk is unskillful in the word, of righteousness: for he is a babe. But strong meat belongs to them that are of full age, even those who by reason of use have their senses exercised to discern both good and evil."

Paul was rebuking these believers because they had not grow in the Word of God. They were still spiritual babes who didn't understand the deeper things of God. They could not endure strong scriptural messages. They should have been teaching the Word of God, but they still hadn't grown beyond the baby Christian stage. Sadly, there are many people who have sat in our churches for years and years; that are still baby Christians. They refuse to read their Bibles. They refuse to study the Word of God. They have no clue what God has to say about anything. They believe the lies of the world; because they do not know the truth of God's Word.

II Timothy 2: 15 "Study to shew yourself approved unto God, a workman that needs not to be ashamed, rightly dividing the word of truth." WE are to study and know what the Bible says. WE are to allow the Holy Spirit to teach us and reveal the scriptures to us as we read them. Read out loud because faith comes by hearing the Word of God. As you read out loud, your ears are hearing the Word of God. Your eyes are reading the Word of God. The scriptures are getting into you both ways.

When you read the Bible ask THE Holy Spirit to teach you the Word of God. He is the best teacher you could have. The Bible was written by holy men of God as they were moved by the Holy Ghost. The Holy Ghost is the real author of the Bible. HE used men to write what He gave them to write. Read the entire chapter and don't take any scripture out of the context it is written in. Rightly divide the Word of Truth. Study the Word. Memorize the scriptures that pertain to you. If you are ever put in prison for the cause of Christ, without a Bible, only the scriptures you know will be there to sustain you. IF you know what the Bible says, you will not be deceived by the devil.

John 14:26 "But the Comforter, which is the Holy Ghost, whom the Father will send in my name, he shall teach you all things, and bring all things to your remembrance, whatsoever I have said unto you." IF we don't study the Word of God, the Holy Ghost has nothing to bring to our remembrance and we have nothing to stand on. WE must study the Word of God to be able to discern God's truth.

LET GOD'S WORD AND GOD'S HOLY SPIRIT CHANGE YOU FROM THE INSIDE OUT. BE A WISE VIRGIN AND A FAITHFUL PRIEST TO GOD. SERVE HIM FAITHFULLY AND HEAR HIM SAY, "WELL DONE MY GOOD AND FAITHFUL SERVANT. STAND STRONG IN THE LORD AND IN THE POWER OF HIS MIGHT. HAVING DONE ALL, STAND. WE DESPERATELY NEED CHURCH GOD'S WAY, NOW!

Kathleen Hollop

ACCREDITATION

All Bible Scripture Verses were taken from The Thompson Chain Reference Bible from the KING JAMES VERSION. ***PLEASE NOTE THAT THE VERBAGES HAVE BEEN CHANGED INTO CURRENT DAY VERBAGE FOR MORE CLARITY FOR THE READERS. Examples of this are as follows: Hearken to hear, thou to you, seethe to see, goest to go, etc…

REFERENCES TO THE REAL HISTORY OF OUR NATION ARE AS FOLLOWS:

"The Light And The Glory" by Peter Marshall and David Manuel

"From Sea To Shining Sea" by Peter Marshall and David Manuel

"Miracles In American History" 32 Amazing Stories of Answered Prayer by Susie Federer adapted from William J Federer's American Minute

"Miracles In American History Volume 2" Amazing Faith That Shaped The Nation by Susie Federer adapted from William J. Federer's American Minute

REFERENCES To Information about Margret Sanger and her ties to the KKK came from the Movie "Hillary's America".

References to the Congress came from the National Legal and Policy Center and their publication of a United States Congress Directory.

References to the Renewal that took place in 1993-1996 came from the Toronto Airport Vineyard Church, Shabbat Chaim, Fountain of Life Church and my own personal experiences attending the Renewal/Revival Meetings.

All word definitions were taken from Websters New World Dictionary Fourth Edition

The Azusa Revival information " Azusa Street They Told Me Their Stories" by Tommy Welchel

THANK YOU

First I want to thank Father God, Jesus Christ and the Holy Spirit/Holy Ghost who inspired me to write this book to bring order and correction to the Body of Christ. Our God is the God of all TRUTH, RIGHTEOUSNESS, LOVE, JOY, PEACE AND JUSTICE. HE IS A HOLY TRINITY. HE IS A GOD OF MERCY AND FAITHFULNESS. WHILE WE WERE YET SINNERS HE TOOK ON HUMAN FORM, LEAD A SINLESS LIFE ,AND BECOME THE ULTIMATE SACRIFICE FOR YOUR SINS AND MINE ON THE CROSS. HE CAME TO REDEEM US BACK TO HIMSELF SO THAT WE CAN BE SAVED AND DWELL WITH HIM FOREVER. JESUS IS THE WAY THE TRUTH AND THE LIFE. NO MAN CAN COME UNTO THE FATHER BUT BY ME. (John 14:6).

Second, I want to thank my Husband Paul who has stood by me and encouraged me to obey the call of God on my life. Thank You Paul for over 50 years of love, support, strength, trust and encouragement. Thank You for releasing me 23 trips 6 weeks at a time to go into Africa, and then years later into Columbia and Venezuela. Thank You for trusting God to bring me home, to you, safe. Thank You for letting me spend our retirement money on mission trips.

Thirdly, I want to thank my Son Brian. Thank you Brian for helping to fund my mission trips into Africa, Columbia and Venezuela. May the Lord bless you and multiply your seed into spreading the Gospel of Jesus Christ into the nations.

I want to Thank all of the Missionaries, Evangelists, Bible Smugglers, apostles, prophets, teachers of God's Word, and faithful pastors who preach the entire Word of God from the pulpits of America (UNCOMPROMISED). Thank You to those who are faithfully serving the Lord. Thank You to those who are suffering persecution for righteousness sake. May the Lord bless you and give you the strength to endure to the end that He may give you the crown of life. May you hear in that day, "WELL DONE MY GOOD AND FAITHFUL SERVANT," in Jesus' Name, Amen!